Living Courageously

Books by
J. ALLEN BLAIR

LIVING RELIANTLY
A Devotional Study of the 23rd Psalm

LIVING PEACEFULLY
A Devotional Study of the First Epistle of Peter

LIVING FAITHFULLY
A Devotional Study of the Second Epistle of Peter

LIVING VICTORIOUSLY
A Devotional Study of Philippians

LIVING OBEDIENTLY
A Devotional Study of the Book of Jonah

LIVING PATIENTLY
A Devotional Study of the Book of Job

LIVING WISELY
A Devotional Study of the First Epistle to the Corinthians

LIVING COURAGEOUSLY
A Devotional Study of the Book of Daniel

Living Courageously

*A Devotional Study
of the
Book of Daniel*

by
J. ALLEN BLAIR

MOODY PRESS
LOIZEAUX BROTHERS

Copyright © 1971 by LOIZEAUX BROTHERS, Inc.

A Nonprofit Organization, Devoted to the Lord's Work
and to the Spread of His Truth

ISBN 0-87213-030-4

Library of Congress Catalog Card Number: 70-140898

PRINTED IN THE UNITED STATES OF AMERICA

Dedicated

to

*my many friends in the ministry
who are faithfully proclaiming
the entire truth of God*

CONTENTS

Introduction	9
1. The Response of Resolution	13
2. The Reliability of Revelation	33
3. The Reward of Righteousness	55
4. The Rebuke of Rationality	75
5. The Reality of Retribution	98
6. The Reaction of Reverence	118
7. The Renunciation of Resistance	136
8. The Restraint of Revolt	156
9. The Retrospect of Repentance	175
10. The Recognition of Renown	192
11. The Reign of Rebellion	213
12. The Record of Recompense	232

INTRODUCTION

Without question, Daniel is one of the most fascinating and intriguing books of the Bible. It is to the Old Testament what the book of the Revelation is to the New Testament. Both of these books are prophetic in nature, stressing with clarity and certainty that grand event for which the entire Body of Christ awaits, the personal, visible return of our Lord.

It has been said that prophecy is history prewritten. Many of the events that have transpired in recent years, as well as those of our present day which have baffled the minds of military strategists, can be traced to God's Word. Daniel foretells the rise and fall of nations and powers. In fact, without a working knowledge of Daniel one cannot fully understand the present course of the world. Daniel gives the history of Jews and Gentiles. Furthermore, in precise detail we are told of the events that will come to pass at the end of the present age as well as the glorious future which will follow Christ's return to rule and reign on the earth.

Considering the importance of the study of prophecy, how disturbing it is to observe the almost complete neglect of this subject in the great majority of our present-day churches. Content to have concern for the present, there is almost complete disregard for the future. The books of Daniel and Revelation are practically ignored. Very often, if they are discussed, it is purely from the figurative standpoint while the great facts of prophecy are either explained away or disregarded.

It was never God's plan that prophecy be neglected in His Church, for we are told by the apostle in 2 Peter 1:19:

"We have also a more sure word of prophecy; whereunto ye do well that ye take heed, as unto a light that shineth in a dark place, until the day dawn, and the day star arise in your hearts." The great books in the Bible dealing with prophecy are not questionable or dubious, as some would have us think. They are, as Peter says, "a more sure word" of the truth of God. Because of this, it is of extreme importance "that ye take heed."

The book of Daniel may be accepted as literal and authentic. It was Sir Isaac Newton who said, "To reject Daniel is to reject the Christian religion." The writer of the book was spoken of and recognized as a historical personage by our Lord in His Olivet discourse in Matthew 24:15 and Mark 13:14. Likewise, Daniel is mentioned in other passages of the Old Testament such as Ezekiel 14:19-20.

The life and character of the author of the book is clearly evidenced in his writings as a man of deep, reliant faith and unshakable, fearless courage. It is difficult to disassociate the writings from the writer. Thus I have given the book the title *Living Courageously*. Not only does Daniel set before us the example of a fearless life, but also a challenge to stand true to our Lord and His teachings regardless of the cost. It is a relatively simple matter for one to fit in with the culture of his environment, with the desire for an "easy road" to Heaven. But Daniel's example would lead us to fix our eyes on our Lord and follow Him, irrespective of the consequences. In a very definite sense, Daniel's goal in life bore a striking resemblance to that of the Apostle Paul, who declared, "But this one thing I do, forgetting those things which are behind, and reaching forth unto those things which are before, I press toward the mark for the prize of the high calling of God in Christ Jesus" (Philippians 3:13-14).

One cannot read the book of Daniel without realizing the mighty power of God at work in overwhelming the forces of evil. No individual or nation could resist His power were it not divinely permitted. God is a God of grace, permitting man to continue in evil, but eventually the sword of judgment must fall. Rather than turn to God, realizing His unlimited grace, often man resists the Lord Jehovah, sealing his own doom. The book of Daniel reveals God in His sovereign power bringing low those who would revolt against His grace and love. So that we might remember this general principle running throughout the book, I offer this simple acrostic of the word "Daniel":

> D ivine
> A ction
> N ullifying
> I rreverent
> E vil
> L awlessness

In all the ages past, God has put down the attempts of man to overthrow righteousness and holiness. And He will continue to do so, as we read in the second Psalm: "The kings of the earth set themselves, and the rulers take counsel together, against the LORD, and against His anointed, saying, Let us break their bands asunder, and cast away their cords from us. He that sitteth in the heavens shall laugh: the LORD shall have them in derision. Then shall He speak unto them in His wrath, and vex them in His sore displeasure" (Psalm 2:2-5). For centuries God has been speaking to rebellious hearts and vexing them in His sore displeasure, but the day will come when Christ will return and all the enemies of the Lord will be destroyed. It will be as God has prophesied in Psalm 2:9, "Thou shalt break them with a rod of iron; Thou shalt dash them in pieces like a potter's vessel." Something of this conflict is seen throughout the book of Daniel as our mighty God brings proud and boastful men to humiliation and judgment.

Just before we begin our verse-by-verse exposition of the book, let me offer this word of caution. Throughout the Bible we find that God gave visions and revelations to spiritual-minded men. Please do not overlook the fact that those who would study and understand the book of Daniel must be in a right relationship with God, fully surrendered to His control and purpose. Let no one think that the carnal mind can understand spiritual truth. Thus it behooves us to permit the Holy Spirit to search us out before we enter into our study.

How is it with you? Are you living in fellowship with our wonderful Lord? If not, yield to His control completely. Should it be that you have never been saved by receiving Christ into your life, call on the Lord Jesus at this moment and receive Him into your heart.

Chapter 1

THE RESPONSE OF RESOLUTION

Key verse, 8: "But Daniel purposed in his heart that he would not defile himself with the portion of the king's meat, nor with the wine which he drank: therefore he requested of the prince of the eunuchs that he might not defile himself."

The first chapter of Daniel provides a worth-while introduction to the rest of the book. But not only is it introductory; the Holy Spirit presents several valuable lessons from the lives of four young Hebrews who walked with God. They were confronted by temptation, but they refused to digress from their fidelity to God. With tenacious determination they chose the Lord's way rather than submit to appeals to the flesh.

1. *The Plight — verses 1-2.* The book of Daniel begins with a sorrowful note. For centuries the chosen people of God had been drifting farther and farther away from the truth. Repeatedly God had spoken to the kings of Judah through His messengers, the prophets, but the pleasure-loving Israelites refused to listen. The Lord Jehovah is a God of grace and mercy. With loving-kindness and long-suffering He patiently appealed to the wavering Jews to repent and turn to Him. It has always been true that when one rejects the Lord continually, sooner or later time runs out and sin must be punished. God says in Genesis 6:3, "My spirit shall not always strive with man." Persistent sin results in promised judgment. Such was the

sad lot of the kingdom of Judah and the capital city Jerusalem in the days of Daniel. "In the third year of the reign of Jehoiakim king of Judah came Nebuchadnezzar the king of Babylon unto Jerusalem, and besieged it." Doubtless the Jews were surprised when Nebuchadnezzar besieged the city. They had no reason to be, however, for Jeremiah had given a specific prophecy of the downfall of Judah many centuries before. In this prophecy (Jeremiah 25:8-11) it is explicitly stated that Nebuchadnezzar would come upon them and carry them to Babylon for a period of seventy years. The wicked king Nebuchadnezzar was the instrument God chose to bring judgment upon the Jews.

Actually there were three attacks made upon Jerusalem: the first in 606 B. C., the one spoken of in our text; the second in 598 B. C., when a much larger number of people were deported; finally in 587 B. C., the third, when the remaining few were carried into captivity and the city was burned.

Daniel indicates that the first attack was in the third year of the reign of Jehoiakim; Jeremiah declares it to be in the fourth year. The reason for this apparent contradiction is clear. Since the attack was made toward the end of the third year of Jehoiakim, Daniel began his reckoning of time at that point; but since it was well into the next year before the first attack was completed, Jeremiah spoke of it as the fourth year of the reign of Jehoiakim.

At the time of the first attack on the Holy City, Nebuchadnezzar planned only a partial overthrow, desiring only to make it a tributary, and leaving only those vessels in the house of God that would be necessary for the continuation of their worship: "And the Lord gave Jehoiakim king of Judah into his hand, with part of the vessels of the house of God: which he carried into the land of Shinar to the house of his god; and he brought the vessels into the treasure house of his god." Later, when

The Response of Resolution

the next attack was made, all the vessels of the house of God were carried away and were consecrated to the Babylonian god, Bel.

Babylon had been well known for its idolatry, but, ironically, this was the sin of Judah that caused her downfall in the judgment wrought through King Nebuchadnezzar. God placed His people in the midst of an idolatrous nation so that they might come to hate that which they dearly loved. Such seems to be the usual course of iniquity. One may choose to drink; rather than heed the warnings of God regarding such a habit, he persists in his drinking and becomes an alcoholic. But later, that which at one time was cherished as an outlet from reality suddenly becomes an abomination. He finds himself helpless with no possibility of escape within his human limitations. God warns of this tragedy in the Word (Proverbs 20:1): "Wine is a mocker, strong drink is raging: and whosoever is deceived thereby is not wise." All goes well for awhile until the drinker realizes suddenly that he has been "deceived" by that which he thought was his friend.

Similar sorrow may befall one who transgresses the truth of God while wandering in the paths of forbidden sensuality. God declares in Exodus 20:14, "Thou shalt not commit adultery." Feeling that he knows more than the Word of God, the sinner continues to transgress. Unconsciously he is ensnared by the devil. Discovering he is in serious trouble, he hates everything and everybody because of his own sin. That which he thought was a thrill proved to be a tragedy.

Oftentimes the Lord permits the rebellious sinner to continue in the ways of the flesh until he sees his evil at its worst and realizes the truth of Scripture: "The way of transgressors is hard" (Proverbs 13:15). Perhaps for the first time he is willing to listen. Considering his foolishness he is ready to respond to the voice of God. This is precisely what happened to God's people in Babylon.

But why wait until judgment comes? Why delay until brought face to face with calamity? Why not come to the Lord now and enjoy the manifold blessings of God? The Israelites could have lived in the fruitfulness and blessing of the Lord, but they chose the broad way that leads to destruction.

2. *The Privilege — verses 3-4.* "And the king spake unto Ashpenaz the master of his eunuchs, that he should bring certain of the children of Israel, and of the king's seed, and of the princes; Children in whom was no blemish, but well favoured, and skilful in all wisdom, and cunning in knowledge, and understanding science, and such as had ability in them to stand in the king's palace, and whom they might teach the learning and the tongue of the Chaldeans." It is interesting to note that what we read here was prophesied a hundred years before, in the words of Hezekiah (2 Kings 20:17-18): "Behold, the days come, that all that is in thine house, and that which thy fathers have laid up in store unto this day, shall be carried unto Babylon: nothing shall be left, saith the LORD. And of thy sons that shall issue from thee, which thou shalt beget, shall they take away; and they shall be eunuchs in the palace of the king of Babylon." Our verses from Daniel reveal the fact that this prophecy was fulfilled to the letter.

King Nebuchadnezzar wanted certain of the young men chosen out of the ranks of the masses who might in the days to come be of use to his government. "Ashpenaz the master of his eunuchs" simply means that he was an official of high rank in the king's court. The word "children" is used in the broad sense, referring to those between the ages of eighteen and twenty. The king desired the very best young men that could be found: good students, who had already acquired a working knowledge of history, philosophy, mathematics, and other essential studies. The men sought after were to be robust in health, able to become good soldiers and ultimately leaders in Nebuchadnezzar's army.

It is obvious that Nebuchadnezzar was a wise man. He recognized the value of training young people and leading them in his way of life. How essential that those of us who call ourselves Christians have a similar concern for youth in our day. Is it not true that the great majority of our churches are geared for adults? Most of our sermons are directed to adult minds. A tragic fact is that all over America today young people are drifting aimlessly and carelessly without the Lord.

Even worse, however, is the fact that many of us who are Christian parents have failed in our chief responsibility, that of instructing and leading our children in the way of the Lord. God says (Proverbs 22:6), "Train up a child in the way he should go: and when he is old, he will not depart from it." Many young people who have been reared in Christian homes have departed from the truth. Whose fault is it? It is not God's, for He says if our children have been reared properly, not by precept only, but by example, they will not depart from the truth. How many parents there are, many of them who go to church every Sunday, who have provided everything for their children, except God. They have clothed, fed, and educated them, but have neglected to provide them with the Saviour; they gave them no family altar, no Bible. I pray that your children will never have to say to God, "I accuse my parents."

On numerous occasions through the years of my ministry I have been urged by parents to call upon their wayward sons and daughters. I can recall talking with some who were living in the lowest depths of sin. But as I counselled with the young people, I often detected that there had been failure on the part of their parents in providing essential spiritual guidance and direction in the years when it was most needed.

Please consider this word of caution, especially if you are a young parent. Do not think you can live carelessly, without the Lord, neglecting to provide a spiritual foundation for your children, and have them turn out all right. The time to train these young ones for God and righteousness is in their early years. And be sure, training means leading; it is more than telling; it is showing. This presupposes that you are in fellowship with God as far as your own life is concerned. Day by day as you walk in fellowship with the Lord, you will teach not only by word but by a holy life as well. Nebuchadnezzar was clever. He recognized the importance of training youth for his government. We need to be even wiser, in that we train our youth for God.

3. *The Problem — verse 5.* All seemed well for the Hebrew boys, but the privilege was not without its problem. "The king appointed them a daily provision of the king's meat, and of the wine which he drank: so nourishing them three years, that at the end thereof they might stand before the king." The word "meat" as used here really means "delicacies" or "dainties." In other words, the young men were to eat not only necessary food but the very best, similar to that which the king ate. Why did the king provide such a benevolent provision for his captives? Doubtless he had an ulterior motive. The mighty monarch saw in them great promise, but he knew they had to be won from their former faith and belief if they were to be useful in Babylon.

On the surface what the king did for the Hebrew boys appears to be advantageous, and it was, if personal comfort can be considered an advantage. But King Nebuchadnezzar was crafty. He knew that if he was to turn the hearts of the Hebrew boys to the Babylonian idols it was necessary first of all to blot out their fidelity to their former teaching of the Jehovah God. Thus, though God intervened to provide the privilege of study and training for the young men, Satan was quick to

The Response of Resolution

respond with the problem of rich food and wine from the king's table.

The great deceiver used one of his age-old methods of laying prosperity and comfort before God's servants in an attempt to get them to supplant the spiritual with the temporal. Satan is well aware that worldly-minded Christians are never spiritually intelligent. God says (James 4:4), "The friendship of the world is enmity with God; whosoever therefore will be a friend of the world is the enemy of God." Satan knows this, and he is ever busy seeking to thrust the pleasures of the world before the child of God.

If the believer is to be effective for God, he must be willing to forsake the world to follow Christ. By "the world" is meant anything that tempts or turns one from following Christ. The world prevents us from following Christ because it caters to the flesh as opposed to the Spirit. John has given us a clear-cut analysis of what the true believer's attitude should be toward the world: "Love not the world, neither the things that are in the world. If any man love the world, the love of the Father is not in him. For all that is in the world, the lust of the flesh, and the lust of the eyes, and the pride of life, is not of the Father, but is of the world. And the world passeth away, and the lust thereof: but he that doeth the will of God abideth for ever" (1 John 2:15-17).

This is not to suggest that the Christian is to withdraw himself from the unsaved, but he is to forsake those things that will hinder his testimony and usefulness among the unsaved.

A yacht at anchor on the Niagara River broke loose from its moorings and drifted with the current, gradually gaining speed as it neared the falls. The panic-stricken passengers tried vainly to stem the speed of the boat and turn it toward shore. Some of them were even accusing one another, trying to fix the blame for their predicament — and this with the sound of the thundering falls plainly to be heard and their destruction only a few minutes away. Then the skipper, a man of intelligence and action, went below and blasted a hole in the hold with dynamite. The crippled craft settled to the shallow bottom in the swift stream — and there it lodged. No lives were lost, and after considerable trouble, the frightened passengers were all rescued.

What a parable this provides for Christians. We are in the world, but at the same time, we are not to be of the world. We must scuttle the ship of worldliness, forsaking her completely, if the purposes of God are to be fulfilled. There can be no compromise, for God declares (Matthew 6:24), "No man can serve two masters."

Let us not be deluded by the wicked one into thinking that personal comfort and enjoyment derived from the things of the world can be interpreted as blessings from God. Every believer needs to pray daily that he may have wisdom in discerning that which comes from God's hand and that which is from the devil. Both the Scriptures and experience teach that Satan is not only a deceiver but an imitator. He is a dangerous foe; he gets us so involved in physical comforts that we completely overlook the essential truth contained in our Lord's words (Matthew 16:24): "If any man will come after Me, let him deny himself, and take up his cross, and follow Me."

Only as we stay close by the side of our living Lord and draw upon His strength and power can we be successful in combating the enemy. Maybe you have been deceived; you are following Christ afar off because you have been eating and drinking of the devil's delicacies rather than standing true to the Lord. Let God have His perfect way in your life!

4. *The Persistence — verses 6-8.* Further attempts were made to abolish any loyalty to the former faith of the Hebrew boys. The God-honoring Hebrew names received at the time of their circumcision were taken from

them and they were given idolatrous Chaldean names: "Now among these were of the children of Judah, Daniel, Hananiah, Mishael, and Azariah: Unto whom the prince of the eunuchs gave names: for he gave unto Daniel the name of Belteshazzar; and to Hananiah, of Shadrach; and to Mishael, of Meshach; and to Azariah, of Abednego." The Hebrew names had real meaning: Daniel — God is my judge; Hananiah — Gift of the Lord; Mishael — He that is a strong God; Azariah — The help of the Lord. How descriptive these names are of God's providential care in each of the four lives. By way of contrast, consider the new names: Belteshazzar — the keeper of the hidden treasures of Bel; Shadrach — the inspiration of the sun; Meshach — of the goddess of Shaca (under which name Venus was worshiped); Abednego — the servant of the shining fire.

By these two subtle methods, the providing of meat and drink from the king's table, and the changing of their names, the king endeavored to destroy the faith of the Hebrew boys. But how mistaken he was. "Daniel purposed in his heart that he would not defile himself with the portion of the king's meat, nor with the wine which he drank: therefore he requested of the prince of the eunuchs that he might not defile himself."

Daniel must have had a wonderful home training. He was only a young lad, but already the foundation for God had been laid in his life. Suppose his parents had been like some we have met, who have said, "We do not believe in thrusting religion upon our children. Let them grow up and make their own choice." What do you think Daniel's choice would have been? There is no doubt about it: he would have succumbed to the many temptations in Babylon.

"Daniel purposed in his heart." The word "purposed" means that he stood with decided determination. He refused to be swayed by popular appeal. The king changed

Daniel's name, but he could not change his morals. Because of the scriptural training Daniel had received from his godly parents, he recognized immediately the pitfalls that were ahead; he knew that the meat and drink from the king's table would be defiling, for this would be food and drink that had been offered to the gods of Babylon. Like Moses of old, he chose "rather to suffer affliction with the people of God, than to enjoy the pleasures of sin for a season" (Hebrews 11:25).

Standing his ground for God, Daniel made a polite request to the prince of the eunuchs, asking that he might be excused from partaking of the king's meat and drink. One cannot help but admire the fortitude and tenacity of this young man. It would have been much easier to say to himself, "For my own welfare, I will go along with what they want me to do, but I will remain true within my heart and mind." Not Daniel! He would have no part in such a sickly faith. The attitude of many present-day Christian students is to drift along with the crowd. We need some Daniels on our high school and college campuses who will refuse to compromise for the sake of popularity. This kind of living demands complete dedication to Jesus Christ.

No young person will ever be effective for the Lord until he is completely yielded to Christ's control. If his life is fully committed to the Lord, he will be willing to say, "No," with firm conviction resulting from the study of the Word of God. He will not say "No" to some sinful practice simply because his parents do not believe in it, nor because his church is against it, but because God is opposed to it. This, I say, demands full dedication to the Lord. Indeed, our lack of conviction and lack of zeal for service can be traced to unsurrendered hearts which are cluttered with worldly and carnal interests.

The late Ruth Paxton, who was greatly used of God as a Victorious Life speaker, used to tell of her visit to a college to conduct evangelistic meetings. She was

The Response of Resolution

entertained in a home where the guest room was over the kitchen and was reached by an outside stairway. Later, when an occasion arose which made it desirable for her to enter another section of the house, she found every other door locked. Seized with a strange sense of loneliness, she returned to the one room which was hers to occupy, and poured her heart out to God in prayer. Later the incident was used very effectively to illustrate to her, and the thousands who were helped by her ministry, how God Himself has in many cases been admitted to some little guest chamber and forced to stay there, while all the while He longed to enter every room and share everything.

Need I remind you that the Holy Spirit has taken up His abode in you? "Know ye not that your body is the temple of the Holy Ghost?" (1 Corinthians 6:19) Do you have Him shut up in one little corner of your heart? If so, this is why you have no inner compulsion to choose holiness when confronted with temptation. Give the Lord the right of way. If you have received salvation through Christ, claim satisfaction in Him also. Let Him have full possession of you, and then, like Daniel, you will purpose in your heart that you will not defile yourself by those things that do not please God.

5. *The Protection — verses 9-10.* Whenever the child of God takes an uncompromising stand for his Lord, it is certain that divine help will be provided. As in the case of Joseph when forsaken by his brothers, so Daniel found a God-prepared friend in his hour of extremity: "Now God had brought Daniel into favour and tender love with the prince of the eunuchs. And the prince of the eunuchs said unto Daniel, I fear my lord the king, who hath appointed your meat and your drink: for why should he see your faces worse liking than the children which are of your sort? then shall ye make me endanger my head to the king."

Obviously, Daniel had a gracious and pleasing personality, though this was not the basic reason why the prince of the eunuchs was attracted to him. It was because God had a plan and purpose for Daniel to be a witness in Babylon. No one could hinder the divine order of things, not even Nebuchadnezzar. Thus God put it into the heart of the prince of eunuchs to be kindly to Daniel. He had to use caution, for any failure to carry out the command of the king would be punishable by death. Thus the prince appealed to Daniel and his three friends to partake of the king's meat and drink, lest they would appear less healthy than the other young people. But the dauntless Daniel was not to be tempted. His eyes were fixed upon the Lord and he was ready to remain true at any cost. Like Peter and his companion, Daniel's approach to the problem was, "We ought to obey God rather than men" (Acts 5:29).

Since Daniel's heart was in tune with God, the Lord would not forsake him at the crisis hour. When the test came, God had already provided the prince of the eunuchs to be Daniel's helper rather than his persecutor. Indeed, the walk of faith always has its rewards. Every true believer is called upon to "walk by faith, not by sight" (2 Corinthians 5:7). But how often we look to our circumstances. Rather than trust God we become fearful and fretful, thinking all is lost. Shame on us that we do not lift "up holy hands, without wrath and doubting" (1 Timothy 2:8).

An eminent naturalist in one of his textbooks describes a marine plant which grows from a depth of 150 to 200 feet and floats on the breakers of the Western Ocean. The stem of this plant is less than an inch thick, yet it grows and thrives and holds its own against the fierce smitings and pressures of the breakers. What is the secret of this marvelous resistance and endurance? How can this slender plant face the fury of the elements so successfully, and in spite of storm and tempest keep its hold and perpetuate itself from century to century? The answer is simple: it reaches down into the still depth of the ocean, where it fixes its grasp, after the fashion of its instinct, to the

The Response of Resolution

naked rocks, and no commotion of the waters can shake it from its fastenings. It was in this same manner that Daniel could face what to him was probably one of the severest trials of his life. His feet were in Babylon, but his heart was in Heaven. He had an unshakable and indestructible faith in his unchangeable God. Like Job, he could say of His Lord, "I know that Thou canst do every thing" (Job 42:2).

Perhaps you are wondering how Daniel could have such a deep-rooted faith. Why do not all believers possess this same dependence and reliance upon God? The depth of one's relationship to the Lord determines to a large degree the extent of his faith. Faith is a spiritual life in action. As one follows wholeheartedly in the will of God, he will rely upon the Lord for everything. When confronted with trial, examine yourself before God. Consider nothing else until you have given due consideration to your spiritual need. In the hour of affliction, you will need all the help you can muster, and especially the help that comes from the hand of God.

The story is told of a wealthy Englishman who had a collection of rare violins. There was one instrument which was of such quality and value that the eminent violinist Fritz Kreisler desired to have it. But the owner was reluctant to let it go. One day Kreisler begged for permission to play the violin just once. The request was granted and the great violinist played as only one of his talent could do. He forgot himself, pouring his soul into his music. As the master artist played, the Englishman stood as one enchanted. When Kreisler finished, not a word was spoken as he loosened the bow and the strings and placed the instrument in its case with all the gentleness of a mother putting her baby to bed. Then the owner exclaimed, "Take the violin, Kreisler, it is yours. I have no right to keep it. It ought to belong to the one who can make such beautiful music upon it."

In those few words we have a sermon of tremendous spiritual import. If you have named Christ as your Saviour from sin, you have no right to keep your life for yourself. It belongs to the Lord of all, who alone can bring forth music from your soul. He expects nothing less than full and complete consecration. If you will give Him everything, you may expect everything from Him.

6. *The Proposition — verses 11-14.* Daniel's faith was not disturbed by what the prince of the eunuchs had to say. When the opportunity came, he proposed a plan to Melzar, one of the underofficers of the prince: "Then said Daniel to Melzar, whom the prince of the eunuchs had set over Daniel, Hananiah, Mishael, and Azariah, Prove thy servants, I beseech thee, ten days; and let them give us pulse to eat, and water to drink. Then let our countenances be looked upon before thee, and the countenance of the children that eat of the portion of the king's meat: and as thou seest, deal with thy servants." Here was a request for common food rather than the rich food from the king's table. This proposition evidenced another great step of faith. The pulse Daniel requested was a vegetable food, composed primarily of legumes such as peas and beans. Though healthful, it was not known to add body weight to any degree. Of course, it was not peas and beans on which Daniel was relying; his confidence was in the Lord Jehovah. He knew his God would not fail. Thus he laid the proposition before the attendant with the request that they might be put on the diet for ten days.

Consider the risk involved in Daniel's request. Suppose in ten days he and his companions were not as healthy nor any heavier? Doubtless the prince of eunuchs would have been slain, along with Melzar, and probably Daniel and his companions, too. Daniel was young and daring, but the odds seemed to be against him. Were they? Ah, no, because God was on Daniel's side. The Bible says, "If God be for us, who can be against us?" (Romans 8:31) Daniel had nothing to fear. The Lord had not failed him in the

The Response of Resolution

past, and certainly He would not fail him in the present situation.

What God did for Daniel, He does for all who love Him and follow Him. Our God is no respecter of persons. He says to each believer (Isaiah 43:2): "When thou passest through the waters, I will be with thee; and through the rivers, they shall not overflow thee: when thou walkest through the fire, thou shalt not be burned; neither shall the flame kindle upon thee." Here is an unequivocal promise of God's unfailing provision. By taking hold of such promises by faith, we soon discover that the promises are really prophecies. Daniel embraced God's promises by faith and with staunch confidence propositioned Melzar. The Lord undertook and Melzar replied favorably: "So he consented to them in this matter, and proved them ten days." A heathen with no practical knowledge of the Lord Jehovah would not endanger his life for the Hebrew boys being held in captivity. It was the Lord who put it into Melzar's heart to accept Daniel's proposition.

How wonderful our God is! He never fails His own. To hear Christians and see the way they act sometimes, one would think that God does fail at times. But He never does! In Jeremiah 32:27 He asks, "Behold, I am the LORD, the God of all flesh: is there any thing too hard for Me?" There is only one answer to this question—*nothing* is too hard for God. Those of us who know Him through His Son Jesus Christ should rely upon Him for all things. Never let us be given to fear or worry, but with unreserved dependence expect Him to do all things.

In Psalm 78 we read of the children of Israel and their doubting during their wilderness journey. With sarcasm and unbelief they asked, "Can God furnish a table in the wilderness?" (Psalm 78:19) What they thought to be an impossibility soon became a reality. God furnished a table in the wilderness, giving quail as well as manna from Heaven. Unbelief asks, "Can God?" Faith says, "God can!" We may not be able to say "God wills," for the choice rests with Him and depends upon His inscrutable wisdom and good pleasure, but the true believer may say always, "God can."

A poor blind woman who had suffered much illness was delighted to have her pastor call one afternoon.

"You seem to be in unusual pain today," said the man of God.

Her answer was amazing: "I once heard Paxton Hood preach, Sir. He told us in his sermon of a visit to a friend who was dying, and when he asked him how he was the answer came, 'My head is resting very sweetly on three pillows — infinite power, infinite love, and infinite wisdom.' And my poor head is on those same pillows now, so that my heart is at rest."

What a marvelous provision God has made for His people, those who belong to Him by faith in Christ. Troubles may come, sorrow may surround us, but inwardly we may enjoy God's perfect peace. Though the burdens weigh upon us heavily, God assures us (Deuteronomy 33:25): "As thy days, so shall thy strength be."

"Well," someone says, "I have faith. Why doesn't God help me? I am trusting in Him, but my situation does not change." Do not overlook the fact that God works according to His time, not ours. The writer to the Hebrews said, "Ye have need of patience" (Hebrews 10:36). Indeed we do. We become so impatient when God does not act at the specific moment we think He should.

In the fifth chapter of John's Gospel is a man who had learned the art of waiting. For thirty-eight years he had sought deliverance from his bodily plague. Think of it, thirty-eight years of waiting! Most of us become discouraged and give up if God does not respond within a week or two, or even several days. Keep in mind that we are subject to the element of time, but God is not. With

The Response of Resolution

Him, a thousand years is as today. He is the eternal I AM, and all eternity to Him is as one great today. The distance between the promise and its fulfillment is negligible in God's sight, even though to us it may be months or even years. But this gap is bridged by faith, knowing with all confidence "that the LORD thy God, He is God, the faithful God, which keepeth covenant and mercy with them that love Him and keep His commandments to a thousand generations" (Deuteronomy 7:9).

Do not give up, child of God. Believe the Lord! Like Daniel, put Him to the test and watch Him work. The same Lord who wrought miracles for Daniel will care for you if you, like Daniel, will lean upon Him wholly and trust Him by faith.

7. *The Pre-eminence — verses 15-21.* What was the result of the ten-day diet of pulse and water? "At the end of ten days their countenances appeared fairer and fatter in flesh than all the children which did eat the portion of the king's meat." There is no doubt about it, the physical excellence described here was not the result of pulse and water only; it was the miraculous intervention of God. Because Daniel trusted the Lord completely, a marvelous result followed. The prophet's concern was more than physical. It was because of his spiritual depth that his body fared so well. How true it is, "Man doth not live by bread only, but by every word that proceedeth out of the mouth of the LORD" (Deuteronomy 8:3).

After what he had seen, Melzar needed no more convincing. Thus he "took away the portion of their meat, and the wine that they should drink; and gave them pulse." Here was another overwhelming victory resulting from the life of faith. Not only did God provide for the bodies of the four young men, but also for their minds: "God gave them knowledge and skill in all learning and wisdom: and Daniel had understanding in all visions and dreams." This is not to suggest that the four Hebrew boys did not study and work hard. They would have been no testimony for God had they shirked their responsibility in preparing their lessons well. However, in addition to the exercise of their own mental acumen, God gave them special wisdom and understanding enabling them to excel.

It is important to distinguish between the wisdom of man and the wisdom of God. One may be an expert in his field, scholarly and intelligent in a particular science; but, on the other hand, he may be totally ignorant of the wisdom that is from above. Every true believer who is right with the Lord is invited by God to be a recipient of divine wisdom: "If any of you lack wisdom, let him ask of God, that giveth to all men liberally, and upbraideth not; and it shall be given him" (James 1:5). Let us not think this wisdom comes always by some extraordinary manifestation. Usually it is received through the study and the searching of the Scriptures. In Psalm 119:130 we are told, "The entrance of Thy words giveth light." Many of God's people stumble about in darkness, confused and perplexed, simply because they do not spend essential time in the study of God's Word. Some of them are prolific readers, but what they read does not feed the heart and inspire the mind.

The story is told of Mark Twain, who planned one evening to take a drive and remain out until late. He told his butler he need not wait up for him, but simply lock the stable when he finished his work and place the key under a certain stone. When Mark Twain reached home, he was surprised to find that the key was not in the place selected. When his patience had been exhausted looking for it, he awakened the butler, who explained as he went to get the missing key, "Mister Clemmons, I found a better place to hide it."

By evident lack of knowledge about the Bible, it would seem that some Christians feel that they have found a better place to get wisdom. "The LORD giveth wisdom: out of His mouth cometh knowledge and understanding" (Proverbs 2:6). If we do not take the proper time to read

The Response of Resolution

and study the Scriptures, we shall be lacking sadly in divine prudence.

The four Hebrew boys worked hard and studied diligently; after three years their course was completed. Again their pre-eminence was demonstrated when brought before the king: "Now at the end of the days that the king had said he should bring them in, then the prince of the eunuchs brought them in before Nebuchadnezzar. And the king communed with them; and among them all was found none like Daniel, Hananiah, Mishael, and Azariah: therefore stood they before the king. And in all matters of wisdom and understanding, that the king enquired of them, he found them ten times better than all the magicians and astrologers that were in all his realm." This is an astounding commentary on the faithfulness of God and obedience of man. Daniel and his three companions had honored the Lord. Though they were *in* Babylon, there was a definite sense in which they were not *of* Babylon. With unflinching courage, they chose God's way as opposed to man's. The result — they were "ten times better than all the magicians and astrologers."

The boys were about twenty years of age at this time, and the king examined them thoroughly in the arts and the sciences and "in all matters of wisdom and understanding." Of course there were others examined at the same time, but the four Hebrew boys excelled them all.

There is still another blessing suggested here that God bestowed upon Daniel — long life: "And Daniel continued even unto the first year of king Cyrus." This does not mean that Daniel did not live beyond the first year of Cyrus, for he lived and prophesied beyond the reign of Cyrus. But "the first year of king Cyrus" is mentioned here to indicate that, though Daniel was one of the first captives rushed off into Babylon, he saw the day when his own people were delivered from this bondage. We are told in the Scriptures, "Rejoice with them that do rejoice, and weep with them that weep" (Romans 12:15). For many years, Daniel wept with his own people in their years of oppression and bondage, but God permitted him to see the day when he could rejoice in their deliverance.

There are many lessons taught in this first chapter of Daniel, but one seems to stand out — it pays to walk with God. Daniel was willing to take an uncompromising stand for the Lord, realizing that lasting happiness is found not in doing as one pleases, but in doing as God pleases. One sin in the life of the believer, if not forsaken through the power of Christ, may be the stumbling block that will keep him from pleasing God. Partial obedience is never satisfying to the Lord. Saul slew all the Amalekites but one, and that single exception in the path of obedience marked the unsoundness of his profession, costing him his throne and bringing him under the awful displeasure of God. There is no such thing as a second-rate Christianity. It is all or none. If it is all, the price is full surrender to Christ's control. Is this the brand of Christianity you possess? This is the only kind the Bible teaches. Maybe you are not a Christian. You thought you were, but the life you are living proves that you are not. Let Christ become real to you. Receive Him as your Saviour and Lord.

Chapter 2

THE RELIABILITY OF REVELATION

Key verse, 28: "But there is a God in heaven that revealeth secrets, and maketh known to the king Nebuchadnezzar what shall be in the latter days."

In its relationship to the rest of the book, chapter two of Daniel is foundational. It provides one of the most concise accounts of prophetic truth to be found anywhere in the Bible. God's divine revelation is seen in triumph over the worthless superstitions of men. One does not read far into the chapter without realizing that "God hath chosen the weak things of the world to confound the things which are mighty" (1 Corinthians 1:27).

1. *The Disturbance — verses 1-3.* "And in the second year of the reign of Nebuchadnezzar Nebuchadnezzar dreamed dreams, wherewith his spirit was troubled, and his sleep brake from him." Does it not seem unreasonable that God would use a heathen king as the medium for one of the greatest prophecies ever given? Would it not be expected that such a revelation would be disclosed to one of the children of Israel rather than to an ungodly monarch? It should be remembered, however, that at the time Israel was little different morally and spiritually than the Chaldeans. God's people had degenerated into gross immorality and idolatry. It was for this reason that judgment was executed, resulting in their Babylonian captivity. Furthermore, the Babylonian captivity under Nebuchadnezzar ushered in a period that will continue

until the return of Christ. This was spoken of by our Lord in Luke 21:24 as "the times of the Gentiles." Thus we may conclude that, because of the sorrowful state of Israel, God chose to use Nebuchadnezzar as His vehicle to convey the prophetic future of the nations of the world, culminating in the return of Christ. We should be reminded, too, that "there is no power but of God: the powers that be are ordained of God" (Romans 13:1). In fulfilling His purposes, the righteous Lord uses anyone He chooses.

When Nebuchadnezzar awakened the morning following his dream, he was greatly disturbed, though he could not recall the details of the dream. Hopeful for a solution to his dilemma, he "commanded to call the magicians, and the astrologers, and the sorcerers, and the Chaldeans, for to shew the king his dreams." The king was so confused and troubled that he commanded that all the wise men of his court be brought before him to provide help at this time of urgent need.

Among those brought before Nebuchadnezzar were the magicians, who declared themselves to be fortune tellers; the astrologers, who pretended to be able to foretell future events by their study of the stars; the sorcerers, who were the spiritualist mediums of their day, professing to have contact with the dead; and the Chaldeans, who were considered the best educated among them, supposedly familiar with all the ancient writings.

Nebuchadnezzar's worst problem was that he did not know the Lord who inspired the dream. How much simpler it would have been for him to go to his knees and beseech God to recall the dream for him as well as give the understanding of it. But not knowing the Lord, he turned in the wrong direction for help. Many in our day are guilty of the same error. In the United States alone, over one hundred twenty-five million dollars is spent every year on superstition — crystal gazers, tea leaf readers, palmists, and astrologers.

The Reliability of Revelation

Houdini is a name associated with magic. I well remember, shortly after my conversion, reading in the newspapers of Mrs. Houdini having given up hope for her husband's return. For ten years she kept a light burning above her husband's photograph. But on the tenth anniversary of his death, with over two hundred interested friends in attendance, his wife staged a final séance, on the roof of a Hollywood hotel, in what she said was a last effort to communicate with him. Nothing happened. After thirty minutes of tearful pleading over a public address system, she cried, "He has not come. I will turn out the light." Mrs. Houdini had agreed with her husband that the first one who died would try to reach the other beyond the grave. A prearranged message in code was memorized by each; but after ten years the hopelessness of these plans was certain.

In spite of this and numerous other failures to reach the dead, gullible humans are still trying. Spiritualist mediums are stuffing their pockets full with money that might otherwise be used for better purposes. People ask me if I think there is anything in spiritualism. I certainly do: the devil is in it, and all of us would do well to stay out of it.

There was an immediate response to Nebuchadnezzar's command: "So they came and stood before the king. And the king said unto them, I have dreamed a dream, and my spirit was troubled to know the dream." These who were brought before Nebuchadnezzar were fakers. But when one is in distress, he is willing to grasp for help of any kind from any direction. Oh, that men and women might know the Lord so they could experience the miracles that God works through prayer. He says, "Call unto Me, and I will answer thee, and shew thee great and mighty things" (Jeremiah 33:3). What a wonderful invitation! But of course, to pray, one needs to know Christ as Saviour and Lord. Prayer is meaningless without conversion. God longs that all come to Him and believe.

Nebuchadnezzar proved the fraudulence of the wise men as he requested them to do something unheard of before. Very often their prophecies were stated in such a manner that they would please the king and protect their own necks. But the king asked them to state the details of the forgotten dream. This was an utter impossibility in their eyes, and consequently their deceit was about to be exposed. God says (Numbers 32:23), "Be sure your sin will find you out." It always does. Lying, cheating, and dishonesty appear to be easy solutions to difficult and embarrassing situations, but the final result is disaster. God's way is always best.

2. *The Deficiency — verses 4-11.* The wise men knew they were ensnared in an impossible predicament. Looking for an escape, they spoke "to the king in Syriack" saying, "O king, live for ever: tell thy servants the dream, and we will shew the interpretation." The king was incensed by their request. Embittered, he threatened them, saying, "The thing is gone from me: if ye will not make known unto me the dream, with the interpretation thereof, ye shall be cut in pieces, and your houses shall be made a dunghill." The severity of this judgment suggests how apprehensive the king actually was.

Nebuchadnezzar was willing however, to give his helpers a fair chance. If they could prove that they were not deceivers by complying with his request, he promised to honor them: "If ye shew the dream, and the interpretation thereof, ye shall receive of me gifts and rewards and great honour: therefore shew me the dream, and the interpretation thereof."

The wise men knew that the hour of their exposure and execution was near at hand. In desperation, they pled again, "Let the king tell his servants the dream, and we will shew the interpretation of it." Nebuchadnezzar accused the miserable deceivers of stalling for time. "I know of certainty that ye would gain the time, because ye see the thing is gone from me." Further, he informed

The Reliability of Revelation

them that their response to his command would be a test of their veracity, for if they could not tell the dream they were surely deceitful liars: "But if ye will not make known unto me the dream, there is but one decree for you: for ye have prepared lying and corrupt words to speak before me, till the time be changed: therefore tell me the dream, and I shall know that ye can shew me the interpretation thereof." The king was adamant. He was unwilling to change his mind. "There is but one decree for you," he declared.

Realizing that death was near, the wise men pled for their justification. They accused the king of demanding an impossibility: "There is not a man upon the earth that can shew the king's matter: therefore there is no king, lord, nor ruler, that asked such things at any magician, or astrologer, or Chaldean. And it is a rare thing that the king requireth, and there is none other that can shew it before the king, except the gods, whose dwelling is not with flesh." By their own acts of deceit, these wicked men brought doom upon themselves. They sought to find a loophole, but their crookedness could not be hidden.

Two partners of a large, prosperous business were both childless. They decided to hire a poor boy, give him every opportunity to advance rapidly, and ultimately have him become a partner and the heir of the business. They found a boy they both liked. He was bright, active, and industrious. The partners agreed to give him six months' trial before informing him of their plan. The last week of the six months' test arrived. One morning the manager happened to see the boy slyly slip something into his pocket. He insisted on knowing what it was, and the boy confessed that he had stolen some money. It was only a small amount, but he was dismissed and never learned how near he had been to a fortune. He had lost splendid prospects for an insignificant sum of money. How many there are who have sold their opportunity for prosperity, or even squandered their privilege of knowing God and walking with Him, because of the sin of dishonesty. No shady business ever produces a sunny life.

Dishonesty and spirituality are never compatible. The truly spiritual man will be extremely careful to avoid any trace of dishonesty. God declares (2 Corinthians 8:21), "Providing for honest things, not only in the sight of the Lord, but also in the sight of men." Everyone who professes to be a follower of Jesus Christ must guard his testimony at all times. Never must room be left for suspicion as to his honesty.

I recall reading about a fire that broke out in a department store in a large city. All of the charge slips for that day were destroyed. A full-page advertisement in each of the newspapers the next day explained that fact to the public and requested all who had bought goods to report their purchases. Although the daily average of charge purchases in the store ran into the thousands of dollars, only one person responded — a man who had bought a pair of gloves. Many clerks remembered making large sales, but the store had no proof and therefore had to stand the loss. Is it any wonder that the proprietor of that store has taken a rather pessimistic view regarding the average person's honesty?

As the wise men of Babylon had to face death because of their dishonesty, how much worse to face an all-righteous God because of this evil. We read in Galatians 6:7-8, "Be not deceived; God is not mocked: for whatsoever a man soweth, that shall he also reap. For he that soweth to his flesh shall of the flesh reap corruption; but he that soweth to the Spirit shall of the Spirit reap life everlasting." One may misrepresent his products, pad his expense account, cheat on his examinations, or be unfaithful to his mate; but one of these days there will come a time of reckoning and then what he has sown must be reaped.

3. *The Decree — verses 12-16.* Because of the failure of the magicians, the astrologers, the sorcerers, and the

The Reliability of Revelation

Chaldeans to recall the dream, the king became extremely angry and issued a decree for their execution: "For this cause the king was angry and very furious, and commanded to destroy all the wise men of Babylon." Not only was the king's violence directed toward the Chaldeans, but against Daniel and his fellow Hebrews as well. This surely evidences the deficiency of anger, for rarely is one reasonable when he is angry. Until this outburst of rage, the king had expressed unusual favor for Daniel and his fellows, claiming them in "all matters of wisdom and understanding" to be "ten times better than all the magicians and astrologers that were in all his realm." But how quickly this attitude of esteem and respect became one of scorn and contempt.

Let us realize the lesson. It is essential that those of us who are in Christ beware of the evil of anger, for rare are the occasions when a Christian can be angry without sinning. Anger is defined as "a sudden, brief, violent displeasure" and wrath is "anger on a large scale, especially when used by those in superior positons." Whenever these emotions are exercised by God, they are, of course, righteous. But He warns His people against their use: "Cease from anger, and forsake wrath: fret not thyself in any wise to do evil" (Psalm 37:8); "Dearly beloved, avenge not yourselves, but rather give place unto wrath: for it is written, Vengeance is mine; I will repay, saith the Lord" (Romans 12:19); "Let all bitterness, and wrath, and anger, and clamour, and evil speaking, be put away from you, with all malice" (Ephesians 4:31).

Soon word reached Daniel concerning the king's decree. Notice his reaction: "Then Daniel answered with counsel and wisdom to Arioch the captain of the king's guard, which was gone forth to slay the wise men of Babylon.... Why is the decree so hasty from the king? Then Arioch made the thing known to Daniel." It is obvious from what we read here that Daniel did not get excited. He knew that his God would be sufficient for this occasion as He had always been in the past. Consequently, with peace and quietness in his heart, he requested more information about the situation from the captain of the king's guard who had the specific responsibility of performing the execution.

Let us not overlook the fact that "Daniel answered with counsel and wisdom." He might easily have become angry. But getting in touch with the Lord for immediate help and direction, with calmness of spirit and a gracious manner Daniel asked a question which received a worth-while answer. Indeed it is true, "A soft answer turneth away wrath: but grievous words stir up anger" (Proverbs 15:1). Daniel had perfect composure not only on the outside but on the inside as well. He kept in contact with God in the face of his adversity and found, as the Lord declared in Isaiah 30:15, "In quietness and in confidence shall be your strength."

Daniel was not like the grim, old Quaker lady who was driving her shiny new car in Philadelphia. Suddenly at a cross street a heavy truck was unable to stop until it had collided with her, crumpling a fender, breaking a window, and gouging a hole in the side of her car. Infuriated, the lady managed to control herself by remembering her Quaker upbringing. She got out, walked over to the truck driver, and said, "When thee gets home to thy kennel tonight, I hope thy mother bites thee." She may have had some composure on the outside, but inwardly she was raging mad.

On the other hand, there was the noble ancestor of Hudson Taylor, who seemed to possess the same composure Daniel had in the face of a very disturbing event. An angry woman with a frying pan in her hand ran after James Taylor, seeking to provoke him into a quarrel. She rubbed it vigorously into his light-colored overcoat, the sooty utensil soiling the back of the garment and her tongue meanwhile lashing the Christian, much to the amusement of onlookers. James Taylor turned around with a smile, suggesting that if it afforded her satisfaction she might grease the front of his coat as well. The woman, covered with confusion, went on her way, but the incident was not easily forgotten in the town.

Of course, our supreme example is our Lord Himself, "Who, when He was reviled, reviled not again; when He suffered, He threatened not; but committed Himself to Him that judgeth righteously" (1 Peter 2:23). This ought to be the spirit of every true follower of the Lord Jesus Christ. In ourselves we cannot face the irritations of life with unruffled composure, but in Christ we can, as we seek His help and strength.

Upon receiving the clear account of the difficulty, "Daniel went in, and desired of the king that he would give him time, and that he would shew the king the interpretation." Why did Daniel want time? Surely it was not for the same reason that the wise men were trying to delay. They wanted time to think of some strategy they might use to outwit the king. Daniel wanted time that he and his companions might go to their knees before God and receive a revelation of the dream. The prophet knew where to turn in his hour of extremity.

It is obvious that God's providence was at work in all of this. Though the king refused to grant the wise men any further time, Daniel's request was granted and his execution was stayed. Again, we are reminded that God takes care of His own. Have you forgotten that God's grace is sufficient for your present trial? He says, "There hath no temptation [testing] taken you but such as is common to man: but God is faithful, who will not suffer you to be tempted [tested] above that ye are able; but will with the temptation [testing] also make a way to escape, that ye may be able to bear it" (1 Corinthians 10:13). Trust God, for there is a way of escape with Him. As He provided for Daniel, He will provide for you.

4. *The Dependence — verses 17-23.* Daniel was granted a brief period of time to determine King

Nebuchadnezzar's forgotten dream. Quickly he hastened "to his house, and made the thing known to Hananiah, Mishael, and Azariah, his companions: That they would desire mercies of the God of heaven concerning this secret; that Daniel and his fellows should not perish with the rest of the wise men of Babylon." Faith led to faithfulness. Daniel's confidence in God prompted him to call a prayer meeting immediately. What a prayer meeting it must have been. Here were men with a real heart burden beseeching God for His answer.

There is no question about it, when believers are serious about prayer they soon see mighty miracles wrought by the power of God. Few of us are willing to claim the precious promises as they are found in the Word relative to prayer. In Isaiah 65:24 we read one of the many unalterable promises of God, "And it shall come to pass, that before they call, I will answer; and while they are yet speaking, I will hear."

One day that great man of prayer, Spurgeon, was visited by a woman who told him that her husband had left her and she did not know where he was. She said, "I want you to pray that the Lord will send my husband home."

"We'll do better than that," said Spurgeon, "we will pray that the Lord will convert him." In simple, believing prayer that great London preacher got down on his knees and poured out his heart to God, asking the Lord to convert the husband.

Only a week had elapsed when the woman returned again to Mr. Spurgeon and said, "My husband is home. He has been converted. As soon as he was converted he came home."

Most of us would look upon this miraculous answer to prayer as being unusual, but if we were to take hold of the mighty promises of God with believing faith, we would soon discover that such answers to prayer are routine with the Lord. We read in Matthew 18:20, "Where two or three

The Reliability of Revelation

are gathered together in My name, there am I in the midst of them." Since God is in our midst, we are assured of His miracle-working power. Let us not miss the blessing of united prayer.

What was the result of Daniel's little prayer meeting with his friends? "Then was the secret revealed unto Daniel in a night vision." Daniel and his Hebrew companions prayed expectantly and they were not disappointed. The answer came at the Lord's appointed hour. Some think Daniel received the vision as he slept. Personally, I feel that the little band of believers remained on their knees calling upon God far into the night until the answer was revealed.

What mighty power there is in believing prayer! Mary, Queen of Scots, once said, "I fear John Knox's prayers more than an army of ten thousand men." The Lord Jesus tells us, "And whatsoever ye shall ask in My name, that will I do, that the Father may be glorified in the Son" (John 14:13). Here is an assuring promise. Lay hold of it by faith for your present need. Do not doubt God for a moment nor be discouraged. He does not always answer as quickly as He did in response to the prayers of the Hebrew boys. But He will always answer, and usually at a time when we most need the answer.

When George Müller was asked how much time he spent in prayer, he replied, "Hours every day. But I live in the spirit of prayer. I pray as I walk, when I lie down, and when I rise. The answers are always coming. Tens of thousands of times have my prayers been answered. When once I am persuaded that a thing is right, I go on praying for it until it comes. I have been praying every day for fifty-two years for two sons of a friend of my youth. They are not converted yet, but they will be. How can it be otherwise? There is the unchanging promise of Jehovah and on that I rest. The great fault," Mr. Müller said, "of the children of God is that they do not continue in prayer. They do not go on praying. They do not persevere. If they desire anything for God's glory, they should pray until they get it."

What happened after Daniel received the vision of the king's dream? Did he jump to his feet and run to make it known unto the king? Ah, no. He knew better than that. "Then Daniel blessed the God of heaven." He remembered an important essential — he gave thanks. He was not like the nine thoughtless lepers, who had been healed by the mercy of Jesus but who neglected to give thanks. The prayer meeting turned into a praise meeting as the four believers lifted their hearts in thanksgiving to the Lord. What a needed lesson for all of us. Even though we may be quick to pray, we are often slow to praise. "Oh that men would praise the LORD for His goodness, and for His wonderful works to the children of men!" (Psalm 107:8)

Daniel's prayer is not recorded, but we are told of that for which he praised God: "Daniel answered and said, Blessed be the name of God for ever and ever: for wisdom and might are His." Daniel knew that Nebuchadnezzar was a mighty monarch, but he knew also that his great God was far more powerful than Nebuchadnezzar. Daniel's God "changeth the times and the seasons." He is not only the Creator but the Sustainer of all things: "He removeth kings, and setteth up kings." "Promotion cometh neither from the east, nor from the west, nor from the south. But God is the judge: He putteth down one, and setteth up another" (Psalm 75:6-7). Likewise, "He giveth wisdom unto the wise, and knowledge to them that know understanding." No one can brag about how much he knows, for all true wisdom comes from God.

Furthermore, the Lord "revealeth the deep and secret things." In Deuteronomy 29:29 we see that "The secret things belong unto the LORD our God: but those things which are revealed belong unto us and to our children for ever, that we may do all the words of this law." Our Lord has not revealed everything, but only that which is essential to man's well-being. His greatest revelation is that which is contained in His Word. This is brought out clearly in this second chapter of Daniel, where the certainty of revelation is seen as opposed to superstition. Five times the word "revealed" is used by Daniel in this chapter: verses 19, 22, 28, 29, and 30. Then in verse 47 King Nebuchadnezzar uses the word.

In offering praise to God, Daniel said, "He knoweth what is in the darkness, and the light dwelleth with Him." Indeed, our God is omniscient. There is no limit to His knowledge. Daniel concluded, "I thank Thee, and praise Thee, O Thou God of my fathers, who hast given me wisdom and might, and hast made known unto me now what we desired of Thee: for Thou hast now made known unto us the king's matter." Let us not forget to give thanks unto the Lord, "who daily loadeth us with benefits, even the God of our salvation" (Psalm 68:19).

5. *The Declaration — verses 24-30.* Daniel came prepared to declare the dream to the king: "Therefore Daniel went in unto Arioch, whom the king had ordained to destroy the wise men of Babylon: he went and said unto him; Destroy not the wise men of Babylon: bring me in before the king, and I will shew unto the king the interpretation." We get some insight here into another side of Daniel's greatness. He knew well that the wise men of Chaldea were fakers, but he also knew they had souls. He expressed his concern for them by requesting Arioch to stay the king's decree of execution. Not only did Daniel have a courageous heart but a loving heart. God's love reaches out to all alike. We are told in Romans 5:6, "in due time Christ died for the ungodly." He gave His life for those who were undeserving. "God commendeth His love toward us, in that, while we were yet sinners, Christ died for us" (Romans 5:8). This was something of the same spirit evidenced by Daniel. He was not obligated to help the wise men, but he realized that they needed the Lord, like all the others in Babylon who had been blinded by idolatry.

With pride, intimating that he deserved credit for what Daniel was about to say, Arioch, the executioner, rushed Daniel to the king: "Then Arioch brought in Daniel before the king in haste, and said thus unto him, I have found a man of the captives of Judah, that will make known unto the king the interpretation." The waiting king asked Daniel anxiously, "Art thou able to make known unto me the dream which I have seen, and the interpretation thereof?" Grasping the opportunity to show the king that revelation supersedes superstition, Daniel replied, "The secret which the king hath demanded cannot the wise men, the astrologers, the magicians, the soothsayers, shew unto the king; But there is a God in heaven that revealeth secrets, and maketh known to the king Nebuchadnezzar what shall be in the latter days." The wise men were helpless to satisfy the king's request, but Daniel informed the king that, in contrast to the gods of wood and stone, "there is a God in heaven that revealeth secrets." Realizing how furious the king had been, the young Hebrew might have said nothing about his God in an attempt to save his own neck, but Daniel was a fearless witness. He grasped the opportunity to give a clear-cut witness for His Lord. The Prophet Isaiah declared, "Fear ye not the reproach of men, neither be ye afraid of their revilings" (Isaiah 51:7). Daniel epitomized the truth of this verse.

Too few Christians have the same earnest desire to witness for God as Daniel did. We read in Acts 8:4 of the zeal of the disciples after Stephen's martyrdom, "Therefore they that were scattered abroad went every where preaching the word." The believers were persecuted, but this did not hinder them. It helped them to strike out in every direction to witness for Christ. They went everywhere preaching the Word. They were filled with the mighty power of their omnipotent Lord and they were possessed by an unshakable faith that enabled them to believe that they would see the "greater works," even

The Reliability of Revelation

as our Lord had promised. They were filled with the Holy Ghost, and though they lacked the media God has given us in our day, they had the burden every Christian needs to tell others about the Lord Jesus.

Old Kim was a tiger hunter. His face was scarred from the claws of more than one tiger. His beard was wild, his face rough from the weather, his neck sun tanned. But Old Kim had heard the gospel of Jesus and had trusted in the Lord for salvation. One day a missionary met Old Kim carrying a little bag.

"What have you in that bag?"

"Ammunition," replied Old Kim, and opened the bag for the missionary to see a New Testament and a hymnbook.

"You can't hunt tigers with that," said the missionary.

"No," replied Old Kim, "I am hunting for men now." Old Kim had experienced a transformation in his heart. He used to hunt for tigers, but now he hunted for men.

Seemingly many of God's people have never had this transformation. Instead of hunting for men, too many of them are hunting for money and the things money can buy. Investing their time and talents in the pursuit of worldly success, they give little thought to witnessing. Do not be deceived by the wicked one who would keep you silent for Christ. Heed the Word of God, as found in Psalm 107:2, "Let the redeemed of the LORD say so."

Daniel warned the king that what he had dreamed was prophetic. "As for thee, O king, thy thoughts came into thy mind upon thy bed, what should come to pass hereafter: and He that revealeth secrets maketh known to thee what shall come to pass." Daniel wanted no credit for what he was about to make known: "But as for me, this secret is not revealed to me for any wisdom that I have more than any living, but for their sakes that shall make known the interpretation to the king, and that thou mightest know the thoughts of thy heart." Daniel had a loving heart, he was courageous, but he was also humble.

He gave God all the praise for the revelation. He realized, like the Apostle Paul, "That no flesh should glory in His presence" (1 Corinthians 1:29).

One of the common dangers that confronts the Lord's people is that of spiritual pride. Because we have a little smattering of truth, we feel ourselves to be superior to others. Paul reminds us in 1 Corinthians 8:1, "Knowledge puffeth up." Indeed it does, unless we stay close to the Lord. There is probably no combination needed more in a saint of God than a hold on God and humility. This was true of Daniel. That is why he was fearless and, as a result, usable. How we need to pray daily that God will keep us humble, that His power may be manifested through us.

6. *The Dream — verses 31-45.* Daniel made known the forgotten dream, informing Nebuchadnezzar that it consisted of "a great image." We read that the "image's head was of fine gold, his breast and his arms of silver, his belly and his thighs of brass, His legs of iron, his feet part of iron and part of clay." But in addition to the image, Daniel informed Nebuchadnezzar of a notable prophecy: "Thou sawest till that a stone was cut out without hands, which smote the image upon his feet that were of iron and clay, and brake them to pieces." Further, after the destruction of the image, "the stone that smote the image became a great mountain, and filled the whole earth."

How startled Nebuchadnezzar must have been as young Daniel recalled the dream for him. How much more startled he must have been as Daniel interpreted the dream. In just a few short statements, Daniel gave a vivid sketch of a period to be known as "the times of the Gentiles," running from Nebuchadnezzar's dream until the Second Coming of Christ. During this period, four great world empires were to exist on earth, all of which are prophesied in Nebuchadnezzar's image vision. Of course, when Daniel declared this amazing prophecy to Nebuchadnezzar only one of these empires had come into existence. Looking back from our present day, history

The Reliability of Revelation

reveals that all four have come and gone, but the concluding event of this prophecy, the "stone . . . cut out without hands." awaits fulfillment in the return of Jesus Christ to rule and reign.

Daniel began his interpretation by saying to Nebuchadnezzar, "Thou, O king, art a king of kings: for the God of heaven hath given thee a kingdom, power, and strength, and glory. And wheresoever the children of men dwell, the beasts of the field and the fowls of the heaven hath He given into thine hand, and hath made thee ruler over them all. Thou art this head of gold." As you can see, there is a steady decline in values from gold to iron mixed with clay. The Babylonian Empire is represented by gold, probably because Nebuchadnezzar's power was derived from God.

The Babylonian Empire continued until 538 B.C., when the next great world empire depicted by the breast and arms of silver came into existence. This was the divided kingdom under the Medes and Persians which came into being under Cyrus, who had been named by Isaiah over a hundred years before he appeared. In speaking of this kingdom, Daniel said to Nebuchadnezzar, "After thee shall arise another kingdom inferior to thee." The Medo-Persian Empire was inferior to Babylon in government but not in culture. It has been said that the kings of Persia were the worst race of men that ever governed an empire. In this sense, it was definitely inferior to the Babylonian form of government.

The empire continued until 330 B.C., when the third great empire came to power, represented by the belly and thighs of brass. This brings us to Alexander the Great. Daniel described this empire as the "Third kingdom of brass, which shall bear rule over all the earth." Alexander was the powerful monarch who, after being successful in many conquests, sat down and wept fearing there would be no more territories to conquer. But according to Nebuchadnezzar's vision of the image, the empire of Greece was to come to an end.

This came to pass in 63 B.C., when another great power swept the earth. Daniel said of this empire,"The fourth kingdom shall be strong as iron: forasmuch as iron breaketh in pieces and subdueth all things: and as iron that breaketh all these, shall it break in pieces and bruise." It is obvious from this description that this kingdom was characterized by unexcelled power and strength. This was true of the Roman Empire, which crushed Greece and every subsequent power that rose up against it. Further in his prophecy of this kingdom Daniel stated, "Whereas thou sawest the feet and toes, part of potters' clay, and part of iron, the kingdom shall be divided; but there shall be in it of the strength of the iron, forasmuch as thou sawest the iron mixed with miry clay. And as the toes of the feet were part of iron, and part of clay, so the kingdom shall be partly strong, and partly broken. And whereas thou sawest iron mixed with miry clay, they shall mingle themselves with the seed of men: but they shall not cleave one to another, even as iron is not mixed with clay." Our history books inform us that, as it was prophesied, the Roman Empire was "divided" into the eastern and western empires.

The Roman Empire has long ago ceased to exist but, according to Daniel's prophecy, it is to continue until the last great event described in this image is fulfilled. There has never been a time in history when there has been a fulfillment of the ten toes, "part of iron and part of clay." Thus it would seem that before the age ends, there will be a revival of the old Roman Empire with a loose coalition of ten kingdoms. It will be during the time of the re-establishment of these ten kingdoms that a sudden calamity will take place, as described by Daniel in verses 44 and 45: "And in the days of these kings shall the God of heaven set up a kingdom, which shall never be destroyed: and the kingdom shall not be left to other people, but it shall break in pieces and consume all these kingdoms, and it shall stand for ever. Forasmuch as thou

The Reliability of Revelation

sawest that the stone was cut out of the mountain without hands, and that it brake in pieces the iron, the brass, the clay, the silver, and the gold; the great God hath made known to the king what shall come to pass hereafter: and the dream is certain, and the interpretation thereof sure."

This prophecy presents clearly the fact of the return of Jesus Christ to rule and reign on this earth. This will be the time described by David in Psalm 72:11, "Yea, all kings shall fall down before Him: all nations shall serve Him." Paul speaks of this time: "At the name of Jesus every knee shall bow, of things in heaven, and things in earth, and things under the earth; And that every tongue should confess that Jesus Christ is Lord, to the glory of God the Father" (Philippians 2:10-11).

When will this take place? At the time of the re-establishment of the Roman Empire, with its ten kings under the control of a dictator. Then will the Lord come to crush this ruler and his satellites, and "The LORD shall be king over all the earth: in that day shall there be one LORD, and His name one" (Zechariah 14:9).

You may ask, can we trust the Word of God to be accurate? Since this dream vision has been fulfilled in every detail from the head to the feet, can we not expect the remaining prophecies to be fulfilled? There is no doubt about the Word of God being reliable. The Psalmist declared, "Thy word is true from the beginning: and every one of Thy righteous judgments endureth for ever" (Psalm 119:160). Let us believe the Word of God. Even though for some these may be days of darkness and discouragement, be sure the Lord is coming and with Him a reign of peace and blessing. If you know Him, you will reign with Him, "heirs of God, and joint-heirs with Christ" (Romans 8:17).

7. *The Deference — verses 46-49.* "Then the king Nebuchadnezzar fell upon his face, and worshipped Daniel, and commanded that they should offer an oblation and sweet odours unto him." This is a rather

surprising response. Having heard the prophecy of doom soon to befall his empire, Nebuchadnezzar might have become furious and had the prophet slain. But it would seem that God was controlling the thinking of Nebuchadnezzar, for his response was gracious and cordial. In fact, he even sought to worship Daniel, as though he were a god. The stately king fell upon his face before the prophet, offering humble gratitude. More than this, he commanded that sacrifices be offered and incense be burned to their heathen gods in honor of Daniel.

Though it is not stated in the passage, it is obvious that Daniel refused all these honors, for we read in verse 47, "The king *answered* unto Daniel, and said, Of a truth it is, that your God is a God of gods, and a Lord of kings, and a revealer of secrets, seeing thou couldest reveal this secret." Daniel, like all true servants of God, gave honor to the One to whom honor was due.

Several similar incidents of man-worship are recorded in the New Testament. Cornelius had heard of the mighty works of God being demonstrated through Peter. He sent for Peter to come to his home, and when he entered, Cornelius met him, and fell down at his feet, and worshipped him" (Acts 10:25). Peter declined to accept any homage for himself, retorting immediately, "Stand up; I myself also am a man" (Acts 10:26).

There was also the case of Paul and Barnabas who were at Lystra, where Paul had been preaching the gospel. In the audience was a man who had been a cripple from birth. Paul said to him, "Stand upright on thy feet. And he leaped and walked" (Acts 14:10). When the people had seen what had happened, they cried out, "The gods are come down to us in the likeness of men" (Acts 14:11). Then with great pomp and ceremony they proceeded to offer sacrifices to their gods in honor of Barnabas and Paul, whom they thought were Jupiter and Mercurius. When Paul and Barnabas realized what the people were doing, they rent their clothes and cried out, "Sirs, why do

The Reliability of Revelation

ye these things? We also are men of like passions with you, and preach unto you that ye should turn from these vanities unto the living God" (Acts 14:15). It is tragic that, when people are moved by some mighty work of God, they are more willing to worship and serve "the creature . . . than the Creator" (Romans 1:25).

King Nebuchadnezzar confessed to the prophet, "Of a truth it is, that your God is a God of gods, and a Lord of kings, and a revealer of secrets." But rather than turn to Daniel's God, he fell down before the prophet and worshiped him. How sad that Nebuchadnezzar did not say, "Your God is *my* God," instead of, "Your God is *a* god." One would expect that, after this startling disclosure of Jehovah's power, Nebuchadnezzar would have readily claimed Him as his own personal God.

Nebuchadnezzar's action was no different from that taken by thousands in our day. They know the way of salvation, they have heard the truth repeatedly, but to them the Lord is objective rather than subjective. He is simply *"a* god." One can never know the assurance of salvation or "the peace of God, which passeth all understanding" until he can say of the Lord, "Thou art *my* God." The Prophet Isaiah could say, "Behold, God is my salvation; I will trust, and not be afraid: for the LORD JEHOVAH is my strength and my song; He also is become my salvation" (Isaiah 12:2). There is no question about it, he had a personal experience with God so that the Lord was his.

It makes all the difference in the world whether one says, "Jesus is *a* Saviour" or "Jesus is *my* Saviour." David did not say, "The LORD is *a* shepherd"; he declared, "The LORD is *my* shepherd" (Psalm 23:1). Thomas could have seen the Saviour in all the clear light of reality and had every doubt removed, as well as touch the scars in His hands, side, and feet. But all of this would have availed nothing unless he had declared, *"My* Lord and *my* God" (John 20:28). Can you say, "Jesus is *mine*"? If you cannot, I beseech you to come to Him and acknowledge Him as your Saviour and Lord.

One readily sees the providence of God at work in caring for Daniel in the midst of Babylon. "The king made Daniel a great man, and gave him many great gifts, and made him ruler over the whole province of Babylon, and chief of the governors over all the wise men of Babylon."

But Daniel did not forget those who faithfully prayed with him in his hour of crisis. He "requested of the king, and he set Shadrach, Meshach, and Abednego, over the affairs of the province of Babylon: but Daniel sat in the gate of the king." The three Hebrew companions, like Daniel, were exalted to key positions in the empire. Certainly God honors those who put Him first in all things. Daniel had his eyes fixed on the Lord, and even though the surrounding circumstances were disturbing, the Lord did not forget Daniel. Thus we see the reliability of revelation over superstition. Daniel depended upon his God, and his God did not fail.

Chapter 3

THE REWARD OF RIGHTEOUSNESS

Key verse, 17: "If it be so, our God whom we serve is able to deliver us from the burning fiery furnace, and He will deliver us out of thine hand, O king."

Nebuchadnezzar had a great image constructed and demanded that everyone in his empire bow down and worship the image. Seemingly everyone responded, with the exception of the three Hebrew boys, Shadrach, Meshach, and Abednego. Word reached King Nebuchadnezzar regarding the disobedience of the three Hebrews. Hailed before the king, they were given another chance to bow and worship the image, but if they refused they would be cast into "a burning fiery furnace." The remaining portion of the chapter evidences "the reward of righteousness" for the three Hebrew boys who trusted their Lord implicitly and were delivered from the furnace of fire. Here is another proof of the fact that God never forsakes those who make Him supreme in their lives.

1. *The Ceremony — verses 1-3.* Where did Nebuchadnezzar get the idea to construct the huge image? Doubtless it was the result of his own pride. While interpreting Nebuchadnezzar's dream, Daniel had declared that the "image's head was of fine gold." Later he said, "Thou art this head of gold." It would seem that Nebuchadnezzar missed the point of the dream vision. Rather than realize that judgment would soon fall upon his empire, he considered only that he was the head of

gold. Thus in his arrogance he constructed the "image of gold, whose height was threescore cubits, and the breadth thereof six cubits."

Possibly this image was designed after the fashion of the image Nebuchadnezzar had seen in his dream. On the other hand, it may have been an image of the king himself, though we are not told that it was the image of a man. It was 90 feet high and 9 feet wide, a ratio of 10 to 1. God has created humans on a ratio of 5 to 1, so it is obvious that Nebuchadnezzar's image was a monstrosity.

The image was set up "in the plain of Dura, in the province of Babylon. Then Nebuchadnezzar the king sent to gather together the princes, the governors, and the captains, the judges, the treasurers, the counsellors, the sheriffs, and all rulers of the provinces, to come to the dedication of the image which Nebuchadnezzar the king had set up." These people had no choice in the matter; they were compelled to assemble for the dedication of Nebuchadnezzar's image. The response was overwhelming; they came from all directions: "Then the princes, the governors, and captains, the judges, the treasurers, the counsellors, the sheriffs, and all the rulers of the provinces, were gathered together unto the dedication of the image that Nebuchadnezzar the king had set up, and they stood before the image that Nebuchadnezzar had set up."

What is the prophetical significance of the image? It will be noted that the image was sixty cubits high and six cubits broad. This reminds us of the number of man as found in the Scriptures, number six. Further we are drawn to Revelation 13, where we read of the dreadful Beast with the number of six hundred threescore and six, who will appear at the consummation of the "times of the Gentiles." Nebuchadnezzar was a type of the Antichrist, who is yet to come and who will cause all men to bow and worship his image. His reign was also the beginning of imperialism that would characterize "the times of the

The Reward of Righteousness

Gentiles" until its consummation in the Antichrist, during the last three and a half years of the tribulation period. Nebuchadnezzar appeared as the first great dictator, who was to be followed by many more and climaxed in the appearance of the Antichrist in the time of the end.

Nebuchadnezzar's image was an attempt on the part of the king to establish man-worship as opposed to the worship of the true God. One would have thought that, after Daniel's interpretation of the dream vision, Nebuchadnezzar would have given deference to the Lord Jehovah. But though he exalted Daniel and the three Hebrew boys out of respect to their God, he gave no thought to his own personal need of the Lord. In fact, sixteen years transpired between chapters 2 and 3 of Daniel, yet the king sought to deify man, another evidence of the pride of his heart. At the same time, he attempted to establish a world religion, causing everyone to worship alike.

Can we not see a striking similarity in the attempts of man in our present day to deify and glorify humanity while ignoring the true God? Are there not attempts on every hand to abolish religious boundaries and have all men worship alike? Indeed, the liberalism of our present day, easily distinguishable in the great majority of churches across our land, is but another result of the pride of the human heart. At the same time, we cannot overlook the fact that communism is seeking to build an image in the world, which all men of every creed and race must fall down and worship. In other words, what Nebuchadnezzar began centuries ago is continuing with marked emphasis in our day and it will continue until the appearance of the Antichrist, who will be an expert in coercing the peoples of the world to worship the image of man.

How important that we ask ourselves, who am I worshiping? Do I know the one true God in my heart? There is only one way to know the Lord Jehovah, the Creator of Heaven and earth, and that is through His Son,

Jesus Christ. "For there is one God, and one mediator between God and men, the man Christ Jesus" (1 Timothy 2:5). The Son of God is the mediator. We approach the Father through the Son, "Neither is there salvation in any other: for there is none other name under heaven given among men, whereby we must be saved" (Acts 4:12).

2. *The Command — verses 4-7.* All the important officials of the kingdom were gathered together before Nebuchadnezzar's image of gold and everything was in readiness for the ensuing ceremony. "Then an herald cried aloud, To you it is commanded, O people, nations, and languages, That at what time ye hear the sound of the cornet, flute, harp, sackbut, psaltery, dulcimer, and all kinds of musick, ye fall down and worship the golden image that Nebuchadnezzar the king hath set up: And whoso falleth not down and worshippeth shall the same hour be cast into the midst of a burning fiery furnace. Therefore at that time, when all the people heard the sound of the cornet, flute, harp, sackbut, psaltery, and all kinds of musick, all the people, the nations, and the languages, fell down and worshipped the golden image that Nebuchadnezzar the king had set up." What a surprise this must have been to those who gathered for the ceremony. Doubtless hundreds of people had come simply to get a look at the great image of gold and witness its dedication. According to verse 2, all who had gathered for the viewing of the image were invited "to come to the dedication of the image." But after they arrived, they were commanded to "fall down and worship the golden image." Any refusal to obey the command would have resulted in immediate death.

Nebuchadnezzar was clever. He undertook in every way possible to provide a proper setting for his idolatrous ceremony. A large orchestra was present to play "all kinds of musick" so the audience might be stirred and moved to respond to any command that might be made. Music

The Reward of Righteousness

often softens and sweetens the mind to receive the poison of false teaching. Satan is aware of this, so he provides excellent music in many of our present-day liberal churches, like Nebuchadnezzar of old. Nebuchadnezzar used music to lure his subjects into his idol worship while he used fear of the fiery furnace to frighten them into obedience.

Nebuchadnezzar commanded everyone to worship his image. There was no choice in the matter. Those who refused were consigned to the furnace of fire. God, on the other hand, does not command anyone to worship Him. Kindly and lovingly, He invites the lost to turn to Him and receive eternal life. If they refuse, there is no choice in the matter; eternal hell is their lot. God longs that everyone come to Him and enjoy the very best in this life, with the promise of eternal life. "The Lord is not slack concerning His promise, as some men count slackness; but is longsuffering to us-ward, not willing that any should perish, but that all should come to repentance" (2 Peter 3:9). God loves you and He wants to save you. Do not reject His invitation.

Before we leave this phase of our study of Daniel, consider the believer's worship of God. Some there are who read the Bible, pray, and witness simply out of a sense of duty and obligation. They have never entered into the real joy and privilege of fellowshiping with God. Even when they serve Him, they do it with a feeling of fear of the consequences if they should not serve Him. Though they worship the true God, their worship stems from compulsion.

We read of John in Revelation 1:17, "And when I saw Him, I fell at His feet as dead." When John got a glimpse of the Lord, this was the end of John. That is what surrender to Christ means. When we get a true vision of the Lord Jesus within our hearts, we shall die to ourselves and Christ will become everything. This is the experience God wants for all of us. How important then that we who know Him say:

> Spirit of our Lord Divine,
> Fill us with Thy living fire,
> Help us know that we are Thine,
> Make Thee our supreme desire.
>
> *Donald A. Fraser*

3. *The Conspiracy — verses 8-12.* It would seem that, with the threat Nebuchadnezzar made concerning the furnace of fire, everyone would have responded to his command to fall down before his golden image, but such was not the case. The three Hebrew boys, Shadrach, Meshach, and Abednego, refused to bow. Standing when everyone else was kneeling and giving homage to the freakish image, the three rebels were easily recognized. The result was that "certain Chaldeans came near, and accused the Jews. They spake and said to the king Nebuchadnezzar, O king, live for ever. Thou, O king, hast made a decree, that every man that shall hear the sound of the cornet, flute, harp, sackbut, psaltery, and dulcimer, and all kinds of musick, shall fall down and worship the golden image: And whoso falleth not down and worshippeth, that he should be cast into the midst of a burning fiery furnace. There are certain Jews whom thou hast set over the affairs of the province of Babylon, Shadrach, Meshach, and Abednego; these men, O king, have not regarded thee: they serve not thy gods, nor worship the golden image which thou hast set up." Whoever these Chaldeans were, it is obvious that they were envious of the high positions given to the Hebrew boys and readily grasped this opportunity to conspire against them.

Envy is an appalling sin. God says in Proverbs 14:30, "A sound heart is the life of the flesh: but envy the rottenness of the bones." Envy in the believer is as rotting bones in the sense that spiritual power and usefulness are

The Reward of Righteousness

curtailed. This was the case in the life of Saul. He had been a great king, anointed of God to be the Lord's witness, but because of the sin of envy, Saul's life degenerated into utter uselessness. Saul heard people singing, "Saul hath slain his thousands, and David his ten thousands" (1 Samuel 18:7). This was only a song, but it awakened in his heart the wicked passion of envy.

"Jealousy is cruel as the grave" (Song of Solomon 8:6). It corrodes the soul like acid. It destroys the beauty of the soul like the grave destroys the beauty of the body. Thus it was with Saul. Envy provoked him to fling a javelin at David. From that time forth he continued in a series of attempts to take the life of this young man. What a miserable existence Saul lived, a man called of God to be used of God but wasting his time; because of his envy seeking to destroy the Lord's anointed. Oh, to what depths the sin of envy will take a man. There seems to be no question that the whining Chaldeans were envious of the three Hebrew boys.

Now the question arises, what has happened to Daniel? There is no mention of him at all in this chapter. It would seem that for some good reason he was not present at the dedication of the image. Had he been there, there would have been no doubt about it, he too would have stood with the three Hebrew boys. Probably he was in another part of the empire, occupied in important business for the state.

It was not easy for the three Hebrews to take the stand they did. It would have been much more convenient to bow to the image. They could have believed the truth in their hearts even though they gave outward respect to Nebuchadnezzar's image. They could have, that is true. But they had convictions and one cannot ignore his convictions without wounding his conscience.

In verse 18 the three Hebrews declared to the king, "We will not serve thy gods, nor worship the golden image which thou hast set up." Why not? Simply because from early childhood they had been taught the commandments as their principal foundation for life and practice. The first and second commandments must have been pre-eminent in their thinking as the command was given to worship the image: "Thou shalt have no other gods before Me. Thou shalt not make unto thee any graven image, or any likeness of any thing that is in heaven above, or that is in the earth beneath, or that is in the water under the earth" (Exodus 20:3-4). Consequently, it was a matter of either breaking the law of God or breaking the law of Nebuchadnezzar. They were not desirous of breaking Nebuchadnezzar's law, but when this involved the breaking of the law of God their convictions demanded that they stand true to their Lord.

Too many people in our day seem to have opinions but few convictions. Opinions are based upon what we think is right or wrong. Convictions rest upon the authority of the Word of God. It is "Thus saith the Lord" that should be our concern.

Though not always evidenced outwardly, even the ungodly respect Christians who remain true to their convictions. Stephen Girard, the infidel millionaire of Philadelphia, told his clerks one Saturday that they had to come the next day and unload a ship which had just arrived.

One young man stepped up to the desk and said nervously, "Mr. Girard, I cannot work on Sunday."

"Well, Sir," replied the employer, "if you cannot do as I wish, we can separate."

"I know that, Sir," said the young man, "and I know too that I have a widowed mother to care for, but I cannot work on Sunday."

"Very well," said Mr. Girard, "go to the cashier's desk and he will settle with you."

For three long weeks the young man tramped the streets looking for work. One day a bank president asked

The Reward of Righteousness 63

Girard to name a suitable person for cashier of a new bank about to be started. After reflection, Girard named the young man he had fired.

"But I thought you discharged him," said the bank president.

"I did," retorted Girard, "because he wouldn't work on Sunday. And I tell you, the man that will lose his job on account of principle is the man to whom you can trust your money."

The three Hebrew boys were possessors of an unshakable confidence and faith in the living God. Regardless of the cost, they stood true, and God honored them for it.

4. *The Coercion — verses 13-15*. The king, Nebuchadnezzar, must have been greatly surprised when he learned of the refusal of the three Hebrews to respect his law. He became extremely angry and demanded that the offenders be brought before him at once: "Then Nebuchadnezzar in his rage and fury commanded to bring Shadrach, Meshach, and Abednego. Then they brought these men before the king." It is pathetic that, though the king could rule an empire, he was not big enough to rule his own passions. The words "rage and fury" mean that he was so angry he was beyond himself. He was so infuriated by the disobedience of the three Hebrew boys that he could hardly get control of himself. Considering all he had done for them in exalting them to positions of authority, and suddenly discovering they refused to cooperate, was too much for him.

Upon seeing the three boys, the king must have had mixed emotions, for his anger seems to have subsided and once again his former generosity was evident: "Nebuchadnezzar spake and said unto them, Is it true, O Shadrach, Meshach, and Abednego, do not ye serve my gods, nor worship the golden image which I have set up?" The king's question, "Is it true?" could also mean, "Is it for this purpose?" That is, "Did you deliberately refuse to bow to the image or was it done inadvertently?"

The king realized how valuable these three men were to him, and desired to give them another chance, declaring, "Now if ye be ready that at what time ye hear the sound of the cornet, flute, harp, sackbut, psaltery, and dulcimer, and all kinds of musick, ye fall down and worship the image which I have made; well: but if ye worship not, ye shall be cast the same hour into the midst of a burning fiery furnace; and who is that God that shall deliver you out of my hands?" The king was willing to go to the trouble of repeating the entire performance to give the three Hebrew boys another chance to bow to the image.

Probably because of other officials, who were gathered in the king's court, it was necessary to state a penalty for refusal to comply. Thus the king made it clear that any resistance to respond to the present opportunity would result in immediate death by being burned alive.

How quickly man forgets. The king asked, "And who is that God that shall deliver you out of my hands?" Sixteen years before, he had been made aware of "that God." He had seen the excellency of the Lord Jehovah manifested through Daniel. In fact, Nebuchadnezzar had come to the conclusion, as he told Daniel previously, "Of a truth it is, that your God is a God of gods, and a Lord of kings, and a revealer of secrets, seeing thou couldest reveal this secret." How slow men are to believe even though God makes every evidence available that they might believe.

Recall the occasion when Moses and Aaron went before Pharaoh, giving him the message of God, saying, "Let My people go, that they may hold a feast unto Me in the wilderness" (Exodus 5:1). With his heart hardened by unbelief, Pharaoh replied, "Who is the LORD, that I should obey His voice to let Israel go? I know not the LORD, neither will I let Israel go" (Exodus 5:2). God sent the various plagues upon Pharaoh and his people that the king might come to know the Lord. But the more severe

The Reward of Righteousness

the plague and the greater the manifestations of the power of God, the harder Pharaoh's heart became.

This same kind of unbelief is still prevalent in our day. On every hand we find those who are hardening their hearts against God, refusing to submit to His lordship and power. In spite of all the evidence God has given, many refuse to believe.

One time an unbeliever said, "I will believe only what I can understand. None of that mystery stuff for me." What a ridiculous statement. Who could begin to understand or explain the thousands of ordinary mysteries we witness day by day? Consider the remarkable transformation that takes place when a caterpillar encases itself in its homemade casket and is changed into a beautiful butterfly. Its hair becomes scales, a million to the square inch. Its many legs become the six legs of a butterfly. The yellow is changed into a beautiful red, and the crawling instinct is supplanted by the flying instinct. Who can begin to explain it? Yet we must believe it.

A handful of sand is deposited by the Lord in the heart of the earth. From underneath great heat is applied; from above, ponderous weight; and lo, when it is finally discovered by man, it is a beautiful, fiery opal. God puts a handful of clay in the earth and from heat beneath and weight above it soon becomes a prized amethyst. A handful of black carbon is planted by the Almighty in the heart of the earth. Over the years as the result of the heat and weight, it becomes a sparkling diamond, fit for a king's crown. We cannot deny these transformations. They must be believed.

But consider something even greater. God takes the life of a sinner, one who for years has lived in sin, and as the result of a simple act of faith in Jesus Christ, the Son of God, the vile life is transformed into one of purity and holiness. Who can doubt the fact of a transformed life? On every hand are walking miracles of lives made new by the transforming power of Christ. Even so, some refuse to believe.

Hear the voice of the Lord before it is too late! "He, that being often reproved hardeneth his neck, shall suddenly be destroyed, and that without remedy" (Proverbs 29:1). There is no second chance after death for those who persist in unbelief. God declares that they "shall suddenly be destroyed." Hear Him as He gently pleads, "O taste and see that the LORD is good: blessed is the man that trusteth in Him" (Psalm 34:8).

5. *The Courage — verses 16-18.* Everyone must have been curious to see what response the Hebrews would give to the king's command. Having listened to the king with the threat of death hanging over them, they were ready to reply. With perfect calmness, offering not even a suggestion of being disturbed or fearful, the answer came, "O Nebuchadnezzar, we are not careful to answer thee in this matter." This was as to say, "We do not need another chance. Our minds are made up. There is no use to gather the orchestra together again, for we have clear-cut guidance as to what we should do." Then they declared, "If it be so, our God whom we serve is able to deliver us from the burning fiery furnace, and He will deliver us out of thine hand, O king."

The three young men had faithfully served King Nebuchadnezzar during their days of captivity, but they had never ceased to honor their God. Though respecting the king, never did the boys compromise in their fidelity to their Lord. What Christ taught many years later was practiced by the three Hebrews, "Render therefore unto Caesar the things which are Caesar's; and unto God the things that are God's" (Matthew 22:21). Over the years of their loyal and conscientious service to the Lord, they had learned to trust Him for His unfailing providence. They knew the reward of putting Him first in everything. Furthermore, they realized that their present calamity was no exception. Thus, with reliant boldness they cried

The Reward of Righteousness 67

out, "If it be so, our God whom we serve is able to deliver us from the burning fiery furnace, and He will deliver us out of thine hand, O king." There is no utterance made by any mortal in all the Bible more sublime than this.

Are you able to say at all times, "My God whom I serve is able to deliver me"? Do you possess this same unshakable reliance in the authority and power of God? Can you say as did the three Hebrews, "He *will* deliver me"? You may be in the midst of the severest trial of your life; but never forget, the God who allowed this trial promises to deliver you. The purpose of this experience is to display the mighty power of God. He will teach you lessons you will never forget and upon which you will reflect for many years to come for strength and encouragement to face ensuing trials. But you must believe God, and be able to say from the depths of your heart, "My God whom I serve is able to deliver me."

In their reply Shadrach, Meshach, and Abednego gave another side to the story as they said,"But if not, be it known unto thee, O king, that we will not serve thy gods, nor worship the golden image which thou hast set up." They knew their God was able to deliver them. They had faith to believe that He would undertake. But if God had other plans, should He choose not to provide deliverance, this would not in any way affect their refusal to give homage to the Babylonian gods or Nebuchadnezzar's image. They would continue to put the Lord Jehovah first in their lives and experience whatever the cost.

It should be kept in mind that though God is able to deliver, He may, for reasons known only to Himself, choose not to do so. This should never in any way change our attitude toward Him. God is good whether or not He heals our bodies. He is good even though He may not provide us with desired funds. He is good whether He answers our prayers today or a year from now. God never makes any mistakes and His plans and purposes are always perfect. If He prefers not to deliver us, we must keep pressing on. With unflinching courage, we must walk in the light as He is in the light, abstaining not only from evil but even from the appearance of it, that the Lord will have the pre-eminence in everything. Like Job we should be able to declare, "Though He slay me, yet will I trust in Him" (Job 13:15). Our walk with the Lord should not be jeopardized by circumstances that surround us.

God tells us in Hebrews 12:11, "no chastening for the present seemeth to be joyous, but grievous: nevertheless afterward it yieldeth the peaceable fruit of righteousness unto them which are exercised thereby." Do not waste your sorrow by letting the precious gifts of disappointment and anxiety *mar* you instead of *mend* you. Let them draw you nearer to God rather than turn you away from Him, for there is no greater failure in life than to receive the pain without the lesson and the sorrow without the softening.

Shadrach, Meshach, and Abednego knew this. Thus with three great facts in mind they answered the king. First, my God "is able to deliver me." Secondly, my God "will deliver me." Thirdly, "But, if not," if He chooses not to deliver me, it is because of His better choice and I will trust Him anyway.

6. *The Condemnation — verses 19-27.* "Then was Nebuchadnezzar full of fury, and the form of his visage was changed against Shadrach, Meshach, and Abednego: therefore he spake, and commanded that they should heat the furnace one seven times more than it was wont to be heated." The king's position of leniency in offering the three young men another chance changed into one of bitter hatred, demanding immediate judgment. Nebuchadnezzar was "full of fury." Thus with uncontrollable anger, the king demanded that the furnace be heated as hot as possible, hotter than it had ever been before. Further, "he commanded the most mighty men

that were in his army to bind Shadrach, Meshach, and Abednego, and to cast them into the burning fiery furnace."

In response to the order given by the king, the "men were bound in their coats, their hosen, and their hats, and their other garments, and were cast into the midst of the burning fiery furnace." No time was lost. The three Hebrews were taken as they were, bound, and thrust into the furnace of fire. We shudder to think of the torture of being cast into a fire that was so hot that it "slew those men" who thrust the Hebrews into the furnace.

The Lord Jesus Christ spoke of another "furnace of fire" in which "there shall be wailing and gnashing of teeth" (Matthew 13:42). This will be the eternal doom of all condemned sinners. It is described by the Apostle Paul as a "flaming fire taking vengeance on them that know not God, and that obey not the gospel of our Lord Jesus Christ: Who shall be punished with everlasting destruction from the presence of the Lord, and from the glory of His power" (2 Thessalonians 1:8-9). This will be far worse than Nebuchadnezzar's furnace of fire. Apart from a miracle of God, the three Hebrews would have been consumed in a matter of seconds and their pain would have been ended. But of those who inhabit hell, God says in Revelation 14:10-11: "The same shall drink of the wine of the wrath of God, which is poured out without mixture into the cup of His indignation; and he shall be tormented with fire and brimstone in the presence of the holy angels, and in the presence of the Lamb: And the smoke of their torment ascendeth up for ever and ever: and they have no rest day nor night, who worship the beast and his image, and whosoever receiveth the mark of his name."

How foolish of anyone to fail to consider eternity. For millions, hell may be closer than they think. God longs for all men to come to Him and be saved. We read in 1 Timothy 2:3-4: "For this is good and acceptable in the sight of God our Saviour; Who will have all men to be saved, and to come unto the knowledge of the truth." No one will ever go to hell because God wanted him there. He will go because he did not receive the Lord Jesus into his heart.

The "three men, Shadrach, Meshach, and Abednego, fell down bound into the midst of the burning fiery furnace." The Scripture says they "fell down." Could it be that they "fell down" on their faces before God in humble supplication, praying that He might preserve them in the midst of their calamity? These faithful saints knew the power of prayer, and even though King Nebuchadnezzar refused to give them any consideration, the King of kings heard them and sustained them.

After the heat of the furnace had subsided to some degree, the anxious king hastened to see what had happened. "Then Nebuchadnezzar the king was astonied, and rose up in haste, and spake, and said unto his counsellors, Did not we cast three men bound into the midst of the fire? They answered and said unto the king, True, O king. He answered and said, Lo, I see four men loose, walking in the midst of the fire, and they have no hurt; and the form of the fourth is like the Son of God." This was not a vision such as the great image he had seen in a dream. What he saw was real. There were not only three men, but four, and the fourth, he declared was "like the Son of God."

Nebuchadnezzar's experience was unusual for him, but not for those who love the Lord. The Son of God always enters the fire with His people. The Lord Jesus has been in many furnaces with believers down through the ages; He will be in many more as well. "I will never leave thee, nor forsake thee," He promises (Hebrews 13:5). It makes no difference how hot the furnace may be or how severe the test, Christ will be there with His own.

"Then Nebuchadnezzar came near to the mouth of the

The Reward of Righteousness

burning fiery furnace, and spake, and said, Shadrach, Meshach, and Abednego, ye servants of the most high God, come forth, and come hither. Then Shadrach, Meshach, and Abednego, came forth of the the midst of the fire. And the princes, governors, and captains, and the king's counsellors, being gathered together, saw these men, upon whose bodies the fire had no power, nor was an hair of their head singed, neither were their coats changed, nor the smell of fire had passed on them." Once again our great God proved Himself to be superior to a proud, selfish king. At the same time, the holy faith of the three obedient Hebrews was rewarded by a mighty miracle of God. Notice God's preservation of His own: "Nor was an hair of their head singed, neither were their coats changed, nor the smell of fire had passed on them." Indeed, the promise of God is true as we find it in Isaiah 43:2, "When thou walkest through the fire, thou shalt not be burned; neither shall the flame kindle upon thee."

Here were three young men who trusted the Lord. They believed the promises of God. How unlike many of us who when, thrust into the fiery trials of life, forget all about the promises of our unchanging Lord. May God grant that we shall believe Him without any shadow of turning and trust Him implicitly for all things.

7. *The Confession — verses 28-30.* A mighty miracle of God preserved the three Hebrew boys in the midst of the fiery furnace. The curious audience which examined the three men after they emerged from the fire stood speechless. Finally Nebuchadnezzar broke the silence: "Blessed be the God of Shadrach, Meshach, and Abednego, who hath sent His angel, and delivered His servants that trusted in Him, and have changed the king's word, and yielded their bodies, that they might not serve nor worship any god, except their own God." What a profound statement coming from the lips of this pagan king. After what he had witnessed, Nebuchadnezzar had

only praise for the Lord Jehovah and admiration for the three young Hebrews.

What is recorded here provides a splendid example of how God can change one's heart. Previous to the furnace experience, Nebuchadnezzar had little or no respect for Jehovah, having been a worshiper of his heathen gods. Now he blesses the God of Shadrach, Meshach, and Abednego. This should be a reminder to all of us that, though one's heart may be hardened against the truth, it is not too hard for God. Some of us have unsaved friends and even dearest loved ones who have not met the Lord. At times we get discouraged because we see very little evidence of any interest in spiritual things. Do not let the wicked one deceive you into thinking, even for an instant, that there is any such thing as an impossible case. God the Holy Spirit will work in His own time. Our responsibility is to be faithful and diligent in prayer, interceding for the salvation of the lost. Furthermore, it is mandatory that we manifest Christ to them by permitting Him to have full control of our lives.

It seems obvious that Nebuchadnezzar had a change of heart not only because of the miracle he witnessed. Doubtless the piety of the three young men had already spoken to his heart. He must have realized for some time that there was something different in the lives of these boys who faithfully followed the Lord Jehovah; even in the face of death they possessed perfect calmness and serenity of mind. This seems to have impressed Nebuchadnezzar for, in praising the Lord Jehovah, Nebuchadnezzar said of the three young men that they "trusted in Him . . . and yielded their bodies, that they might not serve nor worship any god, except their own God." The word "yielded" here embraces the thought of presenting oneself voluntarily without any restraint. This they did because they so firmly trusted in the power of God. What a testimony they were to the king. For years,

The Reward of Righteousness

even before their Babylonian bondage, these boys had lived consistently for the Lord, but their present witness in the midst of severe affliction seemed to be the capstone.

Not only did Nebuchadnezzar bless the Lord Jehovah, he made a decree prohibiting any contentious talk about the God of the three Hebrews: "Therefore I make a decree, That every people, nation, and language, which speak any thing amiss against the God of Shadrach, Meshach, and Abednego, shall be cut in pieces, and their houses shall be made a dunghill: because there is no other God that can deliver after this sort." Bel was the chief god of the Babylonians. There were many loyal worshipers of this god who spoke disparagingly of the Hebrew God. Nebuchadnezzar made it clear that this should never happen again, as the guilty one would be in danger of immediate death. "Because," said Nebuchadnezzar, "there is no other God that can deliver after this sort." He recognized that the gods of the Babylonian Empire, including Bel, were all inferior to the Lord Jehovah.

But not only did the king give due deference and respect to the Lord, he gave special honor to the three young men: "Then the king promoted Shadrach, Meshach, and Abednego, in the province of Babylon." "When a man's ways please the LORD, He maketh even his enemies to be at peace with him" (Proverbs 16:7). How many Christians go to the opposite extreme and while seeking to be men-pleasers they become enemies of the Lord. The Apostle James says of them, "Whosoever therefore will be a friend of the world is the enemy of God" (James 4:4). God says in Titus 2:11-13: "For the grace of God that bringeth salvation hath appeared to all men, Teaching us that, denying ungodliness and worldly lusts, we should live soberly, righteously, and godly, in this present world; Looking for that blessed hope, and the glorious appearing of the great God and our Saviour Jesus Christ."

A teen-age girl was joyously converted. She was filled with love for her Lord and desired to please Him in all that she did.

"I want to be the best kind of a witness for my Lord, but I don't know where to draw the line," she said to her pastor. "There are certain kinds of worldly pleasures that other Christian young people seem to think are all right. I don't want to go any place where I cannot take my Lord."

The pastor replied sympathetically, "Elizabeth, Christ is now your companion. Will your going to questionable places strengthen your daily walk with Him? Can you invite Him to accompany you and take part in these things?"

"Thank you, Pastor," said Elizabeth, "when I am in doubt about anything, I will give Jesus the benefit of the doubt and seek to please Him in all I do."

If we are Christ's, and desire to please Him, we shall not spend our time doing things that do not honor and magnify His name. Ours is a serious responsibility. If we are cross bearers, then we must exemplify Him who died and rose again for us.

Chapter 4

THE REBUKE OF RATIONALITY

Key verse, 33: "The same hour was the thing fulfilled upon Nebuchadnezzar: and he was driven from men, and did eat grass as oxen, and his body was wet with the dew of heaven, till his hairs were grown like eagles' feathers, and his nails like birds' claws."

The Lord dealt with Nebuchadnezzar in mercy but the proud king refused to respond. Thus it became necessary for God to act harshly that the erring monarch might be brought face to face with the greatest issue of life — his own personal salvation. Like many in our day, Nebuchadnezzar sought to rationalize the supernatural, but suffering divine judgment he realized the hopelessness of such action and forsook his rationalism to embrace the revelation of God.

1. *The Impenitence — verses 1-3.* God had spoken to Nebuchadnezzar in several ways, first by the dream vision and then by the remarkable appearance of the Son of God in the fiery furnace. But Nebuchadnezzar's heart was hard and rebellious. He refused to submit to the rulership of God. As an alternative, he blessed God and demanded that no one in his empire should speak against Him. Though this was worth while, it was not conversion.

Now we see the king going further. He issued a proclamation: "Nebuchadnezzar the king, unto all people, nations, and languages, that dwell in all the earth; Peace be multiplied unto you. I thought it good to shew the signs and wonders that the high God hath wrought toward me. How great are His signs! and how mighty are His wonders! His kingdom is an everlasting kingdom, and His dominion is from generation to generation." This statement suggests that there might be some hope, yet it is nothing other than more nice talk about God. Though Nebuchadnezzar was willing to confess to his own people, as well as to all the nations of the world, that God is great and good, mighty in power, and unsurpassed in wisdom, he was unwilling to claim the Lord as his own. For approximately forty-three years Nebuchadnezzar had been in authority; God had spoken but his pride prevented him from submitting to the Lord's control.

How many like Nebuchadnezzar have been shut out from the glories of Heaven because of pride. No truer statement has been made than Proverbs 29:23, "A man's pride shall bring him low." Pride bars the gate to Heaven and closes the door to salvation. But God has His own way of humbling the proud heart. He says in Jeremiah 49:16, "Thy terribleness hath deceived thee, and the pride of thine heart, O thou that dwellest in the clefts of the rock, that holdest the height of the hill: though thou shouldest make thy nest as high as the eagle, I will bring thee down from thence, saith the LORD." It is impossible for one's pride to take him high enough to escape the judgment of God. This fact is portrayed vividly as the Lord deals with the pride of Nebuchadnezzar.

God pleads in mercy for the unrepentant sinner to turn to Him and be saved; but if rebellion persists, it is impossible to escape the judgment of God. One may have "a form of godliness" (2 Timothy 3:5) like Nebuchadnezzar, whose high-sounding platitudes suggested love for God. Those who observe may be deceived into thinking that such is an evidence of conversion, but "The LORD seeth not as man seeth; for man looketh on the outward appearance, but the LORD

The Rebuke of Rationality 77

looketh on the heart" (1 Samuel 16:7). The Lord Jesus declared in Luke 13:3, "Except ye repent, ye shall all likewise perish."

Some years ago a murderer was sentenced to die for his crime. His brother, to whom the state was deeply indebted for former services, besought the governor for his brother's pardon. The pardon was granted and the brother visited the criminal with the pardon in his pocket.

"What would you do," he asked the murderer, "if you received a pardon?"

"The first thing I would do," he replied, "would be to track down the judge who sentenced me and murder him, and the next thing, I would track down the chief witness and murder him."

His brother rose quietly and left the prison with the pardon in his pocket. Here was a man who might have been liberated to enjoy freedom once again, but he condemned himself.

In the spiritual realm there are millions like him in our present day. God has been gracious to them. Repeatedly He has pled with them, "Come unto Me, all ye that labour and are heavy laden, and I will give you rest" (Matthew 11:28). Rather than turn to the Lord, they continue on in their daily pursuits, ignoring the claims of the eternal God. Failing to repent, they live on in sin without experiencing the joy of conversion.

2. *The Incompetence — verses 4-7.* Nebuchadnezzar had enjoyed remarkable success in his wars with other nations. Syria, Phoenicia, Judea, Egypt, and Arabia had been defeated by the powerful Babylonian monarch. With all of his enemies subdued, Nebuchadnezzar relaxed to revel in the glories of his success: "I Nebuchadnezzar was at rest in mine house, and flourishing in my palace." Suddenly, the quiet rest was interrupted. Another enemy arose to disturb the king which seemed to distress him

more than the countries he had conquered. "I saw a dream which made me afraid, and the thoughts upon my bed and the visions of my head troubled me." This enemy came not from outside but from within.

How descriptive this is of the man in the world without God — "at rest" and "flourishing" but "troubled." He trusts in the false security of his riches but inwardly there is an unceasing fear of death and the future. Isaiah described this pathetic condition clearly: "But the wicked are like the troubled sea, when it cannot rest, whose waters cast up mire and dirt. There is no peace, saith my God, to the wicked" (Isaiah 57:20-21).

Apart from the Lord there can be no real "rest." Nebuchadnezzar merely thought he was "at rest." Extremely frightened by the dream, once again he ordered the wise men of his court to appear before him to provide help. "Therefore made I a decree to bring in all the wise men of Babylon before me, that they might make known unto me the interpretation of the dream." Unlike his previous dream, Nebuchadnezzar was able to recall this one. Yet this seemed to be of no greater value to the wise men than on the previous occasion when he could not recall it. "Then came in the magicians, the astrologers, the Chaldeans, and the soothsayers: and I told the dream before them; but they did not make known unto me the interpretation thereof." Over a period of years these deceivers had not improved in their deceptive art. They were still as incompetent as ever.

As we shall see, Daniel had no difficulty providing an adequate interpretation of the dream, even though he made no profession of being a diviner or a "wise man" such as those who were hired for this purpose in the king's court. What was the difference between Daniel and the magicians, the astrologers, the Chaldeans, and the soothsayers? Just this — Daniel was a man of God. He was

The Rebuke of Rationality

in a right relationship with the Lord, filled with the Spirit, able to determine God's plan and will through prayer.

This portion of Scripture suggests vividly the ceaseless conflict between the flesh and the Spirit. Paul declared in Romans 8:8, "They that are in the flesh cannot please God." Until one has been born again by the Spirit, he is in the flesh, living in a state of rebellion against God. On the other hand, even after some trust in Christ for salvation, they continue to cater to the flesh rather than permit the Holy Spirit to control them.

The late Bishop Ryle was heard to say, "The place given to the Holy Ghost in the most decided Christians is altogether out of proportion to that which it occupies in the Word of God." One of the greatest needs among believers is to be filled with the Spirit. We have attractive church buildings, the best of equipment, well-trained choirs, and great preachers. But of what value is all of this without the power of the Holy Spirit?

The Lord Jesus made this fact clear to His disciples following His resurrection. Calling them together He said, "Go ye into all the world, and preach the gospel to every creature" (Mark 16:15). But He told them something else also. He knew it would be useless for them to start on a journey to preach the gospel without the necessary power. For this reason He instructed them: "Tarry ye in the city of Jerusalem, until ye be endued with power from on high" (Luke 24:49). They obeyed their Master and on the day of Pentecost the power came.

How many of us are trying to serve the Lord Jesus without claiming the power from on high. Small wonder that so little is being accomplished. Jesus declared, "Ye shall receive power, after that the Holy Ghost is come upon you: and ye shall be witnesses unto Me" (Acts 1:8). God used Daniel because he was Spirit-controlled. What about you? Is your life governed by the flesh or the Holy

Spirit? God commands every true believer to "be filled with the Spirit" (Ephesians 5:18). Oh, child of God, receive of the Spirit's fullness, that your efforts for the Lord might be blessed by Him. At the same time, your own heart will overflow with joy. You will recognize service for Christ to be not a burden, but a happy privilege.

Recall how Paul and Barnabas were ill treated after their faithful preaching of the gospel at Antioch. They were persecuted and expelled from the city. Immediately after this they "were filled with joy, and with the Holy Ghost" (Acts 13:52). Though suffering physically and having been treated unkindly, their hearts overflowed with joy because they were filled with the Spirit.

3. *The Image — verses 8-18*. Doubtless the king was disturbed greatly by the incompetence of the wise men to interpret his dream, but recalling a similar situation which had taken place some years before, he was confident that Daniel could help. Thus, whether he was sent for or simply appeared in the providence of God, Daniel entered the scene again: "But at the last Daniel came in before me, whose name was Belteshazzar, according to the name of my god, and in whom is the spirit of the holy gods: and before him I told the dream, saying, O Belteshazzar, master of the magicians, because I know that the spirit of the holy gods is in thee, and no secret troubleth thee, tell me the visions of my dream that I have seen, and the interpretation thereof." From what Nebuchadnezzar had to say here it is obvious that over the years he made no spiritual progress. Bel was the chief god of Babylon and it was this god Nebuchadnezzar revered and honored. In fact, he thought he was placing worthy distinction on Daniel when he named him Belteshazzar after the pagan deity Bel.

Though remaining faithful to his pagan god, Nebuchadnezzar did recognize a difference between Bel

The Rebuke of Rationality

and the Hebrew God, for he declared to Daniel, "I know that the spirit of the holy gods is in thee." Here is a notable concession. The king was unaware of the plurality of Jehovah, though he had spoken of the "holy *gods*." He did believe however, that Jehovah was "holy." Rarely were the heathen gods recognized as holy even by their most fanatical adherents. Nebuchadnezzar must have concluded that one as consecrated and saintly as Daniel was that way because of his God.

There is an important lesson here for every follower of the Lord Jesus Christ. Our God is a holy God. It is this same God, however, who declared in Leviticus 19:2, "Ye shall be holy: for I the LORD your God am holy." Daniel respected this fact. It is obvious that not all Christians acknowledge this important truth because their lives do not reflect the holiness of God. Before one comes to Christ, he has no possibility of attaining holiness; but after he receives the Lord Jesus into his life, he is enabled by the indwelling Christ to be holy. In fact, he is duty bound to honor the Lord through a life of holiness (1 Thessalonians 4:7), "God hath not called us unto uncleanness, but unto holiness."

A missionary had a little Hindu orphan living with her. She had taught him much about Christ, and one night when he was six years old she asked him to pray. This was his prayer: "Dear Jesus, make me like what you were when you were six years old." How essential that all of us pray in a similar manner. We need to ask God to make us like Christ, that we shall exemplify His holiness. In so many cases, there seems to be a greater resemblance to the world in which we live than to our Saviour to whom we belong. "Enoch walked with God" (Genesis 5:24). It is difficult to distinguish with whom many of God's people are walking, there is so little evidence of holiness.

Stanley found Livingstone in the heart of Africa and stayed with him for six months. Stanley was a professed skeptic when he went to find Livingstone — he came away a Christian. Asked what Livingstone said that converted him, Stanley replied that it was what Livingstone *was* that brought him to Christ. Livingstone, according to Stanley's report, never asked Stanley if he were a Christian and never preached to him nor seemed to pray for his conversion. But Livingstone was so thoroughly a Christian that it dawned upon Stanley that one who was not a Christian was something less than a Christian. Livingstone was a man of God who permitted the Lord to live through him. Consequently his was a life of victory and blessing. Daniel must have been this same type of man. Nebuchadnezzar realized this. Thus, he spoke of Daniel's God in a manner in which he did not speak of his own pagan deities.

The king described his dream to Daniel: "Thus were the visions of mine head in my bed; I saw, and behold a tree in the midst of the earth, and the height thereof was great. The tree grew, and was strong, and the height thereof reached unto heaven, and the sight thereof to the end of all the earth: The leaves thereof were fair, and the fruit thereof much, and in it was meat for all: the beasts of the field had shadow under it, and the fowls of the heaven dwelt in the boughs thereof, and all flesh was fed of it." Here was a vast flourishing tree planted in the midst of the earth.

It did not flourish for long, for as Nebuchadnezzar said, "I saw in the visions of my head upon my bed, and, behold, a watcher and an holy one came down from heaven; He cried aloud, and said thus, Hew down the tree, and cut off his branches, shake off his leaves, and scatter his fruit: let the beasts get away from under it, and the fowls from his branches: Nevertheless leave the stump of his roots in the earth, even with a band of iron and brass, in the tender grass of the field; and let it be wet with the dew of heaven, and let his portion be with the beasts in the

The Rebuke of Rationality

grass of the earth: Let his heart be changed from man's, and let a beast's heart be given unto him; and let seven times pass over him. This matter is by the decree of the watchers, and the demand by the word of the holy ones: to the intent that the living may know that the most High ruleth in the kingdom of men, and giveth it to whomsoever He will, and setteth up over it the basest of men." It must have been the latter part of this dream that disturbed Nebuchadnezzar the most, for in verses 14 through 16 the prophecy personalizes the tree: "His branches . . . his leaves . . . his fruit . . . his roots . . . his portion . . . his heart."

There seems also to be an important lesson involved in the dream, "that the living may know that the most High ruleth in the kingdom of men, and giveth it to whomsoever He will, and setteth up over it the basest of men." Nebuchadnezzar could not escape the personal application here, for he realized that time and time again God had been dealing with him. But ignoring the Lord's appeals, he centered his interest in ruling his kingdom. Surely he could not escape this clear and pointed application.

Desperate, Nebuchadnezzar pled with Daniel for help: "This dream I king Nebuchadnezzar have seen. Now thou, O Belteshazzar, declare the interpretation thereof, forasmuch as all the wise men of my kingdom are not able to make known unto me the interpretation: but thou art able; for the spirit of the holy gods is in thee." Here was a fearless and courageous king who at the time was the most powerful monarch in the world. He had terrified others, but now he was a terror unto himself, all because of a dream. Indeed it is true, "Pride goeth before destruction, and an haughty spirit before a fall" (Proverbs 16:18). Nebuchadnezzar had gloried in his conquests and achievements, but suddenly he was made aware of the fact that there was One far greater than he. This is a fact every human needs to realize: there is One greater than all of us. How important that we respect Him, giving Him the honor He deserves.

4. *The Interpretation — verses 19-26.* God gave Daniel understanding as to the meaning of the dream, but it was not a simple matter for God's servant to reveal the interpretation to the king. "Then Daniel, whose name was Belteshazzar, was astonied for one hour, and his thoughts troubled him." As the meaning of the dream was unfolded to Daniel's mind, he was greatly disturbed. There were several things that bothered him. One was, how would the king react when he heard that the dream was a prophecy of judgment upon him? Oftentimes tyrants punished their prophets severely for such messages foretelling chastisement or doom. Further, Daniel was saddened because of his heart concern for Nebuchadnezzar's spiritual need. Daniel had spent many years in the empire and had worked closely with the king. No one recognized the king's spiritual need more than Daniel. Doubtless God's servant spent many hours on his knees interceding for this selfish and arrogant monarch. Daniel must have realized the truth of Psalm 49:8, "The redemption of their soul is precious."

God's people need the same holy concern for souls in our day that Daniel had. We read in Psalm 126:6, "He that goeth forth and weepeth, bearing precious seed, shall doubtless come again with rejoicing, bringing his sheaves with him." How few believers in these days are really going forth as God's witnesses to sow the precious seed of life. Even worse, how few of those who are going forth have a sincere heart burden for souls, evoking holy tears that the lost might come to Christ. Oh, that God would come upon us afresh with an unresting compulsion that would move us to grasp the scores of opportunities He gives to point lost souls to Jesus Christ.

The Rebuke of Rationality

Years ago in London there was a large gathering of noted people. Among the invited guests was a famous preacher of his day, Caesar Malan. A young lady played and sang charmingly and everyone was thrilled. Very graciously, tactfully, and yet boldly, the preacher went up to her after the music had ceased.

"I thought as I listened to you tonight how tremendously the cause of Christ would be benefited if your talents were dedicated to His cause," he said. "You know, young lady, you are a sinner in the sight of God, but I am glad to tell you that the blood of Jesus Christ His Son can cleanse you from all sin."

The young lady snapped out a rebuke for his presumption.

"Lady, I mean no offense. I pray God's Spirit will convict you."

They all returned to their homes. The young woman retired but could not sleep. The face of the preacher appeared before her and his words rang through her mind. At two o'clock in the morning she sprang from her bed, took a pencil and paper, and with tears dripping from her face, Charlotte Elliott wrote:

> Just as I am, without one plea,
> But that Thy blood was shed for me,
> And that Thou bidd'st me come to Thee,
> O Lamb of God, I come.

Charlotte Elliott came to Jesus Christ and was wondrously saved because Caesar Malan had a burden and a love for souls. This love comes from Heaven above. "The love of God is shed abroad in our hearts by the Holy Ghost" (Romans 5:5).

The king sensed trouble ahead. He recognized Daniel's anxiety, which could not be hid. But in spite of this, he said, "Belteshazzar, let not the dream, or the interpretation thereof, trouble thee." Nebuchadnezzar was suggesting that he was willing to listen and that no harm would come to Daniel. Thus courageously God's servant lifted his shoulders, and looking the king in the eye said, "My lord, the dream be to them that hate thee, and the interpretation to thine enemies. The tree that thou sawest, which grew, and was strong, whose height reached unto the heaven, and the sight thereof to all the earth; Whose leaves were fair, and the fruit thereof much, and in it was meat for all; under which the beasts of the field dwelt, and upon whose branches the fowls of the heaven had their habitation: It is thou, O king, that art grown and become strong: for thy greatness is grown, and reacheth unto heaven, and thy dominion to the end of the earth." This much of the interpretation must have sounded extremely satisfying to the king, for it catered to his pride as he realized that the huge tree reaching into heaven and as far out as the corners of the earth, covered with leaves and laden with fruit, represented him.

But the king was not at ease for long. The prophet continued with the interpretation, telling of the "watcher and an holy one coming down from heaven" to cut down the tree while leaving the stump in the earth. Daniel declared further that "they shall drive thee from men, and thy dwelling shall be with the beasts of the field, and they shall make thee to eat grass as oxen, and they shall wet thee with the dew of heaven, and seven times shall pass over thee, till thou know that the most High ruleth in the kingdom of men, and giveth it to whomsoever He will. And whereas they commanded to leave the stump of the tree roots; thy kingdom shall be sure unto thee, after that thou shalt have known that the heavens do rule."

Nebuchadnezzar was to be humiliated. He was to lose his rationality and become as a beast of the field, crawling about, eating grass. The stump in the ground was a

The Rebuke of Rationality 87

promise that he would not die, nor would he lose his empire immediately. But all of this was to bring him to a personal experience with the Lord. Nebuchadnezzar had received knowledge of the way of salvation from the Hebrews, but he failed to submit, thus he had to come the hard way. Being a very proud man, he looked within rather than upward, trusting his own rationality rather than the revelation of God.

In spite of the fact that in His mercy God gave another startling revelation, Nebuchadnezzar refused still to bow to the Lord. How hard is the impenitent heart of man. There are many like Nebuchadnezzar. In spite of the mercy of God being showered upon them day by day, they have turned their faces from Him. Oh, if only they could see, which they soon will see if they fail to repent, that "the wages of sin is death" (Rómans 6:23).

5. *The Importunity – verse 27.* Daniel's burden and concern for the spiritual welfare of Nebuchadnezzar was further evidenced as he pled, "Wherefore, O king, let my counsel be acceptable unto thee, and break off thy sins by righteousness, and thine iniquities by shewing mercy to the poor; if it may be a lengthening of thy tranquillity." If Daniel's "counsel" were to "be acceptable" unto the king, it would be necessary for Nebuchadnezzar to act immediately. Daniel stated two things that were imperative. First, the king must break with sin that he might enter into a favorable relationship with the Lord Jehovah. Secondly, he was to show mercy to the poor, revealing the love of God to men. In Daniel's appeal we are reminded of the words of the Lord Jesus as found in Matthew 22:37-39: "Thou shalt love the Lord thy God with all thy heart, and with all thy soul, and with all thy mind. This is the first and great commandment. And the second is like unto it, Thou shalt love thy neighbour as thyself." Christ stressed the importance of a right relationship to God and to men. Daniel did the same.

Anyone desirous of the Lord's best in life must give due consideration to the two essentials described by Daniel and later by the Lord Jesus. No one can have a satisfactory relationship with his neighbor until his heart is right with God. For this reason Daniel urged the king to forsake his sins; though there may be pleasure in sin, there is no peace. If one is to know God's peace and tranquility, there must be a turning from sin unto Him. Isaiah declared, "Let the wicked forsake his way, and the unrighteous man his thoughts: and let him return unto the LORD, and He will have mercy upon him; and to our God, for He will abundantly pardon" (Isaiah 55:7).

Perhaps someone will argue that to be saved it is not enough to turn away from sin, that Daniel should have been more explicit in his appeal to the king. Surely we can agree that Daniel had witnessed to the king repeatedly over the years. The way of truth was not unknown to Nebuchadnezzar, but he refused to forsake his sins, chief of which was his pride. Thus Daniel exclaimed with great anguish of soul, "O king, let my counsel be acceptable unto thee. [Hear me before it is too late. Continue in your sin no longer.]"

It was not knowledge of the Lord that Nebuchadnezzar needed, but action. He had knowledge but he needed to repent and believe. Like Nebuchadnezzar there are many precious souls who have heard the gospel and know the gospel, but they have procrastinated. As Felix of old, they have said, "Go thy way for this time; when I have a convenient season, I will call for thee" (Acts 24:25). For many that "convenient season" will never come, for as they grow older the heart becomes harder.

Living near a church I served in the midwest was an elderly gentleman and his wife. For many years the wife had been a zealous saint of God, but her husband was a professed atheist. I called at that home repeatedly and

The Rebuke of Rationality 89

sought to point this man to Christ, but it seemed as if each visit became more difficult because with the passing months and years his heart became harder and harder. One day, his wife took sick and, after several weeks, died. I am sure the angels rejoiced when this saint of God entered Heaven. Being quite elderly, the husband needed a housekeeper. One of the ladies of the church went to work for him. Shortly after, she felt constrained to speak to him about the Lord.

"You had a wonderful Christian wife," she said, prayerfully. "Now she is in Heaven. Don't you want to meet her there some day?"

Angrily and bitterly he cursed his housekeeper and shouted, "Get away with that foolishness." It was not knowledge of the Lord this man needed, it was the Lord Himself.

God declares in Isaiah 1:18, "Come *now*, and let us reason together, saith the LORD: though your sins be as scarlet, they shall be as white as snow; though they be red like crimson, they shall be as wool." God longs that all men turn to Him and believe. Many desire to wait, but waiting can be very dangerous.

One time, while speaking at the Gull Lake Bible Conference, I preached on the theme of God's wonderful peace. After the service a young lady came to me. "I know what that peace is that you spoke about tonight," she said. "For years, I have been praying for my husband that he might come to Christ. Several weeks ago he was stricken suddenly and died. But I have perfect peace in my heart, for God heard my prayers, and five nights before he died he went to church with me and received Jesus Christ into his heart." Though the tears of sorrow were in this girl's eyes, the joy and peace of the Lord radiated from her face. Her husband waited long, almost too long, but praise God, he responded to the Lord's call and was saved in the nick of time.

No one knows how soon death will strike. It is far better to come to the Lord now, for the Word of God says, "So teach us to number our days, that we may apply our hearts unto wisdom" (Psalm 90:12). If only Nebuchadnezzar had heeded the words of Daniel, he could have been saved from his misery and sorrow.

6. *The Irrationality — verses 28-33.* Did Nebuchadnezzar heed the sound, scriptural advice given by Daniel? It is quite obvious that he did not, for we read, "All this came upon the king Nebuchadnezzar." Then in vivid detail we are told of the fulfillment of the dream. Here is another conclusive evidence that all God has prophesied in His Word will come to pass in God's own time.

Once more we are reminded of the hardness of Nebuchadnezzar's heart: "At the end of twelve months he walked in the palace of the kingdom of Babylon." During all this time, there was no sign of repentance or turning to God. Indeed, "It is of the LORD's mercies that we are not consumed, because His compassions fail not" (Lamentations 3:22). Nebuchadnezzar's pride developed to even greater proportions. We can almost visualize him walking about the palace roof overlooking the great city and saying to himself, "Is not this great Babylon, that I have built for the house of the kingdom by the might of my power, and for the honour of my majesty?"

There was no question about it, Babylon was a great city. It was great in size, in magnificence, and in wealth. But there were many others who had a part in building it. Nebuchadnezzar had no right to claim all the glory.

As Nebuchadnezzar walked about in the height of his glory, he was confronted with a severe tragedy. "While the word was in the king's mouth, there fell a voice from heaven, saying, O king Nebuchadnezzar, to thee it is spoken; The kingdom is departed from thee. And they

The Rebuke of Rationality

shall drive thee from men, and thy dwelling shall be with the beasts of the field: they shall make thee to eat grass as oxen, and seven times shall pass over thee, until thou know that the most High ruleth in the kingdom of men, and giveth it to whomsoever He will." What a shock this must have been to one who by a word had thrust his armies at the sternest foe. Now he was completely helpless. The great builder of Babylon was to become a lowly beast. There was no further grant of time. The king had resisted God and judgment was imminent.

"The same hour was the thing fulfilled upon Nebuchadnezzar: and he was driven from men, and did eat grass as oxen, and his body was wet with the dew of heaven, till his hairs were grown like eagles' feathers, and his nails like birds' claws." In oriental countries, the insane were left to wander about at will. No one interfered with them for fear that they might frighten them. Thus for "seven times," that is, seven years, Nebuchadnezzar went about as a beast, eating grass as oxen. "It is a fearful thing to fall into the hands of the living God" (Hebrews 10:31). Man was created in the likeness and image of God. He was never intended to be an animal. But when man leaves God out of his life, he becomes beastlike, living to satisfy the proud demands of the flesh.

How striking is the resemblance between Nebuchadnezzar and the rich farmer of the New Testament, who "thought within himself, saying, What shall I do, because I have no room where to bestow my fruits? And he said, This will I do: I will pull down my barns, and build greater; and there will I bestow all my fruits and my goods. And I will say to my soul, Soul, thou hast much goods laid up for many years; take thine ease, eat, drink, and be merry. But God said unto him, Thou fool, this night thy soul shall be required of thee: then whose shall those things be, which thou hast provided? So is he that layeth up treasure for himself, and is not rich toward God" (Luke 12:17-21). There are many like Nebuchadnezzar and this rich man who glory in things but ignore the greatest essential of life, their own personal salvation. To them, prominence, achievement, and wealth seem to constitute living at its best. Thousands upon thousands of sin-blinded lives are pouring out their health to gain more wealth. Occasionally someone is brought face to face with some stark tragedy and suddenly he realizes that what he thought was enduring is merely transitory.

The story is told of two young men in California who, in a great fire, went into a room of their warehouse to rescue their books and papers. They closed the iron door after them to keep out the smoke and drafts. Immediately they returned with their important papers in their hands, but the heat had caused the iron door to swell. The men tugged and tugged, but the door would not open. Their voices were heard but help from without could not reach them. They perished with all the evidence of prosperity in their hands.

There are multitudes of men and women who are going into the rooms of their own chosen treasures, closing the door behind them; and the furnace heat of God's violated moral law is swelling the iron door so that it will not open. This was the case with Nebuchadnezzar. "Is not this great Babylon, that I have built for the house of the kingdom by the might of my power, and for the honour of my majesty?"

What is the lesson to be learned? God makes it clear in verse 32. God told Nebuchadnezzar his calamity was to continue "until thou know that the most High ruleth in the kingdom of men, and giveth it to whomsoever He will." Nebuchadnezzar thought he was the ruler, ignoring the one true, holy potentate. Though the Lord had been dealing with him for years and revealing the fact of divine omnipotence, Nebuchadnezzar had closed his ears to

The Rebuke of Rationality

God's gentle chidings. "God resisteth the proud, but giveth grace unto the humble" (James 4:6). He promises further, "Humble yourselves in the sight of the Lord, and He shall lift you up" (James 4:10).

It might be well to look into your own heart to be sure that you are giving God all the honor He deserves. Can you say that the Lord is supreme in your life? God has determined, "That no flesh should glory in His presence" (1 Corinthians 1:29). It is He who deserves all the glory. Let us confess every trace of pride, "That in all things He might have the preeminence" (Colossians 1:18).

7. *The Intimacy — verses 34-37.* God's chastisement of Nebuchadnezzar was severe, but at the same time it was purposeful. This we gather from Nebuchadnezzar's own words, "And at the end of the days I Nebuchadnezzar lifted up mine eyes unto heaven, and mine understanding returned unto me, and I blessed the most High, and I praised and honoured Him that liveth for ever, whose dominion is an everlasting dominion, and His kingdom is from generation to generation: And all the inhabitants of the earth are reputed as nothing: and He doeth according to His will in the army of heaven, and among the inhabitants of the earth: and none can stay His hand, or say unto Him, What doest Thou?" A miraculous change took place in Nebuchadnezzar's heart. On former occasions, following a mighty manifestation of God, the king, though offering lip service to Jehovah, gave all the honor to Daniel and his three Hebrew companions. Nothing is said now regarding Daniel or anyone else; praise is offered to God only.

Seven years had passed, in which Nebuchadnezzar crawled about as a senseless beast, feeding on the grass of the field. The last voice he heard before he lost his rationality was God's, saying, "O king Nebuchadnezzar, to thee it is spoken; The kingdom is departed from thee. And they shall drive thee from men, and thy dwelling shall be with the beasts of the field: they shall make thee to eat grass as oxen, and seven times shall pass over thee, until thou know that the most High ruleth in the kingdom of men, and giveth it to whomsoever He will." The first thing Nebuchadnezzar did after being delivered from his insanity was to look up to the One who had spoken to him from Heaven, to offer praise and honor to "the most High."

We must not overlook the fitting picture here of that which will transpire at the close of this present age of grace. The Scriptures make it clear that there will be seven years of tribulation in which God's judgment will be poured out upon the Gentile nations. They, like Nebuchadnezzar, have resisted God's love and endless pleading. Following this period of judgment, the Lord Jesus will return to this earth to rule and reign. All who have rebelled against Him will bow to Him, for "He shall have dominion also from sea to sea, and from the river unto the ends of the earth. They that dwell in the wilderness shall bow before Him; and His enemies shall lick the dust. Yea, all kings shall fall down before Him: all nations shall serve Him" (Psalm 72:8-9,11). This will begin the millennium, Christ's thousand-year-reign of peace, at which time everyone must give respect and honor to Him. "And He shall judge among many people, and rebuke strong nations afar off; and they shall beat their swords into plowshares, and their spears into pruninghooks: nation shall not lift up a sword against nation, neither shall they learn war any more" (Micah 4:3). During this time Jesus Christ will reign as King of kings and Lord of lords. Indeed, the world is in a mess today. But this will not always be, for the Lord will return and establish His kingdom on the earth.

It should be noted also that before his judgment,

The Rebuke of Rationality 95

Nebuchadnezzar had spoken of God objectively. Now he recognizes Him as his own personal God. "*I* blessed the most High, and *I* praised and honoured Him that liveth for ever." "Now *I* Nebuchadnezzar praise and extol and honour the King of heaven." It makes all the difference in the world if the Lord is one's own. Thomas discovered this only after hopeless doubting. Face to face with the fact of Christ's physical presence after His resurrection, the doubter cried out, "My Lord and my God" (John 20:28). Following years of neglect, Nebuchadnezzar could say the same. The Lord Jehovah, in the estimation of Nebuchadnezzar, had been a great God; but now He was *the* God, his own personal God.

Who is the Lord to you? Have you acknowledged Him as your very own? You may have respect for Him, recognize Him as the Creator of the heavens and the earth. It may be that you even teach about Him or preach about Him. But have you received Him into your heart as your Saviour and Lord? Can you say, Christ is mine, or are you like many who speak of Him simply as a great man, a profound teacher, or a worthy example? Who is Jesus Christ to you?

In her book, *Early Will I Seek Thee*, Eugenia Price tells of an experience she had at a summer conference. A little lady in her fifties told Miss Price the tragic story of her life. She was the unnoticed member of a rather brilliant and talented family. For years she felt unwanted and it twisted her personality out of any resemblance to the one God intended her to have. Her pain of being ignored made her more of a burden to her uncaring family, and so her heartache grew. When it had reached the breaking point, she let it break at the foot of the cross of Jesus Christ. Christ healed her heart. Miss Price says, "I shall never forget the look on her plain but radiant face as she said shyly but with great certainty, 'If no one else in all the world had needed a Saviour but me, Jesus would have died — just for me.'" This heartbroken soul came into the wonderful realization that Jesus was everything to her. She could say with joy in her heart, "Jesus is mine." Can you say this?

Nebuchadnezzar testified not only of his personal relationship to the Lord and of God's mighty power in all the earth, but of the Lord's grace in providing all that the king had lost because of his sin: "At the same time my reason returned unto me; and for the glory of my kingdom, mine honour and brightness returned unto me; and my counsellors and my lords sought unto me; and I was established in my kingdom, and excellent majesty was added unto me." It is very possible that Nebuchadnezzar's son, Evil-merodach, reigned during his father's absence. But Nebuchadnezzar was restored to the throne and assumed his former authority and power. He lost nothing by turning to the Lord, but gained everything.

How clearly Nebuchadnezzar's experience is reflected in the words of our Lord found in Matthew 6:33, "But seek ye first the kingdom of God, and His righteousness; and all these things shall be added unto you." The moment Nebuchadnezzar put God first in his life, all that had meant so much to him was given to him again.

It is heartening to know, however, that the king did not forget the Giver of his blessings. He boldly declared, "Now I Nebuchadnezzar praise and extol and honour the King of heaven, all whose works are truth, and His ways judgment: and those that walk in pride He is able to abase." Nothing more is heard after this from the lips of Nebuchadnezzar, but his final statement assures us that he learned the lesson that was hardest for him to learn: "Those that walk in pride He is able to abase." God has declared in Jeremiah 9:23-24: "Let not the wise man

The Rebuke of Rationality

glory in his wisdom, neither let the mighty man glory in his might, let not the rich man glory in his riches: But let him that glorieth glory in this, that he understandeth and knoweth Me, that I am the LORD which exercise lovingkindness, judgment, and righteousness, in the earth: for in these things I delight, saith the LORD." It took Nebuchadnezzar a long time to come to the realization that Jehovah God is the Lord, but finally he came. I hope you have come. Only Christ can give enduring happiness.

Chapter 5

THE REALITY OF RETRIBUTION

Key verse, 30: "In that night was Belshazzar the king of the Chaldeans slain."

God says, "The soul that sinneth, it shall die" (Ezekiel 18:20). The chapter we are about to study provides a vivid commentary on this verse. Man may ignore the voice of God, but eternal judgment will be the final result. The Babylonian kingdom had gradually degenerated into a low state of debauchery and idolatry over a thirty-year period after the death of Nebuchadnezzar. The kings had gone from bad to worse. Ultimately, under the sovereignty of Belshazzar at approximately 538 B.C., the mighty Babylon came to its doom, effecting the transition from the head of gold to the breast and arms of silver, recorded in chapter 2. Prophetically the downfall of Babylon depicted the coming judgment upon this world as the result of man's continued rejection of Christ. Civilization, like the great Babylon, will drift farther and farther away from the truth until God's cup of wrath is filled, and then judgment will be the result. We are told in 2 Timothy 3:13 that "evil men and seducers shall wax worse and worse, deceiving, and being deceived." This will not continue forever however, for the Lord will return to rule and reign in righteousness.

1. *The Sacrilege — verses 1-4.* The occasion described in these opening verses of the chapter is that of a lavish feast arranged by Belshazzar, to which an enormous

number of nobles were invited. "Belshazzar the king made a great feast to a thousand of his lords, and drank wine before the thousand." Some have supposed this to have been an annual celebration, probably dedicated to certain heathen deities worshiped by Belshazzar. It was a time of unrestrained revelry and gross immorality with little thought being given to the dangers posed by their enemies, the Persians.

Belshazzar was a young, dissolute, impious, unworthy ruler with a heart hardened toward the Lord Jehovah; there were no restraints to his blasphemy. "Belshazzar, whiles he tasted the wine, commanded to bring the golden and silver vessels which his father Nebuchadnezzar had taken out of the temple which was in Jerusalem; that the king, and his princes, his wives, and his concubines, might drink therein." Doubtless, after his conversion, Nebuchadnezzar had respect for these vessels taken from the Temple and put them in places of honor. But Belshazzar commanded that they might be used for the furtherance of their drunken orgy.

Normally in the East women were kept in strict seclusion, but as the revelry progressed, they were brought in. This was the case at Belshazzar's feast. As the king demanded, "they brought the golden vessels that were taken out of the temple of the house of God which was at Jerusalem; and the king and his princes, his wives, and his concubines, drank in them. They drank wine, and praised the gods of gold, and of silver, of brass, of iron, of wood, and of stone." Here we see a vivid picture of the fruits of the unregenerate heart. When one has no relationship to God, all restraints are removed. But regardless of the depths to which one may go, if he turns to the Lord and sincerely repents, God will forgive and lift him up. God says, "I will forgive their iniquity, and I will remember their sin no more" (Jeremiah 31:34). Oh, how marvelous is the mercy of the Lord in blotting out our transgressions when we come to Jesus Christ. In Psalm

86:5 David prayed, "For Thou, Lord, art good, and ready to forgive; and plenteous in mercy unto all them that call upon Thee."

In a cemetery not far from New York City there is a headstone inscribed with just one word, "Forgiven." There is no name, no date of birth or death, no epitaph, no eulogy, just the one word — "Forgiven." How pathetic that Belshazzar, the ruler of an empire, did not choose God's forgiveness. His choice, like many in our day, was sin. He reveled in the pleasures of sin, but it did not last long. Sin never lasts.

There are those who name Christ's name but who continue in bondage to some besetting sin. If you are one of them, why not enter into a victorious deliverance, not only from sin's penalty but from its power? God tells us in Psalm 68:6, "He bringeth out those which are bound with chains." God provides deliverance for those who want to be delivered. This deliverance is a definite part of our redemption. We read of this comforting truth in Colossians 1:13-14, where we are told of God, "Who hath delivered us from the power of darkness, and hath translated us into the kingdom of His dear Son: In whom we have redemption through His blood, even the forgiveness of sins." Victory is ours in the redemption of Christ. But let it be understood that the victorious life is brought about wholly by Christ. It is sustained not by our continued effort, but through our continued receiving. By faith we receive of His victory daily, enabling us by His power to overcome all sin. Let us look to God in praise and exclaim, "Thanks be to God, which giveth us the victory through our Lord Jesus Christ" (1 Corinthians 15:57). Then, moment by moment, let us trust Him for this unquestionable victory.

2. *The Shock — verses 5-6.* Belshazzar's feast was an affront to God. Rarely does God retaliate so quickly, but on this occasion He did. "In the same hour came forth fingers of a man's hand, and wrote over against the

The Reality of Retribution

candlestick upon the plaister of the wall of the king's palace: and the king saw the part of the hand that wrote." No one expected anything like this. Most of those in the crowd were intoxicated, but here was a sobering phenomenon that shook them to their senses. All restraints had been cast aside. The wine flowed freely. The sacred vessels of the Temple were being desecrated and the lifeless idols of paganism were being worshiped. Suddenly everything ceased as the pleasure-mad audience was startled by God's response.

How descriptive this event is of another soul-shaking incident that will take place at the end of our present age. All over the world people will be living carelessly and thoughtlessly ignoring the claims of God. Sin and immorality will be on the increase. Warnings of faithful preachers of the gospel will be ignored as millions continue in their worship of the idol gods of materialism and lust. But suddenly laughter will turn to sorrow, for the Lord Jesus Christ will return to execute judgment. God says in Haggai 2:7, "And I will shake all nations, and the desire of all nations shall come." This will be the Day of the Lord, which God declares to be "a day of wrath, a day of trouble and distress, a day of wasteness and desolation, a day of darkness and gloominess, a day of clouds and thick darkness, A day of the trumpet and alarm against the fenced cities, and against the high towers." At that time God "will bring distress upon men, that they shall walk like blind men, because they have sinned against the LORD: and their blood shall be poured out as dust, and their flesh as the dung. Neither their silver nor their gold shall be able to deliver them in the day of the LORD's wrath; but the whole land shall be devoured by the fire of His jealousy: for He shall make even a speedy riddance of all them that dwell in the land" (Zephaniah 1:15-18).

For centuries God has been warning men through His Word, but proud, indifferent unbelievers refuse to heed the warnings. Many even question and ridicule the idea of the return of Christ. This attitude is prophesied in 2 Peter 3:3-4: "Knowing this first, that there shall come in the last days scoffers, walking after their own lusts, And saying, Where is the promise of His coming? for since the fathers fell asleep, all things continue as they were from the beginning of the creation." Such mockery of the truth of God is but another sign of the soon return of our Lord. At a time when Christ's return will be least expected, He will come, as we are told in 1 Thessalonians 5:2-3: "For yourselves know perfectly that the day of the Lord so cometh as a thief in the night. For when they shall say, Peace and safety; then sudden destruction cometh upon them, as travail upon a woman with child; and they shall not escape." Oh, that blinded, indifferent, sinful men would repent and turn to the Lord before it is too late.

Belshazzar's indifference to the claims of God is descriptive of the end times. Here was this pagan king with his invited guests, enraptured in the pleasures of sin. But suddenly the scene changed as God spoke by means of fingers of a man's hand, writing on the wall. It would seem that this particular wall was visible to all. It was well lighted by a candelabra, probably one that had been carried off from the Temple at Jerusalem. Oftentimes on the wall of such rooms the records of masterful victories were inscribed. It could have been that the writing appeared on one of the same walls on which Belshazzar had listed his victories.

The unusual appearance of a man's handwriting on the wall had a tremendous effect upon the king: "Then the king's countenance was changed, and his thoughts troubled him, so that the joints of his loins were loosed, and his knees smote one against another." Could anyone have been more frightened? Belshazzar's countenance had expressed brightness and gaiety, but in an instant a dying paleness was seen, and "his thoughts troubled him." Did he not have vast armies? Was he not one of the wealthiest men in the world? Yes, but face to face with God and judgment these provided no security. He had a conscience within that suddenly reminded him that he had blasphemed God; even though he could not read what was written on the wall, his conscience told him that because of his sins it could not be good news. The king was so frightened "that the joints of his loins were loosed, and his knees smote one against another." His legs gave way under him, he had no strength, severe pain overtook him. Belshazzar was frightened beyond measure. How fearless and mighty one can be when all is going well, but how terror-stricken and impotent he may become in the face of death. Indeed, we can say, "How are the mighty fallen!" (2 Samuel 1:27) God can humble a proud heart, He can bring low the rebellious. There is no limit to His power.

3. *The Summons — verses 7-9.* It must have been quite a while before the startled king could speak. Forgetting his dignity and position, he "cried aloud to bring in the astrologers, the Chaldeans, and the soothsayers." It would have been much better had the king "cried aloud" to God in repentance, but when one gives no thought to God in times of prosperity, he rarely realizes his need for dependence on God when facing emergencies. Thus Belshazzar did the best he knew how to do — he called on the wise men. Of course, they had been proven in the past to be nothing more than imposters; but the natural mind, while refusing to believe in the Lord, usually turns to a substitute of some kind.

The king made this proposition to the magicians: "Whosoever shall read this writing, and shew me the interpretation thereof, shall be clothed with scarlet, and have a chain of gold about his neck, and shall be the third ruler in the kingdom." Belshazzar knew what would best satisfy these men, so he told them of the attractive reward that would be given for their satisfactory response. To be the "third ruler in the kingdom" was a coveted honor, for the first place belonged to the king and the second to his son or the queen. The distressed king was willing to go to practically any extreme to have the mysterious words interpreted. He was desperate, recognizing that this was a matter of life or death.

The wise men were given their chance. All of them were brought before the wall with the mysterious writing, but not only were they helpless in interpreting the words, "they could not read the writing." This made matters worse than ever for the king. "Then was king Belshazzar greatly troubled, and his countenance was changed in him, and his lords were astonied." Previous to the failure of the wise men, the king was "troubled." Now he was *"greatly* troubled." Furthermore, they who had shared the king's wickedness now became his partners in terror. They, too, were disturbed and confused.

How helpless man is without the Lord when he is face to face with calamity. He may turn to his friends, but very often they are equally helpless. There is one Friend who never fails. We are told in Proverbs 18:24, "There is a friend that sticketh closer than a brother." Sometimes even dearest loved ones fail us; but the Lord Jesus Christ never fails. For this reason the Apostle Paul could write in 2 Corinthians 2:14, "Now thanks be unto God, which always causeth us to triumph in Christ."

The believer will certainly have trials and heartaches like the people of the world. God has not promised freedom from suffering because we are followers of Christ. But those who know the Lord have the promise of His presence and provision in every trial of life. And what is more, our sufferings are only for a short period, and then we have an eternity of endless blessing and joy in the presence of the Lord. "For our light affliction, which is but for a moment, worketh for us a far more exceeding and eternal weight of glory; While we look not at the things which are seen . . . for the things which are seen are temporal; but the things which are not seen are eternal" (2 Corinthians 4:17-18).

The Reality of Retribution

It may be that you are facing a time of deep despair, or are in the midst of a trial such as you have never experienced before. You know not where to go or in which direction to turn. May I urge you to look up. God is still on the throne. He invites you to turn to Him. He says in Isaiah 55:6, "Seek ye the LORD while He may be found, call ye upon Him while He is near." If you have claimed the Lord Jesus as your Saviour from sin, He will undertake for your present calamity. God wants to help you.

During the American Civil War, a meeting was being held in Washington at the time when news of a most serious defeat for the northern forces reached the Capitol. Frederick Douglass, the slave orator, was speaking. When the news reached the platform and Douglass heard it, he gave way to despair and burst into tears. The news passed from seat to seat and the audience was gripped with fear. But in the back gallery was an old Negro woman who, when she saw the meeting falling into something like panic with even Douglass in despair, cried out with a hint of reproach in her tone, "Frederick Douglass, God is not dead." These words changed the course of the whole meeting. Take this message to heart for your present need: "God is not dead." Do not be like Belshazzar and turn to sources that will be of no avail. Look to the living Christ; call upon Him and He will answer.

4. *The Solution — verses 10-17.* News of the abrupt end of the sumptuous feast spread rapidly. Shortly after, a visitor entered the banquet hall. "Now the queen, by reason of the words of the king and his lords, came into the banquet house: and the queen spake and said, O king, live for ever: let not thy thoughts trouble thee, nor let thy countenance be changed." This was the queen mother, probably the wife of Nebuchadnezzar. It was possible that Belshazzar had sent for her out of respect for her wisdom and experience. We might well believe that the queen

mother was not sympathetic about the feast, by the fact that she had not attended. But in a time of emergency she was ready to help.

Not only did she offer solace to the king, but she was ready with a solution: "There is a man in thy kingdom, in whom is the spirit of the holy gods; and in the days of thy father light and understanding and wisdom, like the wisdom of the gods, was found in him; whom the king Nebuchadnezzar thy father, the king, I say, thy father, made master of the magicians, astrologers, Chaldeans, and soothsayers; Forasmuch as an excellent spirit, and knowledge, and understanding, interpreting of dreams, and shewing of hard sentences, and dissolving of doubts, were found in the same Daniel, whom the king named Belteshazzar: now let Daniel be called, and he will shew the interpretation." The queen mother had great respect for Daniel, for she had never forgotten the days of Nebuchadnezzar and how Daniel was used to turn the proud king to the Lord Jehovah. Thus she cried out, "There is a man."

Daniel was the man of the hour. Though near ninety on this occasion, he was still usable in the plan of God. Daniel must have been greatly disturbed because of the condition of the empire and the spiritual degeneracy of the king. But he stayed by, waiting for whatever service the Lord might have for him. How we thank God for men like Daniel, full of faith, courage, and zeal for the Lord. Though living in the polluted atmosphere of a godless court, he walked with the Lord in a life of singular piety and service. What a challenge this is to Christians in our generation to be willing to stand and be counted for Jesus Christ. We read in 1 Peter 4:14, "If ye be reproached for the name of Christ, happy are ye; for the spirit of glory and of God resteth upon you."

Moses discovered the value of reproach as we are told in Hebrews 11:24-26: "By faith Moses, when he was come to years, refused to be called the son of Pharaoh's

The Reality of Retribution 107

daughter; Choosing rather to suffer affliction with the people of God, than to enjoy the pleasures of sin for a season; Esteeming the reproach of Christ greater riches than the treasures in Egypt: for he had respect unto the recompence of the reward." Moses was God's man in his generation as Daniel was in his.

What a tremendous need there is for men of the same fearless courage in our day. Recall the time when the Lord looked for a man filled with a holy zeal and exemplified by a valiant spirit but there was none to be found: "And I sought for a man among them, that should make up the hedge, and stand in the gap before Me for the land, that I should not destroy it: but I found none" (Ezekiel 22:30). Likewise God is looking for men in this age. Wherever you go, in the office, the classroom, the club, on the athletic field, in the home; if you are a Christian, God wants you to be His man.

A college professor assigned a term paper on something having to do with social problems. The students were to submit their topics for the professor's approval. One of them selected the topic, "The Possibilities of Christianity Solving Social Problems." The professor informed the student he did not think it was possible to get a grade on a subject like that. The student protested, and a mild argument ensued.

"Allow me to work on the subject, hand in the paper, and if it is not satisfactory, I will choose another subject," proposed the student.

After some discussion, the professor agreed. The student went to work prayerfully, doing research and spending hours on a five-thousand-word thesis, in which men and women were cited who had been changed from drunkenness and debauchery into those whose lives were turned to usefulness in their respective communities because of the grace and power of God. The paper soon came back with the notation in red ink, "You cannot get a grade on this."

After further discussion with the professor, the student was granted the privilege of doing more work on the paper. He searched history books and encyclopedias, gathered other materials, and revamped the entire paper, resulting in a seven-thousand-word thesis. It was handed in, and later returned with an "A." Not only that, the student was permitted to read it before the class. As Daniel was God's man in the king's court, you may be sure this young student was God's man in his college classroom.

Upon recommendation of the queen mother, "Then was Daniel brought in before the king. And the king spake and said unto Daniel, Art thou that Daniel, which art of the children of the captivity of Judah, whom the king my father brought out of Jewry?" Daniel was not well known to the king because he was not of the king's kind. Furthermore, the prophet was a stranger to the king because Belshazzar had no interest in Daniel's God. It was as John the Apostle wrote years later, "The world knoweth us not, because it knew Him not" (1 John 3:1).

The king proceeded to lament his sad plight before Daniel, stating that "the wise men . . . could not shew the interpretation." Then in desperation he promised Daniel that he would "be clothed with scarlet, and have a chain of gold about thy neck," as well as "be the third ruler in the kingdom" if he could interpret the writing on the wall. Unlike his contemporaries, Daniel replied, "Let thy gifts be to thyself, and give thy rewards to another; yet I will read the writing unto the king, and make known to him the interpretation." As a faithful witness for God, he was not interested in personal gain. His concern was to be a testimony for his Lord. Could any believer have a higher goal than this? Is it your purpose in life to be a testimony for God free from any personal desire for gain? How important for each believer to set his "affection on things above, not on things on the earth" (Colossians 3:2).

The Reality of Retribution

5. *The Sermon* — verses 18-25. Before Daniel read and interpreted the writing on the wall, he evidenced his God-given courage once again by giving Belshazzar a much needed message. He did not speak as the wise men who had failed so miserably, but as God's holy servant, divinely appointed for his task. In 1 Peter 3:15 God's people are admonished by the disciple to "sanctify the Lord God in your hearts: and be ready always to give an answer to every man that asketh you a reason of the hope that is in you, with meekness and fear." Thus with a heart burning with zeal for the Lord, Daniel was ready to give his answer.

There could be no mistake as to the one for whom the prophecy was intended, for Daniel began by saying, "O thou king." Daniel was not evasive. He made it clear that what he had to say was for the young, arrogant, licentious king. First was the reminder of the failure of the king's grandfather, Nebuchadnezzar. "God gave Nebuchadnezzar thy father a kingdom, and majesty, and glory, and honour: And for the majesty that He gave him, all people, nations, and languages, trembled and feared before him: whom he would he slew; and whom he would he kept alive; and whom he would he set up; and whom he would he put down. But when his heart was lifted up, and his mind hardened in pride, he was deposed from his kingly throne, and they took his glory from him: And he was driven from the sons of men; and his heart was made like the beasts, and his dwelling was with the wild asses: they fed him with grass like oxen, and his body was wet with the dew of heaven; till he knew that the most high God ruled in the kingdom of men, and that He appointeth over it whomsoever He will."

Several things were emphasized in this straightforward message from Daniel's heart. First, all the power and authority possessed by Nebuchadnezzar was God-given. He ignored this important fact, however, and selfishly took the praise unto himself, refusing to bow to the Lord.

Judgment was the result. In his extremity Nebuchadnezzar finally turned to God and gave Him praise for all things.

Having given this historical background, Daniel made his application to the king: "And thou his son, O Belshazzar, hast not humbled thine heart, though thou knewest all this; But hast lifted up thyself against the Lord of heaven; and they have brought the vessels of His house before thee, and thou, and thy lords, thy wives, and thy concubines, have drunk wine in them; and thou hast praised the gods of silver, and gold, of brass, iron, wood, and stone, which see not, nor hear, nor know: and the God in whose hand thy breath is, and whose are all thy way, hast thou not glorified." Daniel made it clear that though Nebuchadnezzar had degenerated to a low estate, Belshazzar's condition was far more serious. Not only was he guilty of pride like his grandfather, but worse than that, it was as Daniel declared, "Thou knewest all this." Doubtless Belshazzar had heard the truth time and time again from the queen mother. He had knowledge of God's judgment which was unknown by Nebuchadnezzar until he was humbled and made like the animals of the field. It is bad enough for one to live in sin, but to have knowledge of the judgment of God and to do nothing about it is worse. God says in James 4:17, "Therefore to him that knoweth to do good, and doeth it not, to him it is sin." Belshazzar was aware of the truth. He had knowledge of the consequences of sin, but he neglected to repent and turn to God.

In His mercy and love the Lord gives the sinner scores of opportunities to repent. Rarely does He strike in immediate judgment. But ultimately, if one persists in evil, judgment is certain, as seen in Nebuchadnezzar's experience and, as we shall see, in that of Belshazzar. God's Word is unmistakably clear, "He, that being often reproved hardeneth his neck, shall suddenly be destroyed, and that without remedy" (Proverbs 29:1).

The Reality of Retribution

There was once a judge in England who was called "the sleeping judge." Because of his drowsy posture on the bench, many persons unacquainted with his custom and having cases to be tried before him, gave up all hope, expecting no justice from a dormant judge. Yet all the while he only rested within himself so he could more seriously consider the validity of what was alleged and stated before him. His pronouncements which followed evidenced that he only appeared to be sleeping. There are many who, living in sin, think that God is sleeping, some even declaring that He is dead. But in His own time He will assuredly confute their mistake.

After Daniel gave this pointed message to the king, he proceeded to read the words that had been written on the wall by the mysterious hand. "Then was the part of the hand sent from him; and this writing was written. And this is the writing that was written, MENE, MENE, TEKEL, UPHARSIN." No one else was able even to read the words, let alone interpret them. But Daniel was God's appointed man with the Lord's message. Though the inspired prophet's message was for the king in particular, what he said is for all men in general.

6. *The Significance — verses 26-28.* Everyone in the banquet hall was waiting to hear the meaning of the mysterious words. Finally Daniel proceeded to reveal the secret: "This is the interpretation of the thing: MENE; God hath numbered thy kingdom, and finished it. TEKEL; Thou art weighed in the balances, and art found wanting. PERES; Thy kingdom is divided, and given to the Medes and Persians." Here was the message of doom for the great Babylon. "MENE, MENE," as Daniel made clear, meant that the kingdom of Babylon was numbered and finished. The years and days of its existence were numbered in the counsels of God and now the hour of its end had come. Weighed in the scales of divine justice, the empire was found wanting. "PERES" meant "divided" and was used by Daniel to explain "UPHARSIN," which

meant "dividers." Daniel declared, "Thy kingdom is divided, and given to the Medes and Persians." Babylon was to be overrun by this divided empire in a matter of moments. Even during the interpretation of the words, the Medes and Persians with drawn swords were making their way to overpower the Babylonians.

Let us be reminded that what happened to the Babylonian Empire happens also to individuals. Under the leadership of their pleasure-loving monarch, the Babylonians lived in idolatry and wickedness. As is always true, the end came and they were found wanting. How many there are in our day who are living for themselves, giving no regard to God's great plan of redemption. Suddenly they are confronted with death, only to find themselves "wanting," without hope for the future, without any assurance of salvation.

God has a message for every human in Amos 4:12, "Prepare to meet thy God." One can prepare to meet God only while he is alive. There will be no opportunity after death, and death is certain. We read two important questions in Psalm 89:48, "What man is he that liveth, and shall not see death? shall he deliver his soul from the hand of the grave?" God gives us a clear-cut warning in Hebrews 2:1-3: "Therefore we ought to give the more earnest heed to the things which we have heard, lest at any time we should let them slip. For if the word spoken by angels was stedfast, and every transgression and disobedience received a just recompence of reward; How shall we escape, if we neglect so great salvation." Those who neglect the great salvation made possible in Christ, will find no escape from eternal death.

How well it would have been had Belshazzar given heed to the things he had heard about the conversion of his grandfather, Nebuchadnezzar. It is obvious that he, like many people in our day, gave no thought to eternal things until he was brought face to face with doom.

The Reality of Retribution

Though death was only a matter of minutes from Belshazzar, God gave him time to repent and be saved. But his heart had become so hard that his conscience would not permit him to move toward God. There was no need for him to die in his sins, for God is a God of grace and love, desirous that all men be saved and be prepared for eternity. God says: "Believe on the Lord Jesus Christ, and thou shalt be saved" (Acts 16:31).

The story is told of Nicholas Pastoret, who was a flag maker in his native Luxembourg. While there he made many American flags. When he came to the United States, he became very fond of this country and longed to become a citizen of it. He secured his first papers, but before he received his final papers he was dying of cancer. Unable to appear at Federal court in St. Paul, Minnesota, Judge Dennis Donovan went to him and administered the oath which made the dying man a citizen of the United States of America. "I made many American flags, but this is the first time I can call it my own. God bless America," whispered Pastoret through his cancer-stricken throat.

Grand as it is to be made a citizen of the United States, it is grander — in fact, the grandest thing of all — to become a citizen of Heaven. Do not say "tomorrow," for God says "today." In Hebrews 4:7 He says, "To day if ye will hear His voice, harden not your heart." Many have neglected the frequent opportunities to receive Christ, and ultimately they discovered that their hearts were adamant toward God. Do not let this happen to you.

God's message of doom to Belshazzar was numbered, weighed, and divided. I hope you will never have to hear this message addressed to you personally. How much better it would be to hear the words, "Well done, thou good and faithful servant: thou hast been faithful over a few things, I will make thee ruler over many things: enter thou into the joy of thy lord" (Matthew 25:21). What will God say to you when you die and face Him? Will it be, "Well done, [thou] good and faithful servant," or will it be, "Depart from me, ye cursed, into everlasting fire, prepared for the devil and his angels" (Matthew 25:41)? Let there be no misunderstanding, it will be one or the other. If you have taken Christ into your life and if you are truly saved, you will go to be with the Lord. But if you have not received Christ, there is no other way of salvation.

7. *The Sequel — verses 29-31.* Three results followed after Daniel had given the significance of the words, "MENE, MENE, TEKEL, UPHARSIN"; the exaltation, the expiration, and the extermination. At all times, under all circumstances, God takes care of His own. One would have thought, after this frank rebuff of the rebellious king, that Daniel would have been ordered slain. But it was just the opposite; notice the exaltation: "Then commanded Belshazzar, and they clothed Daniel with scarlet, and put a chain of gold about his neck, and made a proclamation concerning him, that he should be the third ruler in the kingdom." In verse 17, Daniel had rejected these promised honors for he did not want to make merchandise of his prophetic gift. But since the king was still desirous of honoring Daniel following the shocking prophecy, God's servant was willing to receive the gratuities from the king. Even this was providential, for as the "third ruler" in the kingdom, Daniel was given back the position he once held under King Nebuchadnezzar. Doubtless it was because of his position as the "third ruler" that the conquering King Darius respected Daniel, making him the first of the three presidents over the entire kingdom.

Let us pause to reflect for a moment upon an important characteristic so noticeable in Daniel. The prophet had his eyes fixed on God, he was concerned about one thing — God's plan for his life. Thus this fearless servant was God's man. Many Christians in our day are of the Laodicean variety — "neither cold nor hot" (Revelation

The Reality of Retribution 115

3:15). God says of such, "So then because thou art lukewarm, and neither cold nor hot, I will spue thee out of My mouth" (Revelation 3:16). God is looking for believers who, like Caleb, are able to say, "I wholly followed the LORD" (Joshua 14:8). It is not easy to walk the path of separation, for it is an unpopular course in the eyes of the world. Many believers are unwilling to pay the price, even though God commands, "Come out from among them, and be ye separate" (2 Corinthians 6:17). It is of far greater importance to please God than men.

The Prophet Daniel was separated from sin throughout his entire experience in Babylon. At the beginning of his captivity he separated himself from the king's meat and the king's wine. As an elderly man he continued in this life of separation, having nothing to do with the king's feast. How great is the need for believers like Daniel in our day.

There are some who limit the meaning of this word "separation" by applying it to apostasy only. Many organizations and groups have nailed the word to their mastheads as the answer to the fast-growing liberal churches. Certainly such a protest is justifiable, but the meaning of separation goes much deeper than this. We are to separate ourselves from all that displeases Christ, from selfish living, pride, unkindness, immorality, and all the other evils hindering our walk with the Lord. Not only are we to separate ourselves *from* but *to*. Separation *from* evil on the part of the Christian demands full surrender *to* the control of Jesus Christ. Thus it is imperative that we be a separated people if we are to bear an impact for God, which is so greatly needed in our present civilization.

Finally in this chapter we read of the expiration: "In that night was Belshazzar the king of the Chaldeans slain." History tells us how King Cyrus, who was the leader of the assault in the name of King Darius, diverted the River Euphrates into a new channel and with the help of two deserters was able to march through the dry bed with his army to kill the king. Galatians 6:7-8 seems to be applicable here: "Be not deceived; God is not mocked: for whatsoever a man soweth, that shall he also reap. For he that soweth to his flesh shall of the flesh reap corruption; but he that soweth to the Spirit shall of the Spirit reap life everlasting." Belshazzar lived for the flesh and died a horrible death. On that memorable night of the feast he died with no hope for eternity.

More important, consider the extermination of the great Babylon of which Belshazzar had boasted. "And Darius the Median took the kingdom, being about threescore and two years old." In just one short night the kingdom of Babylon ceased to be, never again to be known. The head of gold was superseded by the breast and arms of silver as the Medes and Persians came to power. Here is another exact fulfillment of Scripture according to the words of the Prophet Daniel.

This, like the scores of other prophecies both fulfilled and unfulfilled throughout the Word of God, reminds us of one great truth — the authenticity of the Scriptures. God who cannot lie has declared of His Word in Matthew 24:35, "Heaven and earth shall pass away, but My words shall not pass away." We have in the Scriptures the mind and the message of God written by men who were directed and controlled by the Holy Spirit. This fact is stated clearly in 2 Peter 1:21: "For the prophecy came not in old time by the will of man: but holy men of God spake as they were moved by the Holy Ghost." The Bible has always had its critics but few of them have been able to substantiate their arguments.

The late seminary professor, Robert Dick Wilson, told of an incident regarding five students who came to him with the affirmation that they did not believe that Moses wrote the book of Deuteronomy. Without comment he asked, "Have you ever read the book of Deuteronomy?" Not one of the five had done so, but they were merely repeating what they had heard from some critical

The Reality of Retribution

professor in college. To them Dr. Wilson wisely said, "Young men, go and read the book and I will then be glad to discuss it with you." I contend that if anyone goes to the Bible and reads it carefully and thoughtfully with an open mind, he will be convinced that it is the Word of God.

A judge who was occasionally on circuit at a certain town was always sure of being annoyed by some sneering remarks from a conceited lawyer. After one such occasion someone asked the judge why he did not reply to his adversary.

"Up in our town," said the judge, "there is a dog who, whenever the moon shines, goes out on the steps and barks and barks away at it all night."

"Well, judge, what about the dog and the moon?"

"Oh," replied the judge, "the moon kept on shining — that is all." Men have tried to destroy the Bible but the light of God's Word still shines on.

Have you apprehended the greatest truth that appears in the Bible: "That Christ died for our sins according to the scriptures; And that He was buried, and that He rose again the third day according to the scriptures" (1 Corinthians 15:3-4)? This is the pinnacle fact of the Bible. Christ died as our substitute on the cross for sin. The Lord Jesus is God's way of salvation for all. If you never have, take Christ into your life and be eternally saved. Then read and study the Word and you will find it to be the inspired truth of God. The Lord asks in Jeremiah 23:29, "Is not My word like as a fire? saith the LORD; and like a hammer that breaketh the rock in pieces?" God's Word will be a fire to purge your soul of all dross, and a hammer to crush your stony heart that you may be pliable in the hands of God. Oh, give time to the Book, God's eternal Word.

Chapter 6

THE REACTION OF REVERENCE

Key verse, 10: "Now when Daniel knew that the writing was signed, he went into his house; and his windows being open in his chamber toward Jerusalem, he kneeled upon his knees three times a day, and prayed, and gave thanks before his God, as he did aforetime."

Under Darius, the second great world empire was established about 538 B.C. The Medo-Persian Empire, as it was known, had already been prophesied in Nebuchadnezzar's great image in the arms and chest of silver. Silver being inferior to gold suggests the degeneration of this empire as compared with Babylon.

1. *The Advancement — verses 1-3.* Though a man of tremendous resources and great ability, Darius was only a man. In addition to his former holdings, as well as recent conquests, Darius was suddenly confronted with the responsibility of controlling his vast dominion. In his attempt to do this, we are told that "It pleased Darius to set over the kingdom an hundred and twenty princes, which should be over the whole kingdom." The "hundred and twenty princes" were governors who were charged with the specific responsibilities of administering justice to all the subjects, providing for the peaceful coexistence of the people, and collecting revenue for the king. To be sure that the one hundred and twenty princes discharged their duties properly, three presidents were appointed to be their superiors: "And over these three presidents; of

The Reaction of Reverence

whom Daniel was first: that the princes might give accounts unto them, and the king should have no damage." The three presidents were to hear any complaints from the princes and carefully to watch over the king's revenue to be sure there were no discrepancies or dishonesty.

We are told that Daniel was the first of the three presidents; further, "this Daniel was preferred above the presidents and princes, because an excellent spirit was in him; and the king thought to set him over the whole realm." Daniel had been an extremely valuable man in the former kingdom. Darius must have discovered this, for he lost no time in capitalizing upon Daniel's experience and ability. Daniel was also well known for his integrity. Even unbelievers are careful to choose honest men to carry on their affairs. Daniel was a gifted man, but more than that, "an excellent spirit was in him." The "excellent spirit" was not merely the result of human ability. It was effected by the prophet's full commitment to divine control. Daniel served his superiors well because he served his Lord well.

What a lesson for those of us who know the Lord. In Romans 12:11 the apostle tells us not to be "slothful in business" but rather, "Fervent in spirit; serving the Lord." A splendid way for Christians to exalt Christ and to be a testimony to those around is to be diligent in business. Many Christians consider their employment merely as a necessary evil rather than as an opportunity to glorify Christ. They overlook the fact that an opportune way to witness is to be as painstaking and careful as possible about doing their job. Do you think a man who wastes his employer's time will ever win his employer to Christ?

Surely Darius was not looking for someone to run his kingdom on the ground of his belief in God. He needed a man who had the necessary qualifications to do a good job. Daniel was that man. He had proved himself to be diligent in business. He could be trusted.

Furthermore, Daniel had the leadership ability that qualified him for his position. Daniel's faith resulted in works. We are told in James 2:17, "faith, if it hath not works, is dead, being alone." If one has met Christ and experienced a heart conversion, everyone around will know it, not necessarily because of what is said, but because of the new life which is the result of the new God-given nature. Paul exhorted believers in Ephesians 4:24 to "put on the new man, which after God is created in righteousness and true holiness." Of course we cannot put on "the new man" ourselves. This is the work of God within, but the believer must be willing to let God do the work.

L. H. Hough in one of his articles tells that "while walking along the street one day, I came across an extraordinary window display. It was a clock without hands. The pendulum was moving, the works were in motion. Everything about this clock seemed to be in the very best of condition, with one exception. Its face had numbers of all the hours, but no hands moved upon it. It was doing everything except indicating the time — and that was the one thing for which the clock was made." Can it not be said that many who profess to be Christians are like the clock without hands — there is much activity and movement, but little of the purpose for which they were saved.

2. *The Adversaries — verses 4-9.* One of the most destructive evils among mankind is jealousy. The devil used this tool in an attempt to condemn Daniel unjustly. The aged saint, who was at the time in his eighties, became the subject of a wicked plot on the part of his co-workers. "Then the presidents and princes sought to find occasion against Daniel concerning the kingdom; but they could find none occasion nor fault; forasmuch as he was faithful, neither was there any error or fault found in him." The envious rulers put spies on Daniel's trail,

seeking to find grounds for accusation, but as they could discover nothing worthy of condemnation, they turned to illegitimate means. "Then said these men, We shall not find any occasion against this Daniel, except we find it against him concerning the law of his God."

The authorities of state discussed varied means of achieving their wicked intentions until finally they agreed on a method. Hastening to the king, they presented their subtle plan and urged immediate approval. "Then these presidents and princes assembled together to the king, and said thus unto him, King Darius, live for ever. All the presidents of the kingdom, the governors, and the princes, the counsellors, and the captains, have consulted together to establish a royal statute, and to make a firm decree, that whosoever shall ask a petition of any God or man for thirty days, save of thee, O king, he shall be cast into the den of lions. Now, O king, establish the decree, and sign the writing, that it be not changed, according to the law of the Medes and Persians, which altereth not." The words "assembled together" as used in verse 6 embody the meaning of assembling hastily with the intention of acting so fast that the king would have no time to think on the matter.

Notice the fallacy in the appeal. The presidents and princes declared, "*All* the presidents of the kingdom, the governors, and the princes, the counsellors, and the captains, have consulted together to establish a royal statute." This, of course, was an audacious lie, for Daniel had not been consulted. Of all those named, he was the most important. But is it not true that when wicked men attempt to achieve their diabolical purposes, they usually resort to lying?

Since no wrong could be found in Daniel, his wicked adversaries attacked his God, requesting that no one should pray to any god or man other than the king for a period of thirty days. This was the familiar evil of placing man before God, which is so common in our own day.

Thus flattered, with little thought and unaware of what was behind it all, the king responded as anticipated: "Wherefore king Darius signed the writing and the decree." Unaware of his tragic error, the king was ensnared by men who were mastered by the destructive evil of jealousy.

Not only the ungodly are afflicted with jealousy; often Satan deludes the people of God with this evil. It is written in Proverbs 27:4, "Wrath is cruel, and anger is outrageous: but who is able to stand before envy?" Believers and unbelievers alike fall before envy. Let no one think that because he is a Christian he is immune. Though believers need not be overcome by this sin, many are.

One of the most damaging effects of jealousy in the believer is that it hinders his growth as a child of God. The Apostle Peter said, "Wherefore laying aside all malice, and all guile, and hypocrisies, and *envies*, and all evil speakings, As newborn babes, desire the sincere milk of the word, that ye may grow thereby" (1 Peter 2:1-2). Even though one may study the Word faithfully, unless he claims victory over the envy of his own heart, he will discover soon that he is spiritually retarded. The Apostle Paul made it clear that this was the case of the Corinthian saints: "And I, brethren, could not speak unto you as unto spiritual, but as unto carnal, even as unto babes in Christ. I have fed you with milk, and not with meat: for hitherto ye were not able to bear it, neither yet now are ye able. For ye are yet carnal: for whereas there is among you *envying*, and strife, and divisions, are ye not carnal, and walk as men?" (1 Corinthians 3:1-3) Many of the Corinthian saints failed to grow into the fullness of Christ simply because of the stumbling block of envy in their lives.

There are few sins that create greater torture and unhappiness than envy. To have an envious nature is to be exposed to an incessant gnawing of the heart, which, sad to say, accompanies many through life. Of course, the only One who can give lasting victory over jealousy is the Son of God. Think not that you can face this evil in your own strength. Ask the Lord to give you a permanent victory; He is willing, He desires to do so. Let Him work in your heart and life as you humbly confess the envy of your heart.

3. *The Attitude – verse 10.* How did Daniel react to the new law? "Now when Daniel knew that the writing was signed, he went into his house; and his windows being open in his chamber toward Jerusalem, he kneeled upon his knees three times a day, and prayed, and gave thanks before his God, as he did aforetime." The action of the king did not affect Daniel in the least. When he received knowledge of what had been done, he went to his house at the appointed time and prayed as always. Daniel did not complain, nor did he feel sorry for himself; he simply continued to live as he had always lived. Prayer was as important to Daniel's soul as food to his body. He ate three meals a day, but he also prayed three times a day. He was a man of courage and valor; more than that, he was a man of prayer. Doubtless it was on his knees that he received his fearless courage.

There is a striking similarity between David and Daniel in this respect. David declared in Psalm 55:17, "Evening, and morning, and at noon, will I pray, and cry aloud: and He shall hear my voice." Daniel was likewise gallant and bold. It has been said, "If your knees tremble, kneel on them." Many of us are weak and ineffectual for the Lord because we do not give the proper place to prayer in our lives. In Psalm 46:1-2 David writes, "God is our refuge and strength, a very present help in trouble. Therefore will not we fear, though the earth be removed, and though the mountains be carried into the midst of the sea." Because God was his refuge and strength, David turned to the Lord three times a day to unload all his burdens and cares on

Him. Neither David nor Daniel could live without prayer.

God has promised to show us "great and mighty things," but there is no promise in all the Bible that He will show us the "great and mighty things" without faithful prayer. In 2 Chronicles 7:14 He says, "If My people, which are called by My name, shall humble themselves, and pray, and seek My face, and turn from their wicked ways; then will I hear from heaven, and will forgive their sin, and will heal their land." There are other steps to be taken in our quest for revival, but prayer is basic.

The importance of prayer in revival was proven some years ago in the Telugu-speaking area of India. Over 2,000 people had been baptized in a single day. But as time went on, a coldness moved into the church so that there appeared to be a spiritual dearth. Some of the saints became greatly disturbed by the lack of spiritual power. They banded together in prayer, asking the Lord to revive His work. After much preparation, ten days were set aside to pray specifically for revival.

One of the missionaries told what happened during one of those meetings: "At about 8 o'clock, at what seemed an ordinary meeting, someone was praying, when suddenly there was a sob. One cried out. Like a flash, something came over the meeting and there was a tumult of sound, cries, groans, and beseeching calls on God. One present said it sounded like a rushing mighty wind." Another missionary said, "For the first time in thirty-three years in India we have really seen natives crying for their sins." This feature much impressed the heathen. They crowded the door, saying, "Why, they are crying for their sins. How strange."

What God did in India He wants to do in every country of the world. The church today is cold, indifferent, and powerless. If we are to experience revival, there must be many Daniels who will come to the front and be men of persevering prayer.

The Reaction of Reverence

You will note that Daniel's praying was a matter of habit. His was not the emergency kind of prayer practiced by many. We are not told that he opened his windows in his chamber toward Jerusalem; they were already open. Daily and nightly he had been interceding for his people, the Jews. At the appointed time, he went to his stated place for prayer and called on the Lord, regardless of the consequences. In the face of the immediate danger, for his own welfare, Daniel might have closed the windows and sought another place for prayer. Doubtless there were those who were familiar with Daniel's prayer pattern, having observed him praying before the open windows. Would they not be watching in an attempt to catch the prophet breaking the law? Of course they would! But God was first in Daniel's program. The decree did not deter him. He prayed as he did "aforetime."

Someone may ask, "Are not believers supposed to respect the governmental authorities and their powers? Are we not commanded to do this in Romans 13:1-2, 'Let every soul be subject unto the higher powers. For there is no power but of God: the powers that be are ordained of God. Whosoever therefore resisteth the power, resisteth the ordinance of God: and they that resist shall receive to themselves damnation.'" Under normal circumstances, we must give due respect to authority. But when our right to believe in the Lord and commune with Him is taken from us, we are not obligated to bow to such godless authority. Daniel knew this. Thus he was unchanged and unmoved when confronted with the diabolical decree.

4. *The Accusation — verses 11-13.* Daniel prayed as always before the open windows facing Jerusalem. He was visible to those who were anxious to bring judgment upon him, thus the schemers "assembled, and found Daniel praying and making supplication before his God." The word "assembled" as used here embodies the same thought as expressed in its use in verse 6, "hastening or going quickly." With the unquestionable evidence, the

men "came near, and spake before the king concerning the king's decree; Hast thou not signed a decree, that every man that shall ask a petition of any God or man within thirty days, save of thee, O king, shall be cast into the den of lions? The king answered and said, The thing is true, according to the law of the Medes and Persians, which altereth not."

The king was already in the trap that had been laid by the deceivers, but by his admission he removed any possibility of escape. "Then answered they and said before the king, That Daniel, which is of the children of the captivity of Judah, regardeth not thee, O king, nor the decree that thou hast signed, but maketh his petition three times a day." They were suggesting that Daniel was a traitor, that he should not have been trusted in the first place, that since he was of the "captivity of Judah," this should have been enough to keep him from office. But as King Darius had placed Daniel in office, the wicked plotters were desirous that the king discover his mistake.

Consider the circumstances for a moment. We see the faithful Daniel as the victim of a wicked scheme engineered by selfish and godless swindlers. Was he pacing the floor, overwhelmed with fear? After all, his life was at stake. I am confident that Daniel was praying and resting in the all-sufficiency of his great God. He knew he had to face trial. Daniel was a man of faith who knew that somehow God would provide the solution. We are told in Habakkuk 2:4 that "the just shall live by his faith." By "his faith" is meant complete reliance on the Lord. Daniel knew that nothing could come into his life without his Father's permission, therefore he had nothing to fear. He could say as did the Apostle Paul, "For whether we live, we live unto the Lord; and whether we die, we die unto the Lord: whether we live therefore, or die, we are the Lord's" (Romans 14:8).

God is in everything. Does this mean that God was the instigator of this wicked plan to kill Daniel? God was not

The Reaction of Reverence

the instigator, but surely He could use it for His own glory and Daniel's good. God is never brought to failure by the deeds of the unregenerate. The Creator of the universe is so masterful that He can take the works of the godless and bring forth fruit unto Himself.

David declared in Psalm 76:10, "Surely the wrath of man shall praise Thee." How vividly this was portrayed in the life of Joseph. His brothers turned against him because of jealousy and hatred. They tried to do away with him, and even though they appeared to be successful in their wicked venture, God had other plans for His servant. He preserved his life and exalted him. Later Joseph summed it up in speaking to his brothers: "But as for you, ye thought evil against me; but God meant it unto good, to bring to pass, as it is this day, to save much people alive" (Genesis 50:20).

The Lord's care for Joseph was no exception in His dealing with His own. God always does this. No matter what the extent of the evil may be, the Lord will prove Himself to be sufficient. It is for this reason that we must not allow ourselves to be disturbed by any outward circumstances, but rather receive the marvelous peace of God that will help us through the trial until we reach the glory at the end. Remember, we see things from the human side — God looks at them from the divine. Ours is only a partial vision — His is unlimited. We can trust Him implicitly, knowing that whatever our lot may be, for us it is the very best. Our responsibility is not to try to figure things out, but to rest in God's redeeming grace and trust in His unfailing love.

One evening, father and mother were discussing current events. In the light of the seriousness of recent happenings, doubtless they expressed some anxiety. Later when mother was about to pray with her little daughter, a question was asked.

"Mommy, at supper tonight you and Daddy seemed

awfully worried. Is it because you think bad men will blow up the world?"

The mother, an earnest Christian, felt rebuked by this question and replied, "I guess we did act worried and scared. I am sorry, my dear."

"Well then, Mommy," said the child, "when I'm scared you comfort me. Why don't you tell God you are scared and tell Him you are sorry? I am sure He will tell you He is looking after things just like you tell me. And you know, Mommy, you said Jesus would come when things got too bad in the world. Isn't that true?" In Isaiah 11:6 we read that "a little child shall lead them." That mother was led by her little child.

5. *The Anxiety — verses 14-20.* When the king learned what had happened, he "was sore displeased with himself." Realizing the mess he was in, he "laboured till the going down of the sun" in an attempt to find some means whereby Daniel could be delivered from the lions' den. Assured that their king was ensnared, the crafty schemers said, "Know, O king, that the law of the Medes and Persians is, That no decree nor statute which the king establisheth may be changed." The king knew there was only one thing to do — to cast Daniel into the den of lions.

With great sorrow in his heart because of his regrettable mistake, Darius tried to comfort Daniel as he was being rushed off to the lions' den: "Thy God whom thou servest continually, He will deliver thee." It is not to be supposed that the king really believed this, but he had to say something and this seemed to be appropriate. Quickly Daniel was lowered down into the underground dungeon where the lions were kept. A huge stone was placed over the opening. Next "the king sealed it with his own signet, and with the signet of his lords; that the purpose might not be changed concerning Daniel." Humanly speaking, there was no possible escape for Daniel.

An important observation should be made before going

The Reaction of Reverence

further. The king sought to deliver Daniel from judgment but he was unable to do so; he was helpless to save just one person because of the law. Daniel had to be cast into the den of lions. In contrast, think of the King of kings, who came to provide deliverance not for only one person but for all. Darius was helpless because of the law but the Lord Jesus, being the Son of God, fulfilled the law perfectly and "gave Himself a ransom for all, to be testified in due time" (1 Timothy 2:6).

Christ provided deliverance from sin and judgment because He was more than a man. Darius was a mere man, bound by sinful limitations. Jesus, the Son of God, was "without blemish and without spot" (1 Peter 1:19). Unreservedly, He sacrificed Himself on the cross, that the door to salvation might be opened, that "whosoever believeth in Him should not perish, but have everlasting life" (John 3:16). Darius could not offer Daniel deliverance; Christ, on the other hand, can offer deliverance. He offers it to anyone who will receive Him as Saviour and Lord. Have you received Him?

Joseph Vages of Cuba was picked up by the *S.S. Eldorado*. The lad, when rescued, was lying on the bottom of the boat, naked and delirious, chewing his clothing, part of which he had eaten. It appears that the boy and two others had been fishing off Havana when a storm came up and the boys had no control over the boat. Frightened, his companions swam ashore but Joseph, unable to swim, remained in the boat and drifted to sea. For nearly a week he was exposed to wind and weather. His sufferings were dreadful. When picked up, he had drifted five hundred and thirty miles from Cuba. Unable to do anything about his need, he simply drifted with the tide and the drifting nearly cost him his life. Without God, man is drifting farther and farther away from the truth. Remember, not only does Christ want to save you, He can save you if you let Him be your Saviour and Lord.

After Daniel was cast into the lions' den, the king went to his palace in great mental anguish. He refused to eat. Later he went to bed and tried to sleep but it was useless; he tossed and turned. Very early in the morning he arose and hastened to the lions' den. As he neared, he shouted aloud, "O Daniel, servant of the living God, is thy God, whom thou servest continually, able to deliver thee from the lions?" This question suggests that not only was the king interested in Daniel's welfare, but he was becoming interested in Daniel's God. This was a good question coming from an unsaved man. It is the question asked by unbelievers constantly. Though they may not ask it audibly, yet they watch Christians to see if God is able to deliver them. Frequently by our complaining and worry we give the world the wrong impression. Because we doubt, the unbelievers who watch us fall into worse unbelief.

Consider this question, "Is thy God, whom thou servest continually, able to deliver thee?" Of course He is. Job could testify to this. Think what he endured, how sorely he was afflicted. Yet at the end of it all he could say of the Lord, "I know that Thou canst do every thing" (Job 42:2). Oh, that you and I might say the same and really mean it. What sorrow could be averted. God is as good as His Word. Solomon could say, "There hath not failed one word of all His good promise, which He promised by the hand of Moses His servant" (1 Kings 8:56). It is impossible for the Lord's promises to fail. Let us trust Him and believe that He is able to deliver.

6. *The Assurance — verses 21-24.* How reassuring Daniel's voice must have sounded to the anxious king. Probably Darius had never spent such a restless night. Now his fears were allayed — Daniel was alive. There was no enmity or bitterness whatsoever in Daniel's heart. With deference he replied to Darius' question, "O king, live for ever." Daniel desired to be a testimony to this pagan king, thus he continued: "My God hath sent His angel, and hath

The Reaction of Reverence

shut the lions' mouths, that they have not hurt me: forasmuch as before Him innocency was found in me; and also before thee, O king, have I done no hurt." Darius had spoken of Daniel's God; the prophet gave an immediate response: "Yes, He is my God." Further, Daniel made it known that his God was a faithful God who "sent His angel" to shut the mouths of the lions.

How marvelous is God's care in preserving His people! In His own way, He always undertakes for our needs. Daniel was not kept *from* the lions' den, but he was kept *in* it. The Lord has not promised to keep His children from trial, but He has said, "I will never leave thee, nor forsake thee" (Hebrews 13:5). There are times when the lions stand before us with gaping mouths, but we are assured that "The angel of the LORD encampeth round about them that fear Him, and delivereth them" (Psalm 34:7). In 1 Peter 5:8 we read that our "adversary the devil, as a roaring lion, walketh about, seeking whom he may devour." How frequently you and I are confronted by this one who is "as a roaring lion," with his mouth open, ready to devour us. But we have One who has conquered sin and its power, who has given us the enablement to resist all temptation. How clearly this truth is portrayed in Psalm 97:10: God "preserveth the souls of His saints; He delivereth them out of the hand of the wicked." He never fails.

Do you think Daniel was frightened when they lowered him into the lions' den? Possibly, for Daniel was a man, and man at his best is only a man. Left to ourselves we shall be fearful when facing the enemy. But God assures us in 1 John 4:18 that "perfect love casteth out fear." Perfect love is mature love, the result of a life fully committed to God. Daniel was in possession of this kind of love; fear disappeared and faith produced courage.

Though Daniel is not named in the challenging faith chapter of Hebrews 11, yet there is no question about who is meant in verse 33, "Who through faith . . . stopped the mouths of lions." Daniel was a man of faith. We have observed this in our previous studies, but his experience in the den of lions is noteworthy in this respect. God's perfect love not only banished fear for Daniel, but at the same time produced faith to believe that God would undertake. What God did for Daniel, He desires to do for us. How many of our burdens could be turned into blessings if only we would believe the promises of God.

The story is told of the ant who was dragging a piece of straw almost an inch long. This would be like a human trying to drag a log. The ant pulled and struggled, trying to move his burden. Creeping across the desert of concrete, he came to a crack in the concrete. Here it looked hopeless. How could he drag this straw across the crack? He stopped and ran back and forth. It seemed as though he was about to give up. The burden was too much. But what did he do? He managed to push the straw across the crack and then walked across on the straw, after which he continued to drag the straw along. For the little ant, the burden became a bridge and a blessing.

God says in Proverbs 6:6, "Go to the ant, thou sluggard; consider her ways, and be wise." How much better off we are than the ant. We have Almighty God to bear our burdens for us. But remember, "Without faith it is impossible to please Him" (Hebrews 11:6). Let us trust Him implicitly, knowing that He "is able to do exceeding abundantly above all that we ask or think" (Ephesians 3:20).

After Darius heard Daniel's voice, he was "exceeding glad for him, and commanded that they should take Daniel up out of the den." The servants responded to the king's command immediately: "So Daniel was taken up out of the den, and no manner of hurt was found upon him, because he believed in his God." Daniel believed that his God would provide, and the Lord did not fail him.

But look what happened to those who had accused Daniel: "And the king commanded, and they brought those men which had accused Daniel, and they cast them into the den of lions, them, their children, and their wives; and the lions had the mastery of them, and brake all their bones in pieces or ever they came at the bottom of the den." Those who had thought to trap Daniel were now caught in their own trap. Is it not true, as God has said, "Be not deceived; God is not mocked: for whatsoever a man soweth, that shall he also reap. For he that soweth to his flesh shall of the flesh reap corruption; but he that soweth to the Spirit shall of the Spirit reap life everlasting" (Galatians 6:7-8). God makes it clear that the "wages of sin is death" (Romans 6:23). One may think he is deceiving God, but God sees everything and He is the Judge.

7. *The Announcement – verses 25-28.* Following the judgment on Daniel's accusers, King Darius wrote a new decree. He addressed it to "all people, nations, and languages, that dwell in all the earth." Following the usual salutation, "Peace be multiplied unto you," the decree read as follows: "I make a decree, That in every dominion of my kingdom men tremble and fear before the God of Daniel: for He is the living God, and stedfast for ever, and His kingdom that which shall not be destroyed, and His dominion shall be even unto the end. He delivereth and rescueth, and He worketh signs and wonders in heaven and in earth, who hath delivered Daniel from the power of the lions." This was a remarkable proclamation. What a testimony it bore to the mighty power of our great God. It is obvious that the Lord did a miraculous work in Darius' heart.

In comparing Nebuchadnezzar's decree (3:29) with that of Darius, you will recognize readily the greater spiritual depth in the latter. Nebuchadnezzar pronounced judgment upon any who were to "speak any thing amiss against the God of Shadrach, Meshach, and Abednego," while Darius gave a clear-cut witness to the Lord Jehovah, demanding that his subjects "tremble and fear" before the Lord.

Surely we must agree that God performed a mighty work in the heart of Darius. What encouragement this should provide for all of us who have unsaved friends and loved ones for whom we have been praying. Daniel's first relationship to Darius must have been disheartening, for here was a pagan king with no concern or interest in the Lord Jehovah. Though we are not told in so many words that Daniel was instrumental in pointing the king to the Lord, it seems clear that this was the case. Recall how the king was attracted to Daniel because of "an excellent spirit." Daniel was a man of God. He was well known for his integrity and saintly character. Who could deny that this had a profound effect upon the king? When one is yielded to the control of the Lord, the transformed life will provide convincing proof of God and His power to the hardest heart. The unsaved may offer arguments in opposition to our beliefs. They may even question some of the statements of Scripture. But who can deny the effectiveness of a God-controlled heart and life?

In Isaiah 43:10 the Lord declared, "Ye are My witnesses." It is disturbing to see how much emphasis Christians put on *lip* witnessing, and how little emphasis is put on *life* witnessing. Jesus declared, "Ye are the salt of the earth: but if the salt have lost his savour, wherewith shall it be salted? it is thenceforth good for nothing, but to be cast out, and to be trodden under foot of men" (Matthew 5:13). The moment we cease living for God, we have lost our "savour," and any lip witnessing we do will have little effect. Paul could say, "Be ye followers of me, even as I also am of Christ" (1 Corinthians 11:1). The word "followers" as used here is really the word "imitators." Thus what Paul actually said was, "Imitate me, even as I also imitate Christ." If those around you were to imitate your life, to what extent would they be imitators of Christ?

The Reaction of Reverence

Rae Smith, a missionary teacher in New Guinea, writes: "One day I had written a copy of the capital letters of the alphabet in the writing book of one of the boys and found that I had made a mistake in writing one of the letters. Not having an eraser at hand, I drew a line through the letter and rewrote it correctly beside the one with the mistake. I told the boy that he must try to copy as well as he could what I had written for him. When he handed his book to me at the end of the lesson, I saw that he had copied everything — even the mistake with the line through it. At the time we had a good laugh over it, but what a lesson this incident taught me as I realized once again that the only Christian way of life these people see is that lived by their missionary. I wondered how many mistakes in my life these people had copied."

God's power is not limited. He can crush stony hearts and draw men to repentance. But let us remember, God's witness of His glory is revealed through His people. It is amazing what God can do through "clean hands, and a pure heart" (Psalm 24:4). Because Daniel was such a man, Darius came to the Lord. There are many Dariuses that need to be reached at this moment. Let God speak to them through you.

In the concluding verse of the chapter we read, "So this Daniel prospered in the reign of Darius, and in the reign of Cyrus the Persian." To be sure, the man with "excellent spirit" will be the man with the blessing of the Lord. Let this be a call from God to you to yield your entire self to Him, that the Spirit's ministry will in no way be hindered by the flesh. God desires to work through you; let Him do it. If you are unsaved, He wants you to receive His Son into your heart. You cannot live the Christian life until you are indwelt by Christ. I urge you to open the door of your heart and let Him in!

Chapter 7

THE RENUNCIATION OF RESISTANCE

Key verse, 9: "I beheld till the thrones were cast down, and the Ancient of days did sit, whose garment was white as snow, and the hair of His head like the pure wool: His throne was like the fiery flame, and His wheels as burning fire."

Considering the chapter divisions of the book of Daniel which have been supplied by the translators, the twelve chapters divide easily into two parts. With chapter seven we begin the second important division of Daniel. Generally it could be said that the first six chapters treat the historical aspect of the book, while the latter six deal with the prophetical, though in the strict sense we find both historical and prophetical teachings throughout the entire twelve chapters.

As we commence the study of this momentous section of the book dealing specifically with prophecy, in which there are many things hard to understand, it is essential that we keep in mind the words of God's servant in Deuteronomy 29:29, "The secret things belong unto the LORD our God: but those things which are revealed belong unto us." Do not strain at the unknowable; on the other hand, take to heart readily that which through the Holy Spirit is clear and understandable. Indeed we must pray for wisdom as we delve into these passages in search of the spiritual gems God has placed there for His own blood-bought children.

1. *The Burden — verses 1-3,15-16.* There is a striking similarity between the subject matter of chapter seven and that of chapter two, although the visions and the methods of presentation are different. In chapter two the vision was given to an ungodly man, while in the seventh chapter it was given to a holy man. Chapter two presents the political aspects of the kingdoms involved while in chapter seven consideration is given to the moral characteristics.

We are told, "In the first year of Belshazzar king of Babylon Daniel had a dream and visions of his head upon his bed: then he wrote the dream, and told the sum of the matters." From Daniel's statement regarding "the first year of Belshazzar," we see readily that chapter seven does not follow chapter six chronologically.

Daniel tells about his "dream and visions": "I saw in my vision by night, and, behold, the four winds of the heaven strove upon the great sea. And four great beasts came up from the sea, diverse one from another." The striving of the four winds of the heaven upon the great sea denote political strife, uprisings, wars, and bloodshed among nations. There seems to be no question about the sea referring to the Mediterranean Sea, which is spoken of frequently in the Scriptures as the great sea. It is worthy of note also to realize that all four of the kingdoms depicted in Daniel's vision bordered on the Mediterranean Sea at some time during their existence. Symbolically, the great sea represents the masses of people in the kingdoms that are portrayed in the vision. These masses are lashed by the judgments of God in the "winds of the heaven," even as the sea is stirred by the mighty winds. Daniel describes his vision further: "Four great beasts came up from the sea, diverse one from another." As we shall see, each of these beasts of prey was ravenous, oppressive, and ferocious.

Going to verse 15 we find that Daniel was greatly

burdened because of what he had seen: "I Daniel was grieved in my spirit in the midst of my body, and the visions of my head troubled me." Daniel needed more light and understanding to know the meaning of these visions. Here was a man in his eighties, close to ninety. He had been walking with God for many, many years, yet he never lost his quest for more spiritual food. What a challenge for us. In God's Word we have an inexhaustible Book. If it were possible for any of us to study it eight hours a day throughout an entire lifetime, we would be far from mastering its contents. This should not deter us, but challenge us to spend time with the Book. Let us pray for the spiritual hunger within to seek the truth of God as it has been made known in His flawless revelation. Do not be satisfied with a hasty reading of a chapter or two a day. Do as Jesus said, "Search the scriptures" (John 5:39).

Rarely is there ever one in search of truth who does not find it. Daniel wrote, "I came near unto one of them that stood by, and asked him the truth of all this. So he told me, and made me know the interpretation of the things."

Daniel began the interpretation: "These great beasts, which are four, are four kings, which shall arise out of the earth." Actually, these were "four kingdoms." Throughout the Scriptures, kingdoms and kings are used interchangeably. Frequently we find in the Bible that the name of the sovereign heading up his empire is used to represent his kingdom. For example, Nebuchadnezzar in some instances stands for Babylon and Darius and Cyrus for Medo-Persia. We might also think of Alexander as representing Greece; and Augustus, Rome. The fact that the four beasts seen by Daniel were kingdoms is further substantiated by verse 23: "The fourth beast shall be the fourth kingdom upon earth."

2. *The Beasts — verses 4-7.* Daniel's vision of the "four great beasts" that "came up from the sea, diverse one from another" now is described in greater detail. The

The Renunciation of Resistance   139

first beast "was like a lion, and had eagle's wings." Furthermore, "the wings thereof were plucked, and it was lifted up from the earth, and made stand upon the feet as a man, and a man's heart was given to it." It has been said that all history is *His story*. Indeed, it is. The study of the four beasts of Daniel's vision portrays this fact clearly, for as has already been stated, the "beasts" represented four kingdoms. The lion symbolized the vast empire of Babylon. The "head of gold" becomes a wild lion. This is not without significance, for as gold is the chiefest of metals, the lion is the king of the forest. Babylon was like a lion in the sense that she rose to her zenith of power quickly and mightily. The "eagle's wings" suggest the rapidity of her conquests.

Babylon's greatness, however, was to be short-lived, for she was to be subdued by a second beast. Daniel said further concerning Babylon, "I beheld till the wings thereof were plucked, and it was lifted up from the earth, and made stand upon the feet as a man, and a man's heart was given to it." Here Babylon's humiliation is prophesied. The great nation would not be destroyed, but subdued. The plucking of the wings suggests her utter humiliation. But look at the monstrosity — a lion made to "stand upon the feet as a man, and a man's heart was given to it." Here is a picture of weakness. The powerful king of the forest was weakened by a man's heart rather than a beast's heart. It is believed that this was the case when Belshazzar succeeded Nebuchadnezzar, for after King Nebuchadnezzar's death the empire gradually declined until it was so weakened by debauchery and wickedness that it was no real problem for the second beast to move into control.

The second beast was "like to a bear, and it raised up itself on one side, and it had three ribs in the mouth of it between the teeth of it: and they said thus unto it, Arise, devour much flesh." This prophecy had to do with the Medo-Persian Empire, depicted in Nebuchadnezzar's vision as the chest and arms of silver. The bear "raised up itself on one side," which means that one of its paws was lifted. The Medes and Persians were two empires unified under one head. Babylon was conquered by Darius of the Medes, but soon the Persians under Cyrus became much stronger than the Medes and assumed power and control, as seen in the bear with the one paw raised. The three ribs in the mouth of the bear foretold Persia's strength and further conquests as she was to "arise" and "devour much flesh."

The third beast had the appearance of "a leopard, which had upon the back of it four wings of a fowl; the beast had also four heads; and dominion was given to it." Corresponding to the brass thighs of Nebuchadnezzar's vision, this was the Greco-Macedonian Empire. It has been said, "The lion devours, the bear crushes, but the leopard springs upon its prey." In the third beast we see agility and swiftness. With the wings of the fowl it becomes even more swift. Such was the case in the Grecian Empire under its vigorous and energetic king Alexander. All the well-known books record the swiftness with which he expanded his vast empire. It is said that Alexander the Great sat and wept because he had no more nations to conquer.

But the glory of Greece soon vanished. Following the death of Alexander the Great, who died in his early thirties as the result of his extremely sinful and wicked life, the kingdom was divided into four parts, and the leadership vested in four generals, as prophesied in the "four heads."

The fourth beast was unusually ferocious: "After this I saw in the night visions, and behold a fourth beast, dreadful and terrible, and strong exceedingly; and it had great iron teeth: it devoured and brake in pieces, and stamped the residue with the feet of it . . . and it had ten horns." It is obvious that Daniel had a further vision regarding the fourth beast and additional light was given.

The Renunciation of Resistance 141

It seems, too, that the Holy Spirit would have us concern ourselves with the vision of the fourth beast more than the other three, because what He said regarding the fourth beast has not as yet been fulfilled completely. The other prophecies became history. Much regarding the fourth beast has been fulfilled but not all. This prophecy refers to the Roman Empire which is described as "dreadful and terrible, and strong exceedingly." In Nebuchadnezzar's vision we saw the Roman Empire as "strong as iron: forasmuch as iron breaketh in pieces and subdueth all things: and as iron that breaketh all these, shall it break in pieces and bruise" (Daniel 2:40). The conquests of the Romans were unprecedented. Indeed, "it was diverse from all the beasts that were before it."

Much more will be said about this vision, but let us not overlook the one remaining statement regarding the fourth beast: "It had ten horns." There has never been a time in the history of the Roman Empire when this prophecy was fulfilled. Consequently it is yet to be fulfilled in the last times, as we shall see. The Roman Empire will be re-established during the end time, and what is said here regarding the ferocity of this beast is yet to be fulfilled in the finality of its meaning.

At the end of the present age, during the tribulation period, a "little horn" will arise, the Antichrist, who will seek to destroy all of the work of God. He will reign for a few brief years only, for the "Ancient of days" will come to subdue the forces of evil forever. At that time Paul's thrilling prophecy of 1 Corinthians 15:24-25 will come to pass: "Then cometh the end, when He shall have delivered up the kingdom to God, even the Father; when He shall have put down all rule and all authority and power. For He must reign, till He hath put all the enemies under His feet." The course of history has always been a series of conflicts and upheavals. The future will not change until Christ comes, and then the will of God will be done on earth even as it is in Heaven.

3. *The Blasphemer — verses 8,25a.* Daniel told us of the vision of the "ten horns" representing the ten kingdoms within the Roman Empire. He continued: "I considered the horns, and, behold, there came up among them another little horn, before whom there were three of the first horns plucked up by the roots: and, behold, in this horn were eyes like the eyes of man, and a mouth speaking great things." Note in verse 25 that the little horn "shall speak great words against the most High." The one about whom Daniel speaks will begin as a "little horn," but we see from this chapter that he will become stronger and stronger. First of all, he will take control of three of the kingdoms, for "three of the first horns" were "plucked up by the roots." This one who will rise in the latter days before the return of Christ will possess great power which he will use to gain control over the entire world.

The "little horn" will have eyes like the eyes of man. "Eyes" in the Scriptures symbolize intelligence. He will be a man of unusual wisdom and human ability. There are other characteristics mentioned in this chapter that describe this powerful personage, but notice that he will come "speaking great things." As used here, "great" does not mean notable or praiseworthy, but shameful and profane. He will launch his most venomous attack against God, blaspheming His holy Name. There is no question about the identity of the "little horn," for his attitude toward God positively identifies him as the Antichrist. In many ways he will impersonate Christ and even make promises similar to Christ's. But all his promises will prove to be lies.

The "little horn" of this chapter is easily recognized as the beast of Revelation, chapters 13 and 17. Of all the characters who have lived on the earth, this man will be the worst. In his speeches he will go to every extreme of blasphemy to achieve his diabolical goals. Possessed and

The Renunciation of Resistance

controlled by Satan himself, this ruler will be the personification of evil of the worst sort.

More and more in our day, we can see Satan actively engaged in his pursuit of preparing the world for the Antichrist. The Apostle John warned us of this as he wrote in verse 7 of his Second Epistle, "For many deceivers are entered into the world, who confess not that Jesus Christ is come in the flesh. This is a deceiver and an antichrist." Who are these deceivers? Many of them are in our pulpits today, clothed in ecclesiastical garb. By their high-sounding phrases they impress their congregations with their intelligence and ability. They appear to be pious, but it is all superficial. While professing to be believers, they deny the Christ of the Bible and repudiate the truths of God's Word. They are controlled by the spirit of the "deceiver" and Antichrist who is to come. The Apostle John warns of the spirit of the Antichrist: "Little children, it is the last time: and as ye have heard that antichrist shall come, even now are there many antichrists; whereby we know that it is the last time. They went out from us, but they were not of us; for if they had been of us, they would no doubt have continued with us: but they went out, that they might be made manifest that they were not all of us" (1 John 2:18-19).

The fact that there are so many in our day professing to be ministers of God, while at the same time denying God's Son, assures us conclusively that civilization is drawing near to the end when the Antichrist himself will be revealed to blaspheme the Most High God and to pour his fury upon all who honor and worship the Lord. As we see the traditional denominations being run by ecclesiastical machinery controlled by godless men, it behooves those of us who are followers of Christ to identify ourselves with our Lord not merely by words but by life. In 1 Timothy 5:14-15 God says to us, "Give none occasion to the adversary to speak reproachfully. For some are already turned aside after Satan." How important that each believer give himself afresh to God, that he might "be a vessel unto honour, sanctified, and meet for the master's use, and prepared unto every good work" (2 Timothy 2:21).

4. *The Brutality — verses 23-25.* Not only will the "little horn" of this chapter be recognized by his blasphemy but also by the extreme persecution he will pour out upon the "saints." We are told, "The fourth beast shall be the fourth kingdom upon earth, which shall be diverse from all kingdoms, and shall devour the whole earth, and shall tread it down, and break it in pieces. And the ten horns out of this kingdom are ten kings that shall arise: and another shall rise after them; and he shall be diverse from the first, and he shall subdue three kings. And he shall speak great words against the most High, and shall wear out the saints of the most High, and think to change times and laws: and they shall be given into his hand until a time and times and the dividing of time." There are some who try to interpret this in relationship to the old Roman Empire. There is a sense in which it could be said that the Roman kingdom was "diverse from all kingdoms." In political power as well as many other ways, the Roman Empire was distinguished from the Babylonian, Medo-Persian, and Grecian Empires. But it could never be said that the Roman Empire was divided into ten parts, out of which there arose a leader overcoming three of them and then controlling the entire empire.

It is clear from the Scriptures that it was God's plan that Rome was to have a threefold history. The first has come and gone under the Caesars. The second is the present period while the Roman Empire is nonexistent. The third is yet to come. The mighty empire will be re-established and controlled by ten powerful leaders. Ultimately there will be one indomitable leader who will be more powerful than anyone who has ever ruled the earth. He will be distinguished easily by his brazen blasphemy and his bloodthirsty oppression.

Some expositors have sought to apply the teaching regarding the "little horn" to the pope and Romanism. Here again, though some of the prophecies relative to the little horn could be considered from a historical point of view, yet there is much said that cannot be identified with the pope and the Roman Catholic Church. In the study of prophecy, we must be very careful not to link names with the unnamed characters.

The Antichrist will be operative especially during the seven-year tribulation period. During the first three and a half years his strength will not be fully realized. It may be that during this time he will be continuing in his rise to power. But at the end of three and a half years his fury will be unleashed. No one will be able to stand against this master of men. Anyone who names the name of Jesus Christ will suffer unmercifully at his hand, for he "shall wear out the saints of the most High." There have been times when God's people have been persecuted beyond measure, but throughout the history of the world this has usually occurred provincially rather than world-wide. There have been times when believers were hated and despised. Their blood ran in the streets because of godless men seeking to destroy the testimony of Christ. But when the little horn strikes he will bear no resemblance whatever to any other dictator. He will attempt to destroy everything and everyone that bears even a favorable attitude toward Christ.

Furthermore, the Antichrist will "change times and laws." He will inaugurate his own system of government. Most of all, he will seek to dispose of the laws of God in an attempt to control the universe without any trace of divine intervention. Every possible attempt will be made to abolish moral law. It is almost impossible to imagine such conditions.

We are told that this control will be "given into his hand until a time and times and the dividing of time." This seems to describe clearly a period of three and one half years. It was prophesied regarding Nebuchadnezzar, "That they shall drive thee from men . . . and *seven times* shall pass over thee, till thou know that the most High ruleth in the kingdom of men, and giveth it to whomsoever He will" (Daniel 4:25). The "seven times" refer to seven years. It was for this period that Nebuchadnezzar was under the judgment of God. Thus "a time" being one year, "times" would refer to two, and the "the dividing of time" to a half year. It will be during the latter three and one half years of the tribulation period that the little horn will bring about bloodshed such as has never been known in the history of the world. His wrath will be vented especially on all those who worship and honor Christ.

The little horn's authority will be short-lived, for, as we see from this same chapter of Daniel, "the Ancient of days" will come and subdue the power of the "little horn." The little horn's effort to control the earth will be sinful man's final attempt to resist the Almighty, for at the end of the three and a half years of terrible tribulation Christ will come to reign as King of kings and Lord of lords. There will be many who will quickly and willingly rally to the side of the "little horn," hoping that he will provide deliverance. But how sorrowful they will be when they discover that the "little horn" will be powerless and helpless before the Son of God. Instead of finding refuge, they will be outcasts from God.

5. *The Battle — verses 19-21.* Actually this is a battle between unrighteousness and righteousness, godlessness and holiness, immorality and purity. The reign of the little horn will be marked by gross iniquity. Morals will be abolished and lust will become unbridled. Among other things, the little horn will "change times and laws." He will abolish every law that even suggests morality and

The Renunciation of Resistance

sobriety. Who could begin to describe living conditions in such an environment under the control of the godless monster portrayed in this chapter.

Daniel writes in verses 19-21: "Then I would know the truth of the fourth beast, which was diverse from all the others, exceeding dreadful, whose teeth were of iron, and his nails of brass; which devoured, brake in pieces, and stamped the residue with his feet; And of the ten horns that were in his head, and of the other which came up, and before whom three fell; even of that horn that had eyes, and a mouth that spake very great things, whose look was more stout than his fellows. I beheld, and the same horn made war with the saints, and prevailed against them." The fourth beast will be "diverse from all the others, exceeding dreadful."

Doubtless the domination of the future Roman kingdom will be world wide. It is possible that even America will be a part of it. Because of its extreme might, described by the "teeth of iron, and nails of brass," it "devoured, brake in pieces, and stamped the residue with his feet." When the revived Roman Empire reaches the zenith of its power with its ten vast kingdoms under its control, the eleventh horn will rise, who is described as being "more stout than his fellows." Empowered by Satan, this man will appear to be superhuman. No one will be able to resist him. It seems obvious that he will achieve the world dominion which many have sought in former generations. He will have no time or regard for God nor for "the saints of the most High." He will consider himself god while stamping out morality and blaspheming the name of the Lord Jehovah.

The "saints" of God will endeavor to obey the moral truths of the Scriptures. The profane beast, on the other hand, will not only seek to destroy morality but will launch a concerted effort to spread immorality. As one considers the popular "new morality" being advanced by many clergymen in our day, we wonder if we are not approaching the time when the little horn will begin his rise to power.

In a highly respected women's college in Baltimore, the chaplain, the Rev. Frederic C. Wood, Jr., spoke to the young women in a message entitled, "Sex Within the Created Order." Boldly he declared, "There are no laws attached to sex — there is nothing which you ought to do or ought not to do." He continued, "Sex is good. Sex is fun; it is also funny. Premarital intercourse is not bad or dirty. Indeed, it can be very beautiful ... sex is natural ... we all ought to relax and stop feeling guilty about our sexual activities, thoughts, and desires."

The *Campus Encounter*, the publication of the United Campus Christian Fellowship, campus movement of the Christian Churches (Disciples of Christ), Evangelical United Brethren, United Church of Christ, and United Presbyterian Church U.S.A., printed one of the most blatant pieces of sex propaganda yet. The story, "Love Without Fear," was written by Robert C. Buckle, vice-president of the Cornell University United Religious Work. Written to college young people and strongly advocating premarital and extramarital relations, the article speaks of a "new world" in which marriage vows will no longer be needed. The essence is that youth would be free to live with anyone of their choice.

The Rev. Howard Moody, pastor of the Judson Memorial Church (Baptist) in New York City, authored an article in *Christianity in Crisis*, entitled, "Toward a New Definition of Obscenity." In the article his bold and brazen statements were punctuated by dirty words in his attempt to prove that they were not vulgar. He said, "It is hardly justifiable to make a moral or theological case against raw language as the Church is tending to do." To substantiate his point, the Judson Memorial Church featured nude dancers at a service to prove "that nudity on stage can be almost as prim and proper as a church social."

The Renunciation of Resistance 149

There is no question about it: we are rapidly moving toward the end time. The influence of the "little horn" is at work in the hearts of many posing as religionists. What a challenge this is to those who are truly saints of God in Christ Jesus. Ours is a tremendous responsibility to walk with the Lord in the power of His might. We must not become a part of our age, yielding to the surrounding temptations of our environment. God makes it clear in Colossians 3:1-3 that the evidence of the new birth is a new life: "If ye then be risen with Christ, seek those things which are above, where Christ sitteth on the right hand of God. Set your affection on things above, not on things on the earth. For ye are dead, and your life is hid with Christ in God." There is no room for impurity in the Christian life.

After Paul wrote in Colossians 3 of the believer's call to walk in newness of life, he went on to say, "When Christ, who is our life, shall appear, then shall ye also appear with Him in glory" (Colossians 3:4). He reminded us that we are to walk as a heavenly people in anticipation of the return of our Lord Jesus Christ: "Mortify therefore your members which are upon the earth; fornication, uncleanness, inordinate affection, evil concupiscence, and covetousness, which is idolatry" (verse 5). "Mortify" means to kill, or more literally, to deprive of power. You and I have no strength within ourselves to deprive our body of the lusts of the flesh, but Christ can give the enablement. As we yield continually to His almighty control, we shall be victorious.

It is essential that we claim the Lord's victory for our thinking, since thoughts precede actions. In Philippians 4:8 Paul wrote, "Finally, brethren, whatsoever things are true, whatsoever things are honest, whatsoever things are just, whatsoever things are pure, whatsoever things are lovely, whatsoever things are of good report; if there be any virtue, and if there be any praise, think on these things." Frequently throughout the day we need to pray that God will give us clean hearts and pure minds, that our walk will be well-pleasing unto Him. Let us permit Him to live through us, that we shall be able to stand against the forces of evil with the assurance that when He comes we shall be like Him.

6. *The Blessedness — verses 13,14,18,22,26-27.* The Antichrist will be mighty. But we come now to consider One who is the Almighty, before whom even the Antichrist with his superhuman power will fall. In one of his visions Daniel got a glimpse of the eternal Christ: "I saw in the night visions, and, behold, one like the Son of man came with the clouds of heaven, and came to the Ancient of days, and they brought Him near before Him. And there was given Him dominion, and glory, and a kingdom, that all people, nations, and languages, should serve Him: His dominion is an everlasting dominion, which shall not pass away, and His kingdom that which shall not be destroyed." The reign of the Antichrist will be limited, for at the return of the Lord Jesus even this wicked blasphemer will be brought to his knees to "confess that Jesus Christ is Lord, to the glory of God the Father" (Philippians 2:11). The scene Daniel is describing here will take place in Heaven. The Son of man will confer with the Ancient of days, who of course is God, the Father.

The Father has committed all judgment to the Son. The Lord Jesus made this fact known to the embittered Jews who were angry because He had healed on the Sabbath: "For the Father judgeth no man, but hath committed all judgment unto the Son: That all men should honour the Son, even as they honour the Father. He that honoureth not the Son honoureth not the Father which hath sent Him" (John 5:22-23). Furthermore we are told that Christ was given a kingdom and that He would reign over all the peoples and nations of the world. His kingdom would not be like that of the Babylonians, Medo-Persians, Grecians, or Romans. Rather the fifth and final kingdom

The Renunciation of Resistance

described in the book of Daniel will be an everlasting kingdom which no human will be able to destroy.

In verses 18 and 22 Daniel reveals the place of the saints in Christ's kingdom: "But the saints of the most High shall take the kingdom, and possess the kingdom for ever, even for ever and ever. Until the Ancient of days came, and judgment was given to the saints of the most High; and the time came that the saints possessed the kingdom." Think of it, those who have been downtrodden, persecuted, and martyred in all the ages past will someday be placed in positions of world-wide rulership. Paul assures us in 2 Timothy 2:12, "If we suffer, we shall also reign with Him." Consider all the sufferings the people of God have endured and shall endure at the hands of their godless persecutors. This will not continue forever. All who participate in the first resurrection will be on the Lord's side and will know the blessedness of the millennium John describes in Revelation 20:6, "Blessed and holy is he that hath part in the first resurrection: on such the second death hath no power, but they shall be priests of God and of Christ, and shall reign with Him a thousand years." During the closing three and a half years of the seven-year tribulation period the Antichrist will unleash a reign of terror, but when the Son of man returns to earth, He will establish His kingdom which will be perfect in righteousness and peace.

Daniel writes further of the kingdom in verses 26 and 27: "But the judgment shall sit, and they shall take away his dominion, to consume and to destroy it unto the end. And the kingdom and dominion, and the greatness of the kingdom under the whole heaven, shall be given to the people of the saints of the most High, whose kingdom is an everlasting kingdom, and all dominions shall serve and obey Him." This is practically a repeat of what he has already written in the chapter. It is a confirmation of the assuring fact, stated by the prophet in Habakkuk 2:14, "For the earth shall be filled with the knowledge of the glory of the LORD, as the waters cover the sea." God's chosen people Israel will be brought back to their land and will be re-established in their own country. Ever since their beginning as a nation the Jews have been a persecuted and ridiculed people. But God assures them in Ezekiel 36:24, "For I will take you from among the heathen, and gather you out of all countries, and will bring you into your own land." Never again will the Lord's people know suffering or sadness, for Christ's "name shall endure for ever: His name shall be continued as long as the sun: and men shall be blessed in Him: all nations shall call Him blessed." Though bitter days are coming and though hours of extreme suffering are near, the best is yet to come, and those who will be trodden under foot and slain as animals in the tribulation period because of their belief in Christ, will sit on a throne of glory with the King of kings during the millennium.

How important it is that men and women turn to the Lord now before it is too late. We have the warning by the prophet in Zephaniah 1:14: "The great day of the LORD is near, it is near, and hasteth greatly, even the voice of the day of the LORD: the mighty man shall cry there bitterly." In 2 Thessalonians 1:7-9 God's servant appeals to all who need the Lord: "And to you who are troubled rest with us, when the Lord Jesus shall be revealed from heaven with His mighty angels, In flaming fire taking vengeance on them that know not God, and that obey not the gospel of our Lord Jesus Christ: Who shall be punished with everlasting destruction from the presence of the Lord, and from the glory of His power." Why will anyone choose everlasting destruction when he might as easily have everlasting life? Those who want life must choose Christ, for in Him only can everlasting life be known.

7. *The Books — verses 9-12, 28.* In concluding chapter 7, several remaining statements of supreme importance must not be overlooked. The scene before us is one of judgment. Daniel describes the judge: "I beheld

The Renunciation of Resistance 153

till the thrones were cast down, and the Ancient of days did sit, whose garment was white as snow, and the hair of His head like the pure wool: His throne was like the fiery flame, and His wheels as burning fire. A fiery stream issued and came forth from before Him: thousand thousands ministered unto Him, and ten thousand times ten thousand stood before Him: the judgment was set, and the books were opened." Doubtless this scene is in Heaven immediately before the return of Christ and the destruction of the beast. The "Ancient of days" appears to be God the Father and, as we have seen in other portions of this chapter, the "Son of man" is God the Son. In the description given of the Son of God in Revelation 1:13-16, both seem to be combined into one. Christ is the God-man who comes to execute divine wrath on the enemy of the Lord.

We are told in the King James version that Daniel "beheld till the thrones were cast down." The words "cast down" should be translated "set" or "placed." The prophet is not speaking of the thrones on earth that were soon to be cast down, but the throne of God's judgment that was being set up in Heaven prior to Christ's return. We see also that "the books were opened." Probably the books bore the same judgment for the beast as for Belshazzar: "Thou art weighed in the balances, and art found wanting." Following the opening of the books, the Son of God will leave the glories of Heaven and come to earth, not to appear in a lowly manger, but to reveal Himself as the King of kings and Lord of lords. Immediately the Lord Jesus will judge the beast. Daniel writes, "I beheld then because of the voice of the great words which the horn spake: I beheld even till the beast was slain, and his body destroyed, and given to the burning flame." The beast will be cast into eternal hell where he will remain during the thousand-year reign of Christ, after which he will be raised to appear before the Great White Throne of God. The judgment upon the other beasts who sought to help the Antichrist will not be as severe, "As concerning the rest of the beasts, they had their dominion taken away: yet their lives were prolonged for a season and time." God will permit them to continue to live on the earth for a short season before casting them into hell.

Though the judgment described in this passage takes place in Heaven before the return of Christ, typically it does depict the Great White Throne judgment that will be set up at the close of the millennium. For what is said in verse 10 will certainly be true of Christ when He will sit on the throne of judgment at the close of the millennium: "A fiery stream issued and came forth from before Him: thousand thousands ministered unto Him, and ten thousand times ten thousand stood before Him: the judgment was set, and the books were opened." What an impressive sight this will be, when the books are opened.

Many there are in our day who cheat, steal, and deceive, thinking all is done under cover. They do not realize that everything is being recorded in the annals of Heaven. God declares in Numbers 32:23, "Be sure your sin will find you out." There have been many who thought they were getting ahead in spite of their dishonesty. If only they could realize that they cannot escape the judgment of God. This fact is presented so clearly in Galatians 6:7-8: "Be not deceived; God is not mocked: for whatsoever a man soweth, that shall he also reap. For he that soweth to his flesh shall of the flesh reap corruption; but he that soweth to the Spirit shall of the Spirit reap life everlasting." God assures us that all sin will be judged. There have been those who have been clever in eluding the police while hiding their crimes; but this will not continue forever, for some day the books will be opened. In Romans 2:3 God asks the searching question, "And thinkest thou this, O man . . . that thou shalt escape the judgment of God?" No lost soul will ever escape this judgment, for the Lord Jesus made it clear in John

The Renunciation of Resistance

5:28-29 that "the hour is coming, in the which all that are in the graves shall hear His voice, And shall come forth; they that have done good, unto the resurrection of life; and they that have done evil, unto the resurrection of damnation."

As we have just seen, the Bible teaches two judgments, one for the righteous, at which time the members of His Body will be judged for their works; and the other for the unsaved, the Great White Throne judgment, at which time the books will be opened and the unsaved will be judged on the grounds of their sin and rejection of Christ.

One of our radio listeners wrote telling us of the sudden homegoing of her husband who was only fifty-two years of age. This man was a believer. There is no doubt about it, he went to be with the Lord Jesus Christ. But being reminded of the suddenness by which death may come, his wife wrote, "Please tell all your radio audience how important it is not to wait even five minutes to receive Jesus Christ to be born again. There was no time or warning for my husband, but I know he is safe in the arms of Jesus. Tell your listeners that salvation is today, right now." Indeed, there is no time to wait; tomorrow may be too late. God makes it clear in His Word, "Now is the accepted time; behold, now is the day of salvation" (2 Corinthians 6:2).

Chapter 8

THE RESTRAINT OF REVOLT

Key verse, 25: "And through his policy also he shall cause craft to prosper in his hand; and he shall magnify himself in his heart, and by peace shall destroy many: he shall also stand up against the Prince of princes; but he shall be broken without hand."

A decided change takes place commencing with this chapter, which begins what is known as the Jewish portion of the book, relating primarily to the Jews and Jerusalem. From the early part of chapter 2 through chapter 7, the language employed is Chaldee, having to do largely with the Gentiles. But from chapter 8 through to the concluding verses of the book, Hebrew, the familiar language of the Old Testament, is used.

1. *The Observation — verses 1-3,15-20.* The Prophet Daniel was given another vision. As to the time, it was "In the third year of the reign of king Belshazzar." From this we gather that two years elapsed between chapters 7 and 8. At the time of the vision, Daniel was approximately eighty-eight years of age. "The third year of the reign of king Belshazzar" was the year when Belshazzar, the grandson of Nebuchadnezzar, gave his licentious banquet which preceded his fall. Daniel declared that the vision was given to him, "after that which appeared unto me at the first." Doubtless the first vision was the one described in chapter 7, during the first year of Belshazzar.

The Restraint of Revolt 157

Regarding the place where the prophet received the vision, he said, "I saw in a vision; and it came to pass, when I saw, that I was at Shushan in the palace, which is in the province of Elam; and I saw in a vision, and I was by the river of Ulai." Later Shushan became one of the capital cities of the Medo-Persian Empire. Whether Daniel was actually in the palace in Shushan in his body, or merely transported in the spirit, is not clear. This is of little importance since it is the fact of the vision with which we are concerned.

"Then I lifted up mine eyes, and saw, and, behold, there stood before the river a ram which had two horns: and the two horns were high; but one was higher than the other, and the higher came up last." God's servant was not left in the dark as to the meaning of the vision, for the interpreting angel appeared to him, and, as we see from verses 15-20, the meaning was made clear. First Daniel tells about the angel: "And it came to pass, when I, even Daniel, had seen the vision, and sought for the meaning, then, behold, there stood before me as the appearance of a man. And I heard a man's voice between the banks of Ulai, which called, and said, Gabriel, make this man to understand the vision." The angel had "the appearance of a man," which means obviously that he appeared in human form, specifically the angel Gabriel.

The appearance of the angel had a profound effect upon Daniel: "So he came near where I stood: and when he came, I was afraid, and fell upon my face." The heavenly visitor told Daniel that what he was about to reveal was not merely historical but prophetical, having to do with the "time of the end." The prophet "was in a deep sleep on my face toward the ground." The angel touched God's servant and immediately he arose, ready to listen to the further revelation to be given by Gabriel. Repeating what he had already said, the angel instructed the prophet regarding the relationship of the vision to the end of time.

"Behold, I will make thee know what shall be in the last end of the indignation: for at the time appointed the end shall be." It would seem that "the last end of the indignation" refers especially to the closing days of God's chastisement upon His chosen people, preparing the way for their confession, repentance, and forgiveness, resulting in their deliverance from the beast.

Verse 20 provides important prophetic information. The angel stated plainly, "The ram which thou sawest having two horns are the kings of Media and Persia." How reliable the Scriptures are. We are not left to conjecture as to the meaning of the vision; the details are presented clearly. The ram Daniel saw with the two horns, one higher than the other, represented the Medo-Persian Empire, corresponding to the breast and arms of silver of Nebuchadnezzar's image and the bear that was lifted up on one side in Daniel's previous vision.

This vision was given when Belshazzar was still in power. No one would have suspected that Medo-Persia would soon destroy the reign of the present ruler. But the time of the ram was nearing. Incidently, the ram was the symbol of Persia, which she bore on all her banners. Again, how descriptive the Scriptures are. The "two horns" depict the two nations, Media and Persia, the one "higher than the other, and the higher came up last." Later Persia became the more powerful of the two.

Once again, as we have already seen in this book of prophecy, we have clear-cut evidence of history having been prewritten. Even before the Medo-Persian Empire came into power, the important facts of its ascendancy were given to the Prophet Daniel. In Isaiah 40:8 we read, "The grass withereth, the flower fadeth: but the word of our God shall stand for ever." Because the Word of God "shall stand for ever," those who know the Lord should study the Book, with diligence and concern, and an earnest desire to know the mind of God.

The Restraint of Revolt 159

2. *The Oppression — verse 4.* Daniel has something more to say regarding his vision of the ram which provides further evidence of the inerrant truth of God's Word: "I saw the ram pushing westward, and northward, and southward; so that no beasts might stand before him, neither was there any that could deliver out of his hand; but he did according to his will, and became great." Let us be reminded again that Daniel's vision was given to him while the Babylonians were still in power. All the prophet has written in this chapter relative to the Medo-Persian Empire was definitely prophetic.

Notice the direction in which the Persian Empire launched its attack, "westward, and northward, and southward." Coming from the east they did not press eastward, but only in the three directions. History gives evidence of the complete and detailed fulfillment of this prophecy. The Persians achieved vast conquests in the directions cited by Daniel. The result was that this mighty empire spread from India to Ethiopia, which at the time was the known world.

"The kings of the earth set themselves, and the rulers take counsel together, against the LORD, and against His Anointed, saying, Let us break their bands asunder, and cast away their cords from us" (Psalm 2:2-3). Here is a bold and brazen attack not merely on God's creatures but on God Himself. But how ridiculous on the part of mortal man. Is the Lord disturbed by such foolish and hopeless defiance? Of course not. He is Lord of all. "He that sitteth in the heavens shall laugh: the Lord shall have them in derision" (verse 4). Not only does God laugh at those who openly defy His principles and truth, He pours judgment upon them, that His plans may be brought to fruition: "Then shall He speak unto them in His wrath, and vex them in His sore displeasure" (verse 5). Furthermore the Psalmist declared, "Thou shalt break them with a rod of iron; Thou shalt dash them in pieces like a potter's vessel" (verse 9). For centuries godless, merciless dictators have sought to rule the world, but in every instance they were permitted only limited accomplishment before being stayed. The Lord of all is the ruler of the world. Because He is invisible to the human eye does not mean that He is unreal.

All of the prophetic Scriptures will eventually be fulfilled. Many of them have been already. There are thousands more that are being and will be fulfilled before the Lord comes to this earth to rule and reign with limitless power. Thus let us not be alarmed by the events of the day, for the true believer can rest in the fact that all is being done "according to His will"; that no man, irrespective of military power, can go farther than the divine plan allows. In Joshua 2:11 we read, "The LORD your God, He is God in heaven above, and in earth beneath." This condition never has nor never will change: "The earth is the LORD's, and the fulness thereof; the world, and they that dwell therein" (Psalm 24:1).

God's purposes will be brought to pass, not according to our desires but "according to His will." Whether it be the course of an empire or the direction of one's life, God reigns supreme always. How consoling this truth is amidst the uncertainties and perplexities that confront all believers. In Isaiah 55:8-9 God says, "For My thoughts are not your thoughts, neither are your ways My ways, saith the LORD. For as the heavens are higher than the earth, so are My ways higher than your ways, and My thoughts than your thoughts." In our prayer life, the theme must be, as our Lord said, "Not My will, but Thine, be done" (Luke 22:42). How much of our praying is composed primarily of petitions, beseeching God to do certain things rather than waiting upon Him, seeking His divine guidance.

A wealthy American living in Paris was induced by friends to try for an appointment as a member of the United States Embassy in Paris. They told him it would give him more prestige and "help him greatly socially." So

The Restraint of Revolt 161

he came to Washington and gained an audience with the president, during which he said, "I think I could serve my country if I could have this appointment in Paris." The president interrupted him, saying, "My friend, a man desiring to serve his country does not begin by saying where he is going to serve." So it is when you and I go before God, let us in like manner be submissive, willing to receive orders from Him rather than to tell Him what He should do for us. Let us pray as did the Psalmist, "Teach me to do Thy will" (Psalm 143:10).

3. *The Opposition — verses 5-7,21.* A further vision was to have a definite bearing on Persia. Notice first of all that the prophet said, "As I was considering." This suggests that, as he was waiting before God in quiet meditation, another vision was given. How essential is the practice of waiting upon God if we desire to know more of His truth. We cannot understand prophecy by a casual, hasty reading of the Scriptures. God says, "Wait on the LORD: be of good courage, and He shall strengthen thine heart: wait, I say, on the LORD" (Psalm 27:14). David said in Psalm 39:3, "While I was musing the fire burned." The fire will burn in our hearts only as we meditate on the Scriptures.

While he was waiting before the Lord, this unusual vision came to Daniel: "Behold, an he goat came from the west on the face of the whole earth, and touched not the ground: and the goat had a notable horn between his eyes." We should take special note of the fact that this mighty power came from the west. When Daniel received the vision almost three hundred years before it was fulfilled, such a thing had never been known. The East had always been the center of civilization. But Daniel's vision made it clear that a mighty power would arise in the West and verse 21 identifies that power as Greece: "And the rough goat is the king [kingdom] of Grecia." When this prophecy was made known to Daniel, Greece was nothing more than a group of independent states. But gradually

Greece began to emerge from weakness into strength, until when Persia least expected it this irresistible power thrust forth from the west. Greece came toward her avowed enemy with great swiftness, described by the words, "touched not the ground."

We are told further that "the goat had a notable horn between his eyes." From verse 21 we learn that this "notable horn" symbolized Alexander the Great: "The great horn that is between his eyes is the first king." A description of Alexander's conquest of Persia is given by the prophet: "And he came to the ram that had two horns, which I had seen standing before the river, and ran unto him in the fury of his power. And I saw him come close unto the ram, and he was moved with choler against him, and smote the ram, and brake his two horns: and there was no power in the ram to stand before him, but he cast him down to the ground, and stamped upon him: and there was none that could deliver the ram out of his hand." What is said here in just a few words is confirmed by all of history. Greece was "moved with choler against" Persia. For centuries the Persians had been the object of hatred on the part of the Greeks because of former conquests by the Persians. It seemed that the Greeks were never able to overcome their humiliation received from the hands of the Persians, but finally the time came for revenge. Alexander struck with all his fury and, as stated in the prophecy, "He cast him down to the ground, and stamped upon him: and there was none that could deliver the ram out of his hand."

Here is the description of another remarkable fulfillment of prophecy. History confirms every detail which has been supplied for us regarding the he-goat and his surge to power. All that God has declared in His Word will be brought to pass. We may say, as did Solomon in his prayer, "There hath not failed one word of all His good promise" (1 Kings 8:56). We read in Psalm 119:89, "For ever, O LORD, Thy word is settled in heaven." If God

The Restraint of Revolt

were to fail to keep His Word even once, He would be fallible like the rest of us. But the Word of God is settled once and for all, never to change. Long after the achievements of men have passed away, the Word of God will continue. "Heaven and earth shall pass away, but My words shall not pass away" (Matthew 24:35).

Since the Bible is what it is, the eternal Word of God divinely inspired by the Lord Himself, then those who know the Lord should study this Book; for God has given us in His Word instructions for living not only in this life but for eternity. The Lord promises in Psalm 32:8, "I will instruct thee and teach thee in the way which thou shalt go." Primarily the instruction spoken of here comes from the Bible. Let us give prayerful attention to it.

A chaplain who served in World War II was asked unexpectedly to speak to the men in his area. Not having time to prepare a sermon, while walking to where the men were waiting, wondering what he was going to say to them, He asked God to give him a message. Suddenly his eyes fell upon an empty Jello box, and he picked it up. When he arrived at his destination he held his box up where all could see the large brand name.

"What is this?" he asked.

"An empty Jello box."

"And what is this?" he pointed to some reading matter on one side of the container.

"Directions how to make Jello," someone exclaimed.

"Well," said the chaplain, "suppose I knew nothing about how to make the Jello. Suppose I had never seen anyone make it. What chance would I have of making it successfully if I ignored these directions?" Then holding his Bible up before the men, he continued, "When God put us into this world He sent along a book of directions to tell us how to live successfully. If we ignore these directions, thinking we can run our own lives, we make the most serious mistake possible."

God has given us a Book which has been proved to be infallible. There are many proofs as to its infallibility; fulfilled prophecy is an important one.

4. *The Offender* — *verses 8-10,22-24*. Very quickly the Grecian kingdom came to the top as the supreme power of the day. "Therefore the he goat waxed very great: and when he was strong, the great horn was broken; and for it came up four notable ones toward the four winds of heaven." Though Greece "waxed very great," its power and position did not continue for long. In the midst of its supremacy, "the great horn was broken." This prophecy refers to Alexander the Great, who, as a young man of about twenty, started his conquests and very quickly achieved his goal of world-wide domination. At the youthful age of twenty-six he controlled the entire Persian Empire, but only six or seven years later his power "was broken."

Alexander's pattern of life is evidenced by so many in our present age. The young king was not killed in battle but died as the result of drunkenness and debauchery. His brief span of success suggests the multitudes of unsaved people who live for the flesh with no regard for eternity. They are like the rich fool of Luke 12, who lived for this world only. God had been gracious to him in providing repeated successful and plentiful harvests, but never did he give thought to God. In fact, we are told that "he thought within *himself*" (verse 17), that is, he was concerned only with his own selfish benefits.

As the wealthy farmer "thought within himself" he asked, "What shall I do, because I have no room where to bestow my fruits?" (verse 17) Here was his solution: "This will I do: I will pull down my barns, and build greater; and there will I bestow all my fruits and my goods. And I will say to my soul, Soul, thou hast much goods laid up for many years; take thine ease, eat, drink, and be merry" (verses 18-19). But in the midst of his

The Restraint of Revolt

selfish musing there was a startling interruption: "God said unto him, Thou fool, this night thy soul shall be required of thee: then whose shall those things be, which thou hast provided?" (verse 20) Christ, in relating this incident, made the following application: "So is he that layeth up treasure for himself, and is not rich toward God" (verse 21). How many are duplicating the tragic mistake of the rich farmer! How we need to consider Mark 8:36-37: "What shall it profit a man, if he shall gain the whole world, and lose his own soul? Or what shall a man give in exchange for his soul?"

Many are living for selfish gain, ignoring the claims of Christ on their soul. Jesus said in Luke 12:15, "Beware of covetousness: for a man's life consisteth not in the abundance of the things which he possesseth." Life is not found in things. Real life is found in Christ. Apart from Him there can be no lasting satisfaction.

The Scripture is clear as to what was to follow Alexander's death: "The great horn was broken; and for it came up four notable ones toward the four winds of heaven." Further in the interpretation given by Gabriel we read in verse 22, "Now that being broken, whereas four stood up for it, four kingdoms shall stand up out of the nation, but not in his power." There was a time of uncertainty following Alexander's death regarding the kingdom and its future course, but after a period of time four divisions were set up as foretold in Daniel's vision. Later there came forth out of one of these kingdoms Syria, "a little horn, which waxed exceeding great, toward the south, and toward the east, and toward the pleasant land. And it waxed great, even to the host of heaven; and it cast down some of the host and of the stars to the ground, and stamped upon them." Further we read in verses 23 and 24, "And in the latter time of their kingdom, when the transgressors are come to the full, a king of fierce countenance, and understanding dark sentences, shall stand up. And his power shall be mighty, but not by his own power: and he shall destroy wonderfully, and shall prosper, and practise, and shall destroy the mighty and the holy people." There is no doubt as to the identity of this wicked king. Surely this prophecy applies in part to the wicked Antiochus Epiphanes. Antiochus called himself Epiphanes, which means, "the Illustrious." But he was so vile and heartless that those who knew him changed his name to Epimanes, meaning "the Madman."

Coming from the north, Antiochus Epiphanes struck at Egypt in the south and Persia in the east, but his most oppressive attacks were on the "pleasant land," Palestine. His hatred was poured out on the Jews as on no other people. He "cast down some of the host and of the stars to the ground, and stamped upon them." This prophecy is related to those in authority among the Jews, the priests and leaders. Antiochus' bitter persecutions were not executed "by his own power" but by satanic power. Energized by the devil, this cruel oppressor was prospered and given great liberty in his exploits of destroying "the mighty and the holy people."

But though this prophecy had its partial fulfillment in Antiochus Epiphanes, it can by no means be limited to him. It clearly characterizes the Antichrist, about whom we have already studied in chapter 7. Antiochus Epiphanes poured out his wrath upon the Jews, but what he did was minor in comparison to what the Antichrist will do in the last three and a half years of the tribulation period.

5. *The Oblation — verses 11-14.* More is said in these verses about the bitter oppressor of the Jews, Antiochus Epiphanes. God tells us that "he magnified himself even to the prince of the host." That is, he gave no regard whatsoever to the Lord of Glory, openly defying the God of Heaven and earth. Antiochus was godless and despised all who honored the Lord Jehovah. In an attempt to

The Restraint of Revolt 167

prevent the Jews from worshiping, he forbad the offering of daily sacrifices: "By him the daily sacrifice was taken away." Literally this reads, "*from* him the daily sacrifice was taken away"; that is, Antiochus Epiphanes refused to allow the Jews to offer their sacrifices to their God, "the prince of the host." Furthermore, it was through the diabolical efforts of Antiochus that God's sanctuary was "cast down." "Cast down" does not mean that the Temple was destroyed. Rather, he profaned it, making it the temple of Jupiter Olympium. One wonders why God permitted such abomination to befall His people Israel. Yet when you consider the apostasy of Israel at the time, the next verse becomes understandable: "And an host was given him against the daily sacrifice by reason of transgression, and it cast down the truth to the ground; and it practised, and prospered." For years Israel had lived in disobedience to the law of God, reveling in gross iniquity. As the result, the Lord permitted the severe chastening under the rod of Antiochus Epiphanes "by reason of transgression."

We are told that Antiochus "prospered" in his atrocities. To be sure, his power was delegated power. When God's people turn from the way of the Lord, even the godless may be used to bring God's chosen ones back to Himself. There have been occasions in history when the Lord has used one nation to bring judgment on another as punishment for wickedness and constant neglect of God. One wonders if the same will not be the case in our country, where we have enjoyed so many privileges through God's mercy. In spite of the Lord's marvelous grace, as a nation we are getting farther and farther away from Him.

Daniel heard a conversation: "Then I heard one saint speaking, and another saint said unto that certain saint which spake, How long shall be the vision concerning the daily sacrifice, and the transgression of desolation, to give both the sanctuary and the host to be trodden under foot?" "Saint" means "holy one," and it seems obvious that the holy ones Daniel heard were angels who possessed knowledge of the length of time God's sanctuary would be desecrated and the Jews persecuted. "The transgression of desolation" was referred to by the Lord Jesus years later. We have His words in Matthew 24:15, "When ye therefore shall see the abomination of desolation, spoken of by Daniel the prophet, stand in the holy place, (whoso readeth, let him understand)." "The transgression of desolation" mentioned by Daniel had a partial fulfillment during the purge of Antiochus Epiphanes. From what the Lord Jesus said, it will be more completely fulfilled in the time of the end: "For then shall be great tribulation, such as was not since the beginning of the world to this time, no, nor ever shall be" (Matthew 24:21). It would seem that the greater fulfillment of this prophecy will be realized under the domination of the Antichrist. There are able expositors who teach that the prophecy will be fulfilled by the Assyrian king from the north. They have portions of Scripture to support their teaching. But whether it is the wicked king from the north who will pour fury on the Jews, whom he will hate and despise, or the Antichrist, who will set himself up as Christ, he will be one who will abhor God and His people.

You will notice that one of the saints asked the other question, though it was Daniel who was given the reply: "And he said unto me, Unto two thousand and three hundred days; then shall the sanctuary be cleansed." In other words, the holy sacrifices were to be abolished and the Temple of God was to be desecrated for about twenty-three hundred days. There are some who have interpreted this erroneously as years. The word "days" as used here is literally "evenings – mornings." History bears out the fact that from the time Antiochus Epiphanes sacrificed a sow upon the altar of God, and poured its broth throughout the Temple, as an act of wicked desecration, until the time when this wicked despot was oppressed by the Romans and the Maccabees was a period of twenty-three hundred literal days. Thus here is another of the remarkable fulfilled prophecies that assures us conclusively that the Bible is the inspired Word of God.

We have seen that Antiochus Epiphanes and the Antichrist are guilty of a similar evil — the abuse of God's Temple. But have you ever stopped to consider that many believers also are guilty of this sin? In 1 Corinthians 6:19 the question is asked, "What? know ye not that your body is the temple of the Holy Ghost which is in you, which ye have of God, and ye are not your own?" If you have claimed Christ as your Saviour and Lord, the body in which you dwell is God's temple. In 2 Timothy 2:19-21 God says: "Let every one that nameth the name of Christ depart from iniquity. But in a great house there are not only vessels of gold and silver, but also of wood and of earth; and some to honour, and some to dishonour. If a man therefore purge himself from these, he shall be a vessel unto honour, sanctified, and meet for the master's use, and prepared unto every good work." Call upon the indwelling Holy Spirit to purge you of every evil work and abuse, that you will in no way desecrate God's temple!

6. *The Overthrow — verse 25.* Not only do we find a further description of the satanic control of Antiochus Epiphanes in verse 25, but we see the prophecy of his ultimate doom: "And through his policy also he shall cause craft to prosper in his hand; and he shall magnify himself in his heart, and by peace shall destroy many: he shall also stand up against the Prince of princes; but he shall be broken without hand." This prophecy makes it clear that Antiochus would make many gains and achieve what many might judge to be success. His policies, however, would be questionable and despicable, for he would be fraudulent and deceitful in accomplishing his purposes as he causes "craft to prosper in his hand." He

would also be a man well known for his haughtiness and conceit: "He shall magnify himself in his heart." He was to be so deluded by his pride that he would go so far as to put himself in the place of God, instituting laws and commandments of his own making, advocating his own rules for worship.

Not only would Antiochus be fraudulent in his methods and proud in his actions, he would prove himself to be bloodthirsty and heartless, "By peace" he "shall destroy many." His methods of warfare would be identical with his policies of control. No one would be able to trust him, for he would say one thing and do another. He would pretend to work for peace while striving constantly for destruction. While signing treaties for peace, he would break them with no thought or conviction for his inconsistency. By his crafty methods he would conquer his subjects by trickery rather than bravery. What has been said about Antiochus thus far has been bad enough, but actually these things are as nothing when compared to the fact that "he shall also stand up against the Prince of princes." Could one be so brazen as to try to argue and fight with God? Yes, Antiochus Epiphanes would stop at nothing, even trying to resist the Almighty. He did this primarily in his judgments, which were poured out on God's chosen people, the Jews. He broke their hearts by profaning the Temple and worship, but he also broke their bodies by severe persecution. Openly he defied the Lord of lords.

Antiochus' cruel and selfish rebellion did not continue for long. Prophecy was fulfilled and the despised monarch was "broken without hand." "Without hand" means that it was not by human strength that he was brought low. God humbled Antiochus and brought him face to face with death. "Vengeance is Mine; I will repay, saith the Lord" (Romans 12:19). No one can resist Almighty God without suffering judgment. This is what happened to Antiochus Epiphanes, and the same will happen to the

The Restraint of Revolt

Antichrist. As in the case of Antiochus, so the Antichrist will not be killed in warfare, nor will he be assassinated; he will simply fall into the hands of a holy and all-righteous God and be brought to his end. This prophecy had been given earlier in Nebuchadnezzar's dream, depicting the "great image" in chapter 2. In the interpretation of the dream Daniel declared, "Forasmuch as thou sawest that the stone was cut out of the mountain without hands, and that it brake in pieces the iron, the brass, the clay, the silver, and the gold; the great God hath made known to the king what shall come to pass hereafter: and the dream is certain, and the interpretation thereof sure" (Daniel 2:45). Jesus Christ is the Stone "cut out of the mountain without hands," who will return to earth and by a word subdue the vicious blasphemer, the Antichrist. There will be no warfare nor bloodshed; the Antichrist will be subdued by the power of God and His Word.

Antiochus Epiphanes made great strides in his godless purge until finally, because the Jews had cast the image of Jupiter out of the Temple, which had been placed there by the wicked dictator, he became embittered and claimed that he would make Jerusalem "a common burial place." No sooner had he made this declaration than he was inflicted with an incurable disease. His sufferings were unbearable and the stench from his own body was so horrible that even Antiochus himself could not stand the smell. At first he sought to fulfill his threat but, finding it impossible, he called some of his men together and frankly confessed that he knew he was suffering because of what he had done to the Jews and their worship. Soon he died in misery, a foolish man who sought to resist God.

The Antichrist, of whom Antiochus Epiphanes provided a type, will come to a sorrowful end. He, too, will be proud and crafty, making false claims while breaking treaties and persecuting the people of God. But his reign will be short-lived, for the Lord will come, as He has declared, and both the beast and the false prophet will be "cast alive into a lake of fire burning with brimstone" (Revelation 19:20).

No man can stand against God and live. Judgment must come ultimately. Likewise no man, regardless of his position in society, can expect any less than judgment for his sins unless he repents and turns to Christ. In Amos 4:12 the prophet exhorts all men everywhere to "prepare to meet thy God." The only preparation anyone can make is to acknowledge Jesus Christ, the Son of the living God, as his own personal Saviour and Lord. God's judgment comes quickly at times. His mercies are new every morning and His grace is all-sufficient, but without repentance judgment must come.

7. *The Occupation — verses 26-27.* Here we see two things; first, the angel gives Daniel final instructions regarding the vision he had received; and secondly, Daniel tells of the effect the vision had upon him. The angel states that "the vision of the evening and the morning which was told is true." The "evening and the morning" refer to the twenty-three hundred days which was to be the length of time for the fulfillment of all that was prophesied in the vision. Daniel was assured that this was not merely a dream, but that all he had seen would most certainly come to pass.

What the angel declared about the vision being "true" could certainly be said of all of Scripture. The Psalmist wrote, "Thy word is true from the beginning: and every one of Thy righteous judgments endureth for ever" (Psalm 119:160). How surprised millions will be when in hell they discover that what God has said in His Word from Genesis to Revelation is truth. We who know the truth must spread the message of life and do all possible through the power of the Holy Spirit to awaken the minds of men to the reality of Christ.

The angel said to Daniel, "Shut thou up the vision." There are two inferences here. First, it seems that Daniel

The Restraint of Revolt

was not to make this vision known to anyone else. At the time the Chaldeans were in power but the Persians were moving in. What had been revealed in the vision would doubtless cause the Persians to become incensed if it were known, and they would attack the Jews immediately. For this reason it would not have been practical for the vision to be revealed just then. Furthermore, it would seem that Daniel did not have full understanding of all the ramifications of the vision, but the angel assured him that it was not necessary to understand it completely then since it involved the future. He was further told that the vision "shall be for many days," that is, it would not be fulfilled "for many days." In fact, it was some 300 years from the time the vision was given until it was fulfilled.

Daniel understood enough about the vision so that it had a profound effect upon him: "I Daniel fainted, and was sick certain days." Realizing the judgment that would befall his own people by the hands of the ungodly, Daniel was so disturbed that he became ill. Unselfish as he was, the prophet could not divorce himself from the calamities of others. He had a heart concern for his own people. Well might all of us who are in Christ imitate this worthy attitude of God's servant. There is such a need today for believers with a loving interest not only in the unsaved but in the people of God.

Daniel did more than merely brood over his circumstances; he did all possible to alleviate the situation. Rising from his illness, he went out to do the work that was at hand, much as did the early disciples of whom we read in Acts 8:4, "Therefore they that were scattered abroad went every where preaching the word." The more they were persecuted, the more they sought to serve. Obstacles are to be expected, for there is a living devil who opposes all that is right and holy. Daniel knew this, but he "rose up, and did the king's business."

Daniel "was astonished at the vision, but none understood it." Because he could not understand all that he saw, Daniel was "astonished." We are in a far better position than Daniel to understand the vision. Much of it has been fulfilled, and soon the remainder will be fulfilled; but while we wait, let us work, and like Daniel "rise up to do the king's business." Centuries ago David declared, "The king's business required haste" (1 Samuel 21:8). It requires haste still; you and I must redeem the time and grasp the opportunities to make known the name of Jesus Christ. Millions have not yet heard about Him, yet the judgment of God is coming. The unsaved millions should be given a chance to hear the gospel at least once. God has made it clear in His Word that without Christ there is no hope.

Chapter 9

THE RETROSPECT OF REPENTANCE

Key verse, 7: "O Lord, righteousness belongeth unto Thee, but unto us confusion of faces, as at this day; to the men of Judah, and to the inhabitants of Jerusalem, and unto all Israel, that are near, and that are far off, through all the countries whither Thou hast driven them, because of their trespass that they have trespassed against Thee."

Chapter 8 of the book of Daniel concludes with the prophet being stricken physically because of his extreme burden for his people Israel. The prophecies he had received from God, which dealt primarily with the Lord's chosen people, created further distress in the prophet's heart and mind. In chapter 9 we see him as God's compassionate servant interceding for his people whom he loved so well. As he recalls the events of the past and the waywardness of Israel, he lays his heart bare before God in humble repentance, beseeching the Lord to show mercy to the Jews.

Realizing Daniel's great concern for his people, we may well conclude that the visions he received from God were not mechanical. The entire personality of the prophet was involved. Though he did not understand everything, it is evident that he felt anxiety for what he did understand. Because of the anguish within, Daniel was prompted to depend not merely upon his own revelations but also upon those that had been given through other prophets.

1. *The Examination — verses 1, 2.* "In the first year of Darius the son of Ahasuerus, of the seed of the Medes, which was made king over the realm of the Chaldeans." This would fix the date of the chapter at about 537 B.C., one year before the Jews were permitted to return from exile under Cyrus. It was 69 years prior to this that Daniel was taken into captivity. We are told that Darius was the son of Ahasuerus. Though Ahasuerus is declared by many historians to be unknown, Xenophon designates him as Astyhees. Many of the kings of Medo-Persia bore the title of Ahasuerus.

Though Daniel was an instrument through whom God revealed future events, this did not thwart the attempts on the part of God's servant to know more about prophecy. He was a keen student of the Word, and as we find him in the opening portion of this chapter, he was making a careful examination of prophecies concerning Israel's captivity: "In the first year of his reign I Daniel understood by books the number of the years, whereof the word of the LORD came to Jeremiah the prophet, that He would accomplish seventy years in the desolations of Jerusalem." The word "books" as used here might rather be translated "letters." "Book" when appearing in the plural frequently means letters in the Old Testament. Thus Daniel was giving special attention to Jeremiah's letters. Various portions of the Scriptures were available for Daniel's use, such as the Pentateuch, some of the historical books, and including many of the Psalms, Isaiah, Micah, Joel, Obadiah, Amos, Jeremiah, and others. But as we find him here, he is particularly interested in the prophecies of Jeremiah relative to the seventy years of captivity.

There are two specific passages that present this prophetic truth. First, Jeremiah 25:11-12: "And this whole land shall be a desolation, and an astonishment; and these nations shall serve the king of Babylon seventy years. And it shall come to pass, when seventy years are

The Retrospect of Repentance

accomplished, that I will punish the king of Babylon, and that nation, saith the LORD, for their iniquity, and the land of the Chaldeans, and will make it perpetual desolations." Secondly, Jeremiah 29:10, "For thus saith the LORD, That after seventy years be accomplished at Babylon I will visit you, and perform My good work toward you, in causing you to return to this place." Quite familiar with these prophecies and yet realizing that the time was near for their complete fulfillment, doubtless Daniel wanted to reassure himself from God's Word.

Having come through a time of severe stress as the future sufferings of Israel were revealed to him, Daniel found consolation in God's holy Word. Where could one get greater consolation? We are told in Romans 15:4, "Whatsoever things were written aforetime were written for our learning, that we through patience and comfort of the scriptures might have hope." How marvelous is the comfort received from the Scriptures in times of anxiety and adversity.

David, the man after God's own heart, suffered severe trials and afflictions at the hands of his persecutors, but he knew where to turn in the hour of his extremity. In Psalm 119:71 he wrote, "It is good for me that I have been afflicted; that I might learn Thy statutes." His afflictions were used of God to drive him to the Word, through which his own heart was strengthened and encouraged.

There are times when God permits testings to befall in order that we might find essential food for our weary soul. We seem to be so busy with the mundane things of life that we overlook the importance and value of God's Word and fail to give it the place it should have in our daily experience. David declared, "Thy word have I hid in mine heart" (Psalm 119:11). Do the same and you will be far better prepared to cope with the many disturbing vicissitudes of life.

2. *The Effect — verse 3.* Daniel did not ask for a new revelation from God. He faithfully searched the Scriptures to understand the meaning of the revelations already given. We too have the Word of God in which we can find all that we need to know regarding the past, present, and future. God's entire revelation is contained in the Bible. Daniel knew this. The study of the Scriptures had a profound effect upon the prophet. He declared, "And I set my face unto the Lord God, to seek by prayer and supplications, with fasting, and sackcloth, and ashes." This is the effect the study of God's Word should always have upon His sincere saints. As in the case of the Prophet Daniel, Spirit-directed study of the Word should drive us to our knees in humble submission, recognizing the greatness and glory of the Lord of all.

Someone has said there are three stages of Bible study: the cod liver oil stage, when you take it like medicine because it is good for you; the shredded wheat biscuit stage, dry but nourishing; and finally, the peaches and cream stage. It is the last stage with which true believers should be concerned. This kind of Bible study produces the necessary changes within us, enabling us to be more and more like the glorious Christ. Doubtless Daniel could say of God's truth as David did long before, "The law of Thy mouth is better unto me than thousands of gold and silver" (Psalm 119:72).

The Holy Spirit has revealed in these few verses a lesson that we must not overlook. One who loves the Word of God and spends time in it will also give much time to prayer. The two are inseparable — diligent Bible study and reliant prayer. If one is not a student of the Scriptures, he will have only a passing interest in prayer, for it is the Word of God that not only challenges us to pray but assures us of the value of prayer.

Several years ago a little boy was stricken with spinal meningitis at the age of three and a half. His well-to-do Christian parents pled with the Lord and begged God to

The Retrospect of Repentance

heal the child. In fact, as they prayed they actually demanded that God spare the life of the child to prove His divine power. Later they regretted this kind of praying, which is certainly not scriptural, for in answer to their demands, God did spare the child's life; but when he recovered from spinal meningitis his mind was blank and remained so. For eleven long years the mother and father had to care for this afflicted child until the Lord took him home. Any student of the Word knows that when he prays he must always qualify his petitions with, "Thy will be done," and really mean it, knowing full well that God makes no mistakes.

As Daniel searched the Scriptures, he went to his knees with a desire to enter into a fresh experience with the Lord. This is the thought of verse three, "I set my face unto the Lord God." "Sackcloth, and ashes" indicated the deep humiliation of the prophet as he committed himself to the Lord's control. Prayer is a time of soul searching, to permit God to speak to us about personal sin. It demands repentance and renewal of commitment to Christ's control.

3. *The Evil — verses 4-6.* Some Bible students consider this to be one of the greatest prayers of the Bible. One cannot read it without sensing the burden that was on Daniel's heart, mindful that the conclusion of the seventy-year captivity for the Jews was near. But notice what he prayed about first of all: "I prayed unto the LORD my God, and made my confession." Though anxious for the deliverance of his people, he was far more concerned about their evil. He realized, too, that if the deliverance was to be effective and if the Jews were to be kept from further calamity, it was essential that they deal with their sins. In their captivity many of them had taken their eyes from God and His guidance. Living in the midst of pagans, the Jews to a large degree had duplicated the evils of their captors.

Daniel next offered praise and adoration to God: "O

Lord, the great and dreadful God, keeping the covenant and mercy to them that love Him, and to them that keep His commandments." Daniel recognized God's greatness in the sense that He is loving, kind, and merciful. On the other hand, he named Him as the "dreadful God," realizing His dreadful abhorrence of sin and wickedness. God is not only a God of love, but a just God who because of His holiness must punish unconfessed and unforgiven sin. He keeps His "covenant and mercy to them that love Him, and to them that keep His commandments." God's promises are certain, for He never changes. He declares in Malachi 3:6, "I am the LORD, I change not." He never fails His Word. We may depend upon Him faithfully to fulfill what He has promised.

Daniel stated two reasons why the Jews were suffering chastisement: first, because of their sin which was the result of their departure from the Word of God: "We have sinned, and have committed iniquity, and have done wickedly, and have rebelled, even by departing from Thy precepts and from Thy judgments"; secondly, by their failure to hearken to the prophets who had proclaimed the message of God to them: "Neither have we hearkened unto Thy servants the prophets, which spake in Thy name to our kings, our princes, and our fathers, and to all the people of the land." In confessing the sinfulness of the Jewish people, Daniel did not pray "they," but "we."

Of all the humans who are named in the Old Testament, in my thinking no one appears closer to God than Daniel. This is not to say that he was not a sinner, but he walked with the Lord, day in and day out. He seemed to have a character beyond reproach. We read of Abraham, Moses, Aaron, David, and others and we can easily pick out their flaws. Not so with Daniel. Yet when he went before God to confess the sins of his people, the prophet numbered himself among the transgressors. How often the lives of critics evidence the same evils which they condemn in others. Of such persons God declares in Romans 2:1,

The Retrospect of Repentance 181

"Therefore thou art inexcusable, O man, whosoever thou art that judgest: for wherein thou judgest another, thou condemnest thyself; for thou that judgest doest the same things."

So few of God's people are like Daniel in identifying themselves with the sins of other believers. We are reminded in Romans 14:10: "But why dost thou judge thy brother? or why dost thou set at nought thy brother? for we shall all stand before the judgment seat of Christ." Daniel had every reason to divorce himself from the sins of the people, but he realized there could be no blessing from God without an honest confession of sin. Numbers 32:23 makes this clear, "Be sure your sin will find you out."

Every life has been marred by a besetting sin. What is the Christian supposed to do with his besetting sin? "Let us lay aside every weight, and the sin which doth so easily beset us" (Hebrews 12:1). It is not optional that we "lay aside" the besetting sin, it is obligatory. How does one do this? Confess to God! If you do, He will forgive. We are told in Hebrews 12:2, "Looking unto Jesus the author and finisher of our faith." David could say in Psalm 139:5, "Thou hast beset me behind and before." With such a promise, what right do we have to succumb to evil of any kind?

4. *The Extremity — verses 7-14.* Daniel made it clear in his prayer that the Jews were suffering judgment because they were disobedient to the Lord's holy command as well as refusing to listen to His messenger. "O Lord, righteousness belongeth unto Thee, but unto us confusion of faces, as at this day; to the men of Judah, and to the inhabitants of Jerusalem, and unto all Israel, that are near, and that are far off, through all the countries whither Thou hast driven them, because of their trespass that they have trespassed against Thee." In other words, there was not a single Jew who escaped the present

judgment that had befallen the people of God because of their rebellion. Not only were the common people suffering but those in the highest positions: "O Lord, to us belongeth confusion of face, to our kings, to our princes, and to our fathers, because we have sinned against Thee." When God's judgment strikes, no one is able to talk or buy his way out. The wealthy and the poor suffer alike. No one will ever escape the righteous judgment of God.

The Lord Jesus said in Matthew 7:21-23: "Not every one that saith unto Me, Lord, Lord, shall enter into the kingdom of heaven; but he that doeth the will of My Father which is in heaven. Many will say to Me in that day, Lord, Lord, have we not prophesied in Thy name? and in Thy name have cast out devils? and in Thy name done many wonderful works? And then will I profess unto them, I never knew you: depart from Me, ye that work iniquity." God's standard is holiness. Nothing else will suffice.

Daniel continued, "To the Lord our God belong mercies and forgivenesses, though we have rebelled against Him." How we can thank the Lord that "mercies and forgivenesses" belong to Him. Previously in verse 7 Daniel had prayed, "O Lord, righteousness belongeth unto Thee." God is righteous, desiring to produce righteousness through His people, but He is also merciful, willing to forgive when we fail. David wrote in Psalm 86:5, "For Thou, Lord, art good, and ready to forgive; and plenteous in mercy unto all them that call upon Thee."

Daniel prayed, "Neither have we obeyed the voice of the LORD our God, to walk in His laws, which He set before us by His servants the prophets. Yea, all Israel have transgressed Thy law, even by departing, that they might not obey Thy voice; therefore the curse is poured upon us, and the oath that is written in the law of Moses the servant of God, because we have sinned against Him." Notice that

The Retrospect of Repentance

nothing is said regarding the achievements of the Jewish people, likewise there is no mention of the remnant walking in the paths of God's grace, because when a nation suffers, all must suffer. When a nation rebels against God, all the subjects are involved in the judgment.

As he prayed, Daniel had no word of complaint. He did not consider the bondage of his people as a mistake or a tragedy. He called it by its rightful name, "the curse." Read Deuteronomy 27 and notice parts of the law that were made known to the people through Moses. Yet the children of Israel had broken these laws repeatedly, so much so that Daniel confessed to God that no one under all the heaven above had been as guilty of breaking God's laws as the Jews of His day. "And He hath confirmed His words, which He spake against us, and against our judges that judged us, by bringing upon us a great evil: for under the whole heaven hath not been done as hath been done upon Jerusalem." It is one thing to sin against God, but quite another thing to confess and claim forgiveness. Daniel's people were guilty of sinning but they failed to confess. The ensuing consequence was judgment: "As it is written in the law of Moses, all this evil is come upon us: yet made we not our prayer before the LORD our God, that we might turn from our iniquities, and understand Thy truth." God is gracious and is ever willing to forgive, but there must be sincere repentance and a turning unto Him. Israel had sinned and continued in sin as she drifted farther and farther away from God. "Therefore," Daniel prayed in his extremity, "hath the LORD watched upon the evil, and brought it upon us: for the LORD our God is righteous in all His works which He doeth: for we obeyed not His voice."

5. *The Entreaty — verses 15-19.* Daniel's entire prayer is one of entreaty, but in the closing petitions the burden of the sinfulness of his people becomes an even greater concern. Daniel beseeches the Lord to intercede

on the ground of His mercies to Israel in the past: "And now, O Lord our God, that hast brought Thy people forth out of the land of Egypt with a mighty hand, and hast gotten Thee renown, as at this day; we have sinned, we have done wickedly." The phrase "and hast gotten Thee renown" could also be translated, "and Thou has gotten Thee a name."

All the peoples of the known world had heard of the miraculous way in which the Lord delivered Israel from their bondage in Egypt. Though the pagan nations did not acknowledge the Lord Jehovah as their God, Israel's miraculous deliverance created respect for the Lord whereby He was known as the "Jewish God." As Daniel prayed, he stressed the fact that the Lord had a name He must uphold. Were He to permit the Jewish people to go into oblivion, this would not help the lost to turn to Jehovah. Daniel's prayer seemed to be in the spirit of Jacob's, "I will not let Thee go, except Thou bless me" (Genesis 32:26).

With fervency Daniel continued, "O Lord, according to all Thy righteousness, I beseech Thee, let Thine anger and Thy fury be turned away from Thy city Jerusalem, Thy holy mountain: because for our sins, and for the iniquities of our fathers, Jerusalem and Thy people are become a reproach to all that are about us." Here the prophet begged God to preserve the testimony that had been established down through the years by the faithful servants of the Lord. The witness of the true saints was rapidly becoming a reproach because of the sins of the people. God tells us in Proverbs 14:34 that "sin is a reproach" to the people of God. The greater the responsibility before the Lord, the greater the reproach if the believer fails. Christians must keep close to Him who died for sin, that we might live in the power of His victory. Daily we must pray that He will give us a holy hatred of sin as well as a sensitivity to recognize it when it comes in our direction.

The Retrospect of Repentance 185

God has given the little dandelion the enablement to close up tight like a knob and then to open again to protect itself from the storms and wind. The dandelion is sensitive to atmospheric disturbances so that it can close for protection or it can open to the glories of the sun. God can give His people a sensitivity toward sin if we ask Him for it and if we really want it.

As Daniel prayed on, he besought God for the restoration of the "sanctuary": "Now therefore, O our God, hear the prayer of Thy servant, and his supplications, and cause Thy face to shine upon Thy sanctuary that is desolate, for the Lord's sake." Next, God's servant asked for the restoration of Jerusalem: "O my God, incline Thine ear, and hear; open Thine eyes, and behold our desolations, and the city which is called by Thy name: for we do not present our supplications before Thee for our righteousnesses, but for Thy great mercies." Daniel confessed that he prayed not because of anything righteous in the Jewish people, but on the ground of the mercy of God. Then in his concluding petition we sense once again the burden of his heart, as with great fervency the prophet called on God to intervene: "O Lord, hear; O Lord, forgive; O Lord, hearken and do; defer not, for Thine own sake, O my God: for Thy city and Thy people are called by Thy name."

There are many lessons to be gleaned from Daniel's prayer but I think the one all of us need especially is that of Daniel's fervency. He really prayed. He was serious, his petitions were not idle words — each one came from a heart torn by stress and trial, with a holy concern to see God work. How we need this kind of praying in our day. Without question it was this kind of praying the Lord Jesus spoke about when He said, "If ye have faith as a grain of mustard seed, ye shall say unto this mountain, Remove hence to yonder place; and it shall remove; and nothing shall be impossible unto you" (Matthew 17:20).

Dr. Len G. Broughton once said, "It may be our prayers are ineffective because we have been asking God to do His part and ours, too." What is our part in prayer? First of all, we must take the time to pray. Let us not think we can move mountains by a few hasty minutes on our knees; we need to "wait on the LORD" (Psalm 27:14). In addition to this, we must be in a right spiritual relationship with the Lord. All known sin must be confessed and forgiven, for it is true, as David said in Psalm 66:18, "If I regard iniquity in my heart, the Lord will not hear me." Let us call on God as Daniel did, asking Him to cleanse us and make us a holy people.

6. *The Encouragement — verses 20-23*. When one prays as Daniel prayed, something will happen. Daniel wrote, "And whiles I was speaking, and praying, and confessing my sin and the sin of my people Israel, and presenting my supplication before the LORD my God for the holy mountain of my God; Yea, whiles I was speaking in prayer, even the man Gabriel, whom I had seen in the vision at the beginning, being caused to fly swiftly, touched me about the time of the evening oblation." The prophet did not finish his prayer. While he was interceding for his own people Israel and confessing his and their sins, he was interrupted by the touch of someone standing near. Startled, he opened his eyes to find Gabriel, who had appeared to him previously.

Daniel's experience was a living proof of Isaiah 65:24, "And it shall come to pass, that before they call, I will answer; and while they are yet speaking, I will hear." Daniel stated twice that Gabriel came "whiles I was speaking." What a challenge to every believer. To many Christians prayer is a matter of little importance, but to those who have a hold on God, it is recognized as a privilege of supreme importance. Several hundred years ago, William Cowper wrote these descriptive words:

> Here we may prove the power of prayer
> To strengthen faith and sweeten care,
> To teach our faint desires to rise
> And bring all Heaven before our eyes.

It was George Müller who said, "I live in the spirit of prayer. I pray as I walk, when I lie down, and when I arise. The answers are always coming. Thousands and ten thousands of times have my prayers been answered." God desires this experience for all His people, but we must be willing to yield our lives to the control of Christ and spend time in His presence praying earnestly, as Daniel did.

Gabriel touched Daniel "about the time of the evening oblation." Here is another intimation that Daniel was a holy man, walking with God by faith. The evening oblation was offered about three o'clock in the afternoon by the Jews, but was it being offered in Babylon? Decidedly not. It had not been offered since the Temple had been burned and the Jews rushed off into captivity seventy years before. But Daniel never deviated; in his own heart he continued to offer the evening oblation. This particular sacrifice typified Christ and the offering He would make for the sin of the world. To many, Christ, the true "Evening Oblation," means everything, but millions of lost men and women give no respect whatsoever to Him who laid down His life for them.

It is obvious that Daniel was deeply moved and disturbed by the conditions of his day, but the angel appeared to bring encouragement. Daniel says, "He informed me, and talked with me, and said, O Daniel, I am now come forth to give thee skill and understanding. At the beginning of thy supplications the commandment came forth, and I am come to shew thee; for thou art greatly beloved: therefore understand the matter, and consider the vision." Daniel had been praying for His people, that they might get right with the Lord and once again return to a place in God's favor. The angel encouraged Daniel by giving him understanding regarding a vision which he had already seen. It appears that this vision is the one in chapter 8, about which Daniel said, "I was astonished at the vision." But as he prayed the answer came, and Daniel was about to look into the future regarding the great hope for his people Israel.

Notice what the angel said about Daniel: "Thou art greatly beloved." The attitude of the Lord toward Daniel was like that of Jesus toward the Apostle John, the beloved disciple. Could one receive any greater approbation than to be beloved of God? No wonder Daniel's prayer was answered in such a marvelous way, for prayer is not merely a matter of the lips; it is a condition of the heart. This is made clear in James 5:16: "The effectual fervent prayer of a righteous man availeth much." "A righteous man" is one who has surrendered himself to the Lord's control and lordship. He is one through whom God works.

What about you? What is your relationship to God? Are your prayers being answered? Are you privileged to see the hand of God moving in your life? Is there anything between? Oh, give the Lord His way. Let Him be Master of all. Be one of those dear saints who are "greatly beloved" of God.

7. *The Enlightenment — verses 24-27.* The angel Gabriel declared to Daniel, "understand the matter, and consider the vision." The angel revealed one of the most profound prophecies to be found in the Bible. Someone has declared this to be "the backbone of all prophecy."

We read in verse 24: "Seventy weeks are determined upon Thy people and upon Thy holy city, to finish the transgression, and to make an end of sins, and to make reconciliation for iniquity, and to bring in everlasting righteousness, and to seal up the vision and prophecy, and to anoint the most Holy." Here are six accomplishments to be fulfilled: (1) the transgression to be finished; (2) an

The Retrospect of Repentance

end to be made for sins; (3) iniquity to be covered; (4) the righteousness of the ages to be brought in; (5) the vision and the prophecy to be sealed up; (6) the Holy of holies to be anointed.

The time given for these accomplishments was "seventy weeks," or more literally, "seventy sevens." The word "sevens" could refer either to "days" or "years." Daniel had been praying about the seventy-*year* captivity, thus it seems obvious that the "sevens" refer to weeks of years or a total of 490 years.

It appears that 490 years was the time limit prophesied for the six accomplishments to be completed. "The transgression" of the Jews will be finished and there will be "an end of sins" at the time of their national repentance when Christ returns. All of their sinfulness will be covered over by the blood of Christ, providing "reconciliation for iniquity." "Everlasting righteousness" will reign and the millennial kingdom will begin. At the return of Christ "the vision and [the] prophecy" will be sealed up. That is, the "seventy weeks" will be completed. Also, a new Temple will be established for the millennial kingdom where "the most Holy [place]" will be anointed.

In the ensuing three verses greater detail is given regarding the "seventy weeks" of years: "Know therefore and understand, that from the going forth of the commandment to restore and to build Jerusalem unto the Messiah the Prince shall be seven weeks, and threescore and two weeks: the street shall be built again, and the wall, even in troublous times. And after threescore and two weeks shall Messiah be cut off, but not for Himself: and the people of the prince that shall come shall destroy the city and the sanctuary; and the end thereof shall be with a flood, and unto the end of the war desolations are determined. And he shall confirm the covenant with many for one week: and in the midst of the week he shall cause the sacrifice and the oblation to cease, and for the overspreading of abominations he shall make it desolate, even until the consummation, and that determined shall be poured upon the desolate."

According to these verses the "seventy weeks" of years of 490 years are divided into three parts: the "seven weeks" or forty-nine years, "threescore and two weeks" or 434 years, "one week" or seven years.

The question is, when were these 490 years to begin? This must be determined to understand the meaning of the prophecy. The angel made it clear that the 490 years were to begin with "the commandment to restore and build Jerusalem." This command was issued by Artaxerxes in 445 B.C., the twentieth year of his reign (Nehemiah 1:1-3; 2:1-8).

Let us consider the three divisions of the 490 years in greater detail. The first period, spoken of by the angel as "troublous times," began with the decree permitting God's people to return to Jerusalem and continued for 49 years until the city of Jerusalem and its walls were rebuilt. This period was followed by 434 years when Messiah the Prince would appear, who would be "cut off, but not for Himself."

Consider the remarkable fulfillment of this prophecy regarding the Messiah. From the time of the command permitting God's chosen people to return to Jerusalem to rebuild the city until the time the Lord Jesus made his official entry into the Holy City to be crucified was a period of exactly 483 years. Here is an amazing prophecy confirmed by the facts of history.

The third period remains to be fulfilled. We are told that there is a "prince that shall come" who "shall destroy the city and the sanctuary." Who is this prince? Some consider him to be Titus who in 70 A.D. partially fulfilled this prophecy. But there is no doubt about it, the prince spoken of here is the one identical with the "little horn"

The Retrospect of Repentance

of Daniel 7, the Beast of Revelation 13, who will make a covenant with the Jewish people during the seventieth week of this prophecy, the seven-year tribulation period. This covenant will probably grant the Jews the privilege to rebuild their Temple and to possess their land. But in the middle of the seven-year period, this wicked ruler "shall cause the sacrifice and the oblation to cease." Unrestrained wrath such as they have never experienced will be poured out upon the Jews. Since the first two divisions of this prophecy have been fulfilled in every detail, we may expect the same of the third.

Perhaps you have noticed that there is practically nothing said in the prophecy concerning the period from the crucifixion of the Messiah until the seventieth week. Only a brief statement is made in verse 26 that "unto the end . . . desolations are determined." We are not told anything about the length of time to the end, nor are we given any further details. The New Testament gives additional light, however, as the mystery of the Church, which was unknown to the Old Testament prophets, is revealed. During the present church age, God is calling unto Himself a people from all kindreds and nations, building His Church on the ground of belief in Jesus Christ His Son. God's special dealings with Israel will be renewed at the end of the church age, but presently He is especially concerned with His Church.

The prophecies recorded by Daniel may be accepted as truth: but also all that is said in the Bible regarding salvation through Jesus Christ is truth. The most important decision for one to make is to receive Christ as Saviour and Lord, and thus be prepared to face God in eternity. If you have never come to this decision, receive Christ into your life now.

Chapter 10

THE RECOGNITION OF RENOWN

Key verse, 8: "Therefore I was left alone, and saw this great vision, and there remained no strength in me: for my comeliness was turned in me into corruption, and I retained no strength."

We come now to the concluding portion of the book of Daniel which contains the last vision communicated to the aged prophet. Chapters 10, 11, and 12 should be considered together, for a continuous thought runs throughout, presenting one of the most remarkable prophecies ever given. Nowhere else in the Bible do we have such a complete account of history prewritten, embracing the time from Daniel's day up until the Second Advent of Christ when "Every knee should bow, of things in heaven, and things in earth, and things under the earth; And that every tongue should confess that Jesus Christ is Lord, to the glory of God the Father" (Philippians 2:10-11).

1. *The Mystery — verse 1.* Daniel received another vision from God, and though it was not altogether shrouded in mystery, yet the prophet found it necessary to wait before the Lord for a further revelation. The time given was "the third year of Cyrus king of Persia." By now the prophet was well advanced in age, probably in his nineties. Some of the Jews had returned from their captivity to begin the long task of rebuilding the Holy City, Jerusalem, for in the first year of his reign, Cyrus had

The Recognition of Renown 193

issued a decree permitting the Jews to begin the rebuilding of the Temple and their former capital. Only a few Jews returned to their homeland, which suggests the low estate of Israel at the time. The Jews had become so much a part of the pagan culture of Babylon that few of them had any real concern to see the work of the Lord prosper.

We might ask why Daniel did not take the opportunity to return. Guided by the hand of the Lord, probably he felt he could be a greater help to the Jews who remained among the Gentiles through his position of leadership, which he had held for many years. He had a consuming passion to help his own people who were living in wickedness, and was unwilling to leave them to their sins. His prayer recorded in the previous chapter evidenced his soul concern for those he loved so well.

It is refreshing to think of a man like Daniel in this respect. Considering his utter selflessness, how few there are like him in our day. How many Christians do you know who have such a burden for needy hearts that they are willing to forego selfish interests and pleasures? Even clergymen and church leaders are putting materialistic comforts and delights before the work of God. Few there are who are burdened with an anxious desire to see lost men turn to Christ.

Looking through the yellowed pages of the journals and biographies of those of several generations ago, we learn something of the compassion that filled the hearts of our fathers in the faith. Said Bunyan, "In my preaching I could not be satisfied unless some fruits did appear in my work. If I were fruitless it mattered not who commended me; but if I were fruitful I cared not who did condemn." Bishop Patrick wrote of the learned John Smith, "He had resolved very much to lay aside other studies and to travail in the salvation of men's souls, after whose good he most earnestly thirsted." Alleine was "infinitely and insatiably greedy of the conversion of souls, and to this end he poured out his very heart in prayer and in preaching. He imparted not the gospel of God only, but his own soul. His supplications and his exhortations many times were so affectionate, so full of holy zeal, life, and vigor that they quite overcame his hearers. He melted over them so that he mollified and sometimes dissolved the hardest heart."

Wrote Matthew Henry, "I would think it a greater happiness to gain one soul to Christ than mountains of silver and gold to myself. If God suffers me to labor in vain, though I should get hundreds a year by my labor, it would be the constant grief and trouble of my soul, and if I do not gain souls, I shall enjoy all my other gains with very little satisfaction." Dr. Doddridge wrote to a friend, "I long for the conversion of souls more sensibly than anything else. Methinks I cannot only labor but die for it with pleasure. The love of Christ constraineth me." Should these statements be confined merely to the lips of those of former generations? We who are in Christ need this same holy regard to see men and women won to the Lord. Daniel was a man with a burdened heart. How we need men like him today.

The prophet saw that the vision "was true." This was nothing fanciful. What he heard and saw was an authentic vision from God. Furthermore, "the time appointed was long." Not only was the period of time involved in the vision "long," but another meaning of the word "long" as used here suggests a "great calamity." This "great calamity" was to be the experience of the Jewish people for many centuries until their ultimate deliverance through the King of kings when He returns.

Daniel "understood the thing, and had understanding of the vision." He knew it was a definite answer to his prayers regarding Israel, even though some of the details were mysterious. Thus he wanted the complete unfolding of the truths of the vision.

How we need to pray that God will give us understanding of this important portion of Scripture, which to many is mysterious. Thank God we have the Teacher of all teachers, the Holy Spirit. Of Him Jesus said, "He shall teach you all things, and bring all things to your remembrance, whatsoever I have said unto you" (John 14:26). Let us rely upon Him and seek His direction as we continue our study of the remaining chapters of Daniel.

2. *The Meditation — verses 2, 3.* Here again we sense Daniel's complete surrender to God while at the same time overcoming any trace of selfishness in his life: "In those days I Daniel was mourning three full weeks. I ate no pleasant bread, neither came flesh nor wine in my mouth, neither did I anoint myself at all, till three whole weeks were fulfilled." Daniel was mourning for the sins of his people. He had no rest because of the iniquity within the Israelitish camp. Furthermore, he was disturbed because of obstacles that were confronting the labors of the faithful remnant in Jerusalem. How sensitive Daniel was to the needs of others.

How many believers are, like Daniel, living for others rather than self? Indeed, the prophet was unusual in this respect. But should it be unusual for us? Why should we be any different; Has not God said in Philippians 2:4, "Look not every man on his own things, but every man also on the things of others"? It would seem that this exhortation is meaningless as far as many Christians are concerned. The common evil of selfishness seen in most Christians proves it. Surely we can agree that the genuineness of one's conversion is most readily proved by the effect it has on others. Christ saved us to live not for ourselves; He transformed us and came to indwell us that He might live through us. The essence of the Christian life is the outliving of the inliving Christ. Christ lived for others constantly. Ultimately He went to the cross for others. The hymn writer bids us to count our blessings and name them one by one; but we must do more than simply count our blessings. We must utilize them to bless others, for God blesses us that we may be a blessing to others.

Furthermore, He blesses us the second time when we pass His blessings on to others. We are alive in this world to be useful. When we fail to be a blessing to others, we fail largely in our mission here on this earth.

When General William Booth of the Salvation Army was an old man in London, handicapped with blindness, he was unable to be present at a great convention. He was asked for a message that might be read to the assembled delegates. In the midst of one of the meetings, someone brought a letter and handed it to the moderator. He held it up and shouted, "A message from General Booth!" He opened it and his countenance changed as he said quietly and reverently, "My comrades, it contains just one word — 'Others.' " That one word was extremely meaningful in General Booth's life. That is why he was able to help thousands in their distress. He did not live for himself but for others.

Daniel must have been the same kind of man. He had a heart for his own people as well as for the Gentiles all around him. He gave little attention to his own needs while pouring out his life for others. Even in his eating, like the Apostle Paul, he was unwilling to permit the flesh to rule over the spirit. Paul declared in 1 Corinthians 9:27, "But I keep under my body, and bring it into subjection." Daniel did likewise.

For three full weeks God's servant fasted as he thought on the vision that had been given him. This was not a fast of no food but of plain food: "I ate no pleasant bread, neither came flesh nor wine in my mouth." Surrounded by pleasure-mad people who lived lavishly while freely gratifying the lusts of the flesh, it would have been easy to follow the crowd. But Daniel chose a better way of life. To him, life consisted of pleasing God and doing His work. The prophet knew this would be impossible if he were to cater to the whims and desires of his flesh.

Daniel did not fast to be seen of men, as was often the case with many others: "Neither did I anoint myself at all,

The Recognition of Renown

till three whole weeks were fulfilled." That is, he did not anoint his head, which to the Jews was an outward sign of fasting. What he did he kept within his heart, that he should receive no praise or glory from men. Centuries later our Lord warned His own of the evil of doing their alms before men: "And when thou prayest, thou shalt not be as the hypocrites are: for they love to pray standing in the synagogues and in the corners of the streets, that they may be seen of men. Verily I say unto you, They have their reward. But thou, when thou prayest, enter into thy closet, and when thou hast shut thy door, pray to thy Father which is in secret; and thy Father which seeth in secret shall reward thee openly" (Matthew 6:5-6).

We need not wonder that God chose Daniel to receive the vision we have read about in this prophecy. He was God's man. His heart was prepared to receive blessing from the Lord. He was willing to sacrifice for his Lord at any price. How great the need is for men and women who will do the same in this materialistic age, when millions are concerned about leisure and luxury. The Apostle Paul could say, "I bear in my body the marks of the Lord Jesus" (Galatians 6:17). Paul had been mutilated for the glory of Christ. He could have escaped all this if he chose to do so. He could have settled down into a nice, comfortable, cozy existence like many Christians of our day, but this kind of fruitless living was not for Paul. Consider his impassioned plea to the saints at Rome, "I beseech you therefore, brethren, by the mercies of God, that ye present your bodies a living sacrifice" (Romans 12:1). Not only did the apostle urge others to do this; he did it himself. Like Daniel of old, he was "a living sacrifice" for God. He had one object and goal in life — to live for the Lord. Show your gratitude and appreciation to your gracious Lord for all He has done by giving yourself to Him to be a channel of blessing to the millions who need to hear the glorious gospel of Jesus Christ.

3. *The manifestation — verses 4-7.* Whenever a true believer takes time to wait on God as Daniel did, the results will be overwhelming. It was so in Daniel's case. The time was "the four and twentieth day of the first month." He "was by the side of the great river, which is Hiddekel." It would seem that he was walking by the river, meditating on the things of God while interceding for his own people, the Jews. His eyes were downcast as he mourned their sorrowful state. But suddenly, he was lifted from the depths of despair into the realms of glory by the appearance of a heavenly visitor. "I lifted up mine eyes, and looked, and behold a certain man clothed in linen, whose loins were girded with fine gold of Uphaz: His body also was like the beryl, and his face as the appearance of lightning, and his eyes as lamps of fire, and his arms and his feet like in colour to polished brass, and the voice of his words like the voice of a multitude."

What Daniel saw was not a dream nor a vision, but an actual visit of a celestial personage. The question is, who was this "certain man"? There are some who believe that it must have been Gabriel, Michael, or another of the angelic beings. It seems, however, that it was the Lord Jesus Christ Himself who appeared unto Daniel. Those who disagree with this conclusion claim that verse 13 makes it clear that the "certain man" Daniel saw was dependent upon Michael for help. This, they say, could not possibly have been the Lord Jesus, for He is not dependent on anyone for help. But it is questionable if the one described in verses 5-7 is the same as the one who needed help from Michael, according to verse 13.

The description of the one described by the prophet is almost identical with the one given by the Apostle John in Revelation 1, the difference being that Daniel saw the Lord before His birth into the world, while John saw Him as the risen, glorious King of kings. In spite of this, there is a striking similarity in the details that must not be overlooked.

The Recognition of Renown

In His appearance to Daniel, Christ appeared in His high priestly garb. "Linen" was the material used in the high priest's garment worn on the Day of Atonement as he offered the sacrifice for the sins of the people. His "loins were girded with fine gold of Uphaz," signifying His walk of obedience to the Father which characterized His willingness to go to the cross to die for our sins. "His body . . . like the beryl, and his face as the appearance of lightning, and his eyes as lamps of fire, and his arms and his feet like in colour to polished brass, and the voice of his words like the voice of a multitude" all suggest that He is a just God who will visit judgment upon all who neglect to obey His truth. What a privilege Daniel had, to see our Lord in this awesome appearance.

Keep in mind that while the prophet had been praying for his people Israel, his thoughts had been directed to the end time. Receiving a glimpse of the "High Priest of our profession" (Hebrews 3:1), doubtless God's faithful servant was reminded that deliverance and national repentance would come to the Jew eventually. This provided a ray of hope for the burdened prophet. His heart had been heavy, but God did not leave him comfortless. What an assuring truth this is for all of us. The cares and sorrows of life may weigh heavily upon us, but the unfailing hand of God always provides. As Abraham trudged the difficult way to the place of sacrifice on Mount Moriah, he must have been torn asunder within when Isaac asked, "My father . . . behold the fire and the wood: but where is the lamb for a burnt offering?" (Genesis 22:7) With assurance and confidence, Abraham replied, "My son, God will provide Himself a lamb for a burnt offering" (Genesis 22:8). How did Abraham know this? He walked "by faith, not by sight" (2 Corinthians 5:7).

How can we know with certainty that God will provide? As God sent His beloved Son to commune with Daniel, so He communes with us. As we prayerfully read

His Word, He speaks to our hearts. When we study the Scriptures, it is as though Christ is standing in our midst speaking words of comfort while providing us with confidence to face the future. In Hebrews 13:5 God says, "I will never leave thee, nor forsake thee." Could it be that Daniel as an old man was getting discouraged as he "mourned" for his people? This seems possible. Seventy years of captivity was a long time. Yet, as Daniel neared the breaking point, the Lord Jesus came to him. The Lord never forsakes His own. "There hath no temptation taken you but such as is common to man: but God is faithful, who will not suffer you to be tempted above that ye are able; but will with the temptation also make a way to escape, that ye may be able to bear it" (1 Corinthians 10:13). Take those words to heart! "God is faithful." He will "make a way to escape, that ye may be able to bear it." Oh, suffering saint, troubled child of God, look up. The Lord will undertake.

Daniel tells us further that he was the only one who saw the "certain man clothed in linen." His companions were unable to behold the unusual appearance, "And I Daniel alone saw the vision: for the men that were with me saw not the vision; but a great quaking fell upon them, so that they fled to hide themselves." This suggests a similar experience in Paul's life when he had his transforming vision on the Damascus highway. Those present with him heard a voice but they saw no man.

The Lord Jesus taught in His Sermon on the Mount, "Blessed are they which do hunger and thirst after righteousness: for they shall be filled" (Matthew 5:6). How many times we have known this to be true — in the Scriptures as well as many contemporary examples. Angrily, the learned Saul was persecuting Christians when God subdued him. What Saul did was done in sincerity. The Lord understood this and intervened, that the deluded persecutor might be brought to the truth. In a sense, Daniel's case was different in that he was walking with the Lord in obedience to the truth. Daniel and Saul were alike in that they were both sincere. Those who were with them were evidently not of the same attitude, thus they missed God's blessing. The Lord reveals Himself to those who want to know Him. We are told in Isaiah 55:6, "Seek ye the LORD while He may be found, call ye upon Him while He is near." It may be that there is uncertainty in your heart about your relationship to the Lord. You may be sincere, but why not go all the way with God? Believe on Christ as He is revealed in God's Word and surrender your heart and life to His control.

4. *The Mastery — verses 8-9.* What effect did the unusual visitation from Heaven have upon the prophet? "Therefore I was left alone, and saw this great vision, and there remained no strength in me: for my comeliness was turned in me into corruption, and I retained no strength. Yet heard I the voice of His words: and when I heard the voice of His words, then was I in a deep sleep on my face, and my face toward the ground." After the vision of the Prince of Glory, Daniel fell prostrate before God in deep humiliation. "There remained no strength in me." When one sees Christ as Lord of all, he will recognize his own personal unworthiness. A glimpse of the Son of God should cause the child of God to realize his own limitations and failures. But even mature saints sometimes find it difficult to come to this place of complete helplessness before God. So often we look to our talents and abilities, feeling that we are not wholly bad.

Daniel said, "For my comeliness was turned in me into corruption, and I retained no strength." The word "comeliness" as used here is the word for "vigor," while "corruption" means "deadliness." One cannot read the opening chapters of the book of Daniel without recognizing Daniel's vigor. He was energetic and wise, but when he saw the Lord in all His glory, his confession was, "Though I was vigorous, I became as a dead man." A dead body is not only helpless but useless. In other words,

Daniel came to the end of himself. He was broken completely.

Perhaps you will recall that the Apostle John reacted in a similar manner after seeing the resurrected Christ. He declared, "And when I saw Him, I fell at His feet as dead" (Revelation 1:17). He, too, was as a dead man before God. This is the kind of man God uses, one who is dead to himself but alive unto Jesus Christ. It is for this reason that the apostle wrote in Romans 6:11, "Likewise reckon ye also yourselves to be dead indeed unto sin, but alive unto God through Jesus Christ our Lord." It is not your personality God desires to use, but "Christ in you" who is "the hope of glory" (Colossians 1:27).

The Apostle Paul knew all about the experience of death. He wrote to the Corinthian saints, "I die daily" (1 Corinthians 15:31). He said to the Galatians, "I am crucified with Christ" (Galatians 2:20). Doubtless this is one of the reasons we have at least twelve Epistles from the pen of this saintly ambassador of God. There were other Christians in Paul's day but God chose a "dead man" who would be a usable instrument in the hands of His Lord. The need has not changed. God uses dead men. We must be willing to die to ourselves so we might be usable to Him.

A young woman, an honor student through all her four years of university work, went to Mexico as a missionary. She lived and worked among an Indian tribe where there were few of the comforts of life. A commercial traveler, recognizing her ability, was surprised that she would live in such surroundings.

"Don't you love life? Why waste your talents here?" he asked.

"I know Someone," she replied, "who can change the love of life into a life of love."

God has greatly honored that life of love through the years. She has translated a portion of the New Testament into the language of a people that never before knew the Word of God. The entrance of God's Word is giving light and life to many who otherwise would still be walking in the darkness of superstition and sin. Indeed this young woman is a living witness to Paul's words, "What things were gain to me, those I counted loss for Christ. Yea doubtless, and I count all things but loss for the excellency of the knowledge of Christ Jesus my Lord: for whom I have suffered the loss of all things, and do count them but dung, that I may win Christ" (Philippians 3:7-8). This young missionary is as "dead" before Him whom she serves. Christ has control of her life. She has laid aside earthly ambition to be possessed by Him who is being permitted to direct and lead her in His will. This is what God wants for all Christians.

Daniel said, "Yet heard I the voice of His words: and when I heard the voice of His words, then was I in a deep sleep on my face, and my face toward the ground." What does one see as he looks toward the ground? Nothing! If one is lying prostrate, looking toward the ground, everything else is shut out. Do you see the picture? Jesus Christ wants His followers to come to the place where their eyes will be turned from worldliness, money making, lust, and all the many other things that hinder the spreading of the gospel of the grace of God.

There was a day in the life of Philip Doddridge when he came to this place of unreserved commitment to Christ. It is impossible to read his words without sensing something of the enriching victory that became his: "Henceforth I am dying, blessed God. It is with the utmost solemnity that I make this surrender of myself unto Thee. Henceforth I am Thine, entirely Thine. I would not merely consecrate unto Thee some of my powers or some of my possessions or give Thee a certain proportion of my services or all I am capable of for a limited time. But I would be wholly Thine and Thine forever. From this day I would solemnly renounce every sin and every lust and bid in Thy Name an eternal defiance to all the powers of hell which have most unjustly usurped the empire over my soul and to all the corruptions which their fatal temptations have entered into it. The whole frame of my nature, all the faculties of my mind and all the members of my body, would I present before Thee this day as 'a living sacrifice, holy, acceptable unto God' which I know to be my most 'reasonable service'" (Romans 12:1). Oh, that the Spirit of God might draw all believers to this place, that they might fall before the Lord Jesus as "dead," to be His instruments, His witnesses in a world of spiritual darkness and godless unbelief.

5. *The Messenger — verses 10-11.* "Behold, an hand touched me, which set me upon my knees and upon the palms of my hands." It does not appear that the hand that touched Daniel was the hand of the Lord whom he had just seen. Possibly it was the angel Gabriel or another of the heavenly messengers. As the result of the vision he had witnessed, Daniel had fallen into a "deep sleep." The touch of the angel awakened him and brought him to his knees. "O Daniel, a man greatly beloved, understand the words that I speak unto thee, and stand upright: for unto thee am I now sent."

Consider how the angel addressed Daniel, "A man greatly beloved." What a marvelous commendation. Could one receive any greater honor than to be known as "a man greatly beloved"? This was God's appraisal of Daniel. David enjoyed a similar honor when God spoke of him as "a man after His own heart." Oh, to be such a man, well pleasing in the sight of the Lord, filled with the fullness of God. God has such men scattered here and there in our day, but they are few in number. Some are in our pulpits proclaiming the truth. Others are out on the far-flung mission fields of the world. Still others are businessmen who have determined to put God first in everything. But there are so few believers who will really yield all to the lordship of Jesus Christ. There are many

The Recognition of Renown

Christians, but a comparatively small number who have experienced God's mighty power.

As we consider the great host of believers who are powerless, I am reminded of an incident reported by the Associated Press, describing a man who left his car on a vacant lot one night. In the morning he tried to start the car but there was no response. He raised the hood, and to his great surprise the engine had been stolen. Here was a late model car, beautiful in design, with every possible comfort, but it lacked one thing of greatest importance — power.

This is a parable of many a man and woman who have acknowledged Christ as Saviour but have never known Him as Lord. When one submits to Christ to the extent that all known sin is confessed, so that there is nothing between the Saviour and the saint, that one will be empowered by the Holy Spirit for usefulness. The Lord Jesus said in Acts 1:8, "Ye shall receive power, after that the Holy Ghost is come upon you." As it concerns us, our Lord was not speaking here of a unique emotional experience resulting from days and nights of tarrying and seeking. Rather it is the experience that may be the possession of every believer the moment he yields his life to the full and complete control of Jesus Christ. As long as we are controlled by self and the desires of the flesh, there will be no room for the fullness of the Holy Spirit, but if we bow in complete submission to the Son of God, we shall know His power as we have never known it before. The Apostle Paul described many of our present-day Christians well: "Having a form of godliness, but denying the power thereof" (2 Timothy 3:5).

The angel besought Daniel to get up off his knees and stand upon his feet to receive a special divinely-sent message. The prophet responded immediately, but as he arose and stood before the angel, we find that he "stood trembling." Do you think Daniel "stood trembling" because he was afraid of the angel? Surely not. He had been in the presence of angels before and gave no indication of fear. Doubtless he was still under the influence of seeing the Lord of glory. Daniel could not get over it. Daniel had seen a visible appearance of Christ.

When one sees Christ in a spiritual experience, there will be a similar result. He will be broken before God in humility and self-abnegation. He will seek to make Christ known to everyone. No longer will he live for self and this world, but he will have a burning compassion within to tell the lost of the One who came to seek and to save. David declared in Psalm 71:24, "My tongue also shall talk of Thy righteousness all the day long." What prompted him to make such a statement as this? The first verse of the psalm gives the answer, "In thee, O LORD, do I put my trust." Here was total yieldedness, an unreserved commitment to the Lord's control. God covets this for every one of His people. Do not be satisfied with a mere profession of faith. Make your experience real in every sense of the word. Ask God to give you spiritual depth and breadth, that you might have a sincere love for needy and unregenerate men.

6. *The Message – verses 14-19, 21.* Let us think now of the angel's particular purpose in appearing to Daniel: "Now I am come to make thee understand what shall befall thy people in the latter days: for yet the vision is for many days." Here we are prepared for what is to follow on through to the end of the book of Daniel. Though it has some reference to the wars of the Ptolemies and others, and though Antiochus Epiphanes is characterized, in its finality the prophecy looks forward to the concluding three and a half years of the tribulation period. Thus we have a clear statement as to what God's chosen people would face during the latter days before the return of the Lord.

Consider the effect this message had on Daniel: "And when he had spoken such words unto me, I set my face toward the ground, and I became dumb." With great humility of heart and mind, Daniel bowed in holy reverence as he realized that he was chosen to receive such a revelation.

It would seem that at this point another heavenly messenger appeared, of whom Daniel writes in verse 16, "And, behold, one like the similitude of the sons of men touched my lips: then I opened my mouth, and spake, and said unto him that stood before me, O my lord, by the vision my sorrows are turned upon me, and I have retained no strength." There are important details in this statement that must not be overlooked. Until this angel touched Daniel's lips, he had not spoken a word since his vision of the Lord of glory. He was so overcome with the splendor and glory of Christ that he could not speak. Enabled by the angel to speak, Daniel's first words were a confession of his utter helplessness and weakness: "For how can the servant of this my lord talk with this my lord? for as for me, straightway there remaineth no strength in me, neither is there breath left in me."

Another angelic touch was given the prophet and as the first opened his lips, this one provided strength, "Then there came again and touched me one like the appearance of a man, and he strengthened me." Further, a message of encouragement and comfort was given to Daniel: "O man greatly beloved, fear not: peace be unto thee, be strong, yea, be strong." How wonderful it is that God always has the right message at the right time. Daniel had been experiencing a time of stress and turmoil within his heart and soul as he agonized before God on behalf of his people. Hearing his earnest pleading, God's reply was, "Fear not." Faithful saints of every generation have heard these same words from the lips of our gracious God as they have passed through the hard and difficult places of life. Indeed, "The LORD is good, a strong hold in the day of trouble; and He knoweth them that trust in Him (Nahum 1:7).

Maybe at this moment you need to hear one of the Lord's sweet, comforting "fear not's." May I suggest that, like Daniel, you humbly bow before Him in complete commitment calling upon Him for help. I assure you that He will hear and undertake for you.

> Doth He not know how weak we are, to meet
> life's fevered rush?
> Has He removed Himself afar? Would He our
> spirits crush?
> Doth He not care when nerves are taut? When
> heart and flesh may fail?
> Has He for tired ones no thought, when doubts
> their faith assail?
> Oh yes, He calls us as of old — the weary and
> distressed —
> To enter in within His fold and find in Him
> our rest.
> We bear naught but the common load apportioned
> unto all,
> And those who trust a faithful God, He'll
> suffer not to fall.
>
> Author Unknown

In His Word, God gives us this assuring promise in Isaiah 43:2, "When thou passest through the waters, I will be with thee; and through the rivers, they shall not overflow thee." How marvelous is His provision. But rarely does He provide paths for us before we need them. He promises help, but only as it is needed. Likewise obstacles are not removed out of our way prior to reaching them, but the very moment we face the need, God's hand is stretched out. Some of us forget this and are guilty of worrying about imagined future difficulties. You must get to the waters before God will open the way through. For example, there are many believers who dread death and lament the fact that they do not have "dying grace." Naturally they will not have dying grace while they are in good health, busily engaged in life's duties and activities.

The Recognition of Renown 209

Why should they have dying grace now? Grace for duty, grace for living; that's what they need now. When it comes time to die, then the Lord will shower them with dying grace. Thus, we must live by faith and trust the Lord for all things, confident that whatever the need, He will supply.

Before departing, the angel said to Daniel, "I will shew thee that which is noted in the scripture of truth: and there is none that holdeth with me in these things, but Michael your prince." What is meant by the expression, "the scripture of truth"? It is the eternal Word of God which was written in Heaven but was to be revealed to Daniel so it might be recorded on earth. For those who regard the book of Daniel as nothing more than myths, how surprised they will be at the time of God's judgment to discover that it is one portion of the inspired Word of God. Indeed, "All scripture is given by inspiration of God, and is profitable" (2 Timothy 3:16). There is nothing in the Bible that is not inspired. The Holy Spirit declares all of Scripture to be "profitable." For this reason you and I should give ourselves to constant, diligent study of the Word, realizing that when we open this Book we have before us the eternal truth of God.

7. *The Mischief — verses 12-13,20.* After the heavenly messenger touched Daniel, who had been in a deep sleep, the prophet arose to his knees. The angel urged him to "stand upright." Then said the angel, "Fear not, Daniel: for from the first day that thou didst set thine heart to understand, and to chasten thyself before thy God, thy words were heard, and I am come for thy words." You will recall that for three weeks Daniel was meditating and praying. He interceded for his beloved people, but no answer came. Now he hears the assuring words from the angel that his prayers were heard from the first word he uttered to God three weeks before. Blessed truth! This is a fact that has been enjoyed not only by Daniel but by all of God's saints in every age. David said in

Psalm 116:1, "I love the LORD, because He hath heard my voice and my supplications."

There is never a time when God does not hear. Because our prayers are not answered immediately or answered as we desire is no indication that God does not hear us when we pray. Though Daniel had been praying three weeks with no sign of an answer, God heard every prayerful utterance. The Lord is more ready to hear than we are to pray. Oh, what a mighty potential we have in our possession if only we would make full use of it.

Those who have prayed faithfully have been privileged to see God work. Abraham prayed and Lot was delivered. Jacob prayed and Esau's wrath subsided. Moses prayed and the Red Sea was divided. Joshua prayed and the walls of Jericho fell. Manoah prayed and Samson was born. David prayed and became victor over Goliath. Hezekiah prayed and Sennacherib's army was dispersed. Elijah prayed and the widow's son was restored. Paul and Silas prayed and the prison doors were opened. The Lord Jesus said in Luke 18:1, "Men ought always to pray, and not to faint." We must not give up, for there are no limits to the resources of God. Claim the promises and plead them in the name of Jesus Christ, realizing that nothing lies beyond the reach of prayer except that which lies outside the will of God.

The angel told Daniel why the answer to his prayers was delayed: "But the prince of the kingdom of Persia withstood me one and twenty days: but, lo. Michael, one of the chief princes, came to help me; and I remained there with the kings of Persia." Here God permits us to peer into the unseen world in order that we might get some idea as to the conflict existing in the heavenly places. Daniel's first prayer was offered to God three weeks before; the angel was sent to answer but was prevented from doing so by the prince of the kingdom of Persia. The angel's mission was not completed until given assistance by Michael the archangel. Who was the prince of the kingdom of Persia? Some think that it was Cyrus. How could an earthly monarch curtail the plan of a heavenly being? Thus it would seem that the prince of the kingdom of Persia was one of Satan's wicked fallen angels who had been assigned to the kingdom of Persia. We are told in 2 Corinthians 4:4 that Satan is "the god of this world" who "hath blinded the minds of them which believe not."

The devil is not omnipresent but he has an innumerable host of fallen angels to assist him in his wicked machinations. He is the constant enemy and deceiver of mankind who "walketh about, seeking whom he may devour" (1 Peter 5:8). This wicked deceiver works frequently through his fallen angels to influence the leadership of the nations of the world. It seems obvious from what we are told in this chapter of Daniel that Satan assigns the evil spirits to guide nations into destruction. Thus when the angel Gabriel was on his way to provide the answer to Daniel's prayer, the wicked spirit controlling the godless leaders of Persia arose to resist him.

After three weeks, Michael, spoken of by Jude as "the archangel," or more literally, "the chief angel" (Jude 9), came to liberate Gabriel from the resistance of the prince of the kingdom of Persia. Further conflicts are described in verse 20 where the angel said to Daniel, "Knowest thou wherefore I come unto thee? and now will I return to fight with the prince of Persia: and when I am gone forth, lo, the prince of Grecia shall come." Much of this is very mysterious. All that we know about the unseen world is what God has declared in His Word. Enough is written that all of us might realize the supernatural power of the forces of evil. No Christian is free from the influence of these wicked spirits. It is for this reason that Christ interceded on behalf of Peter: "The Lord said, Simon, Simon, behold, Satan hath desired to have you, that he may sift you as wheat: But I have prayed for thee, that thy faith fail not: and when thou art converted, strengthen thy brethren" (Luke 22:31-32). Satan desires to sift every believer as wheat. It is his ambition to ruin our testimony and cause us to fall into sin. Paul wrote in Ephesians 6:12, "For we wrestle not against flesh and blood, but against principalities, against powers, against the rulers of the darkness of this world, against spiritual wickedness in high places."

No human in himself is equipped to resist Satan. Only as we clothe ourselves with the "whole armour of God," are we able to resist the attacks of the wicked one. As daily we commit ourselves to the control of Christ and walk in His strength and power, spending time in His Word, finding refuge on our knees, then and only then can we stand against "the prince of the power of the air" (Ephesians 2:2). Without Christ, no man is equipped to face the devil. In fact, without Christ man is hopelessly defeated. It is Satan's desire to force every human into hell. For centuries he has been successful in keeping men and women blind in their sin. He is determined that you be lost for eternity. But you can break his control; you can thwart all his attempts if you will invite the Son of God to come into your life to be your Saviour and Lord. You are no match for Satan, but on the other hand, Satan is no match for Christ. If you never have, let Christ become your shield and defender by receiving Him into your life.

Chapter 11

THE REIGN OF REBELLION

Key verse, 36: "And the king shall do according to his will; and he shall exalt himself, and magnify himself above every god, and shall speak marvellous things against the God of gods, and shall prosper till the indignation be accomplished: for that that is determined shall be done."

In chapter 11 of Daniel we see man's final attempt, in the person of the Antichrist, to rebel against the rule of God. Our key verse makes it clear that this wicked ruler is dominated solely by the flesh, for he "shall do according to his will." In addition to the end time, this chapter depicts most accurately history prewritten for a period of some two hundred years following the time of Daniel. The prophecies given in the opening verses of this chapter are so accurate that the critics claim it is impossible that they could have been written previous to the occurrence of the events. Of course, these unbelievers do not realize that "all scripture is given by inspiration of God" (2 Timothy 3:16).

1. *The Tension — verses 1-20.* To consider these verses in detail would involve hundreds of pages, consequently we shall confine ourselves to a rapid summary of events in the light of the prophecies given. Actually verse 1 belongs to the previous chapter as again we are reminded that the angel "stood to confirm and to strengthen" Daniel. What he declared to the prophet would be "the truth."

"There shall stand up yet three kings in Persia; and the fourth shall be far richer than they all: and by his strength through his riches he shall stir up all against the realm of Grecia." These three kings were Ahasuerus, Artaxerxes, and Darius. In history they are named as Cambyses (529-522 B.C.), Pseudo-Smerdis (522-521 B.C.), and Darius Hystaspis (521-485 B.C.). We are told also of "the fourth" who would be "far richer than they all." This was Xerxes (485-465 B.C.) who, as prophesied, was extremely rich. It was he who invaded Greece according to prophecy and fought at Salamis and Thermopylae in 480 B.C.

Events move quickly in this chapter. Between verses 2 and 3 about a century and a half elapsed until the "mighty king" came to power, who stood up and ruled "with great dominion." This "mighty king" was Alexander the Great, who overthrew Persia in 331 B.C. The prophecy states that "when he shall stand up, his kingdom shall be broken." Later the kingdom was broken by the death of Alexander. Further, the kingdom was to "be divided toward the four winds of heaven; and not to his posterity, nor according to his dominion which he ruled: for his kingdom shall be plucked up, even for others beside those." After much disputing and inner strife, the Grecian Empire was partitioned into four parts under four generals following the battle of Ipsus in 301 B.C. The divisions and their leaders were as follows: Ptolemy taking Egypt, Palestine, and Syria; Seleucus taking Syria proper, Mesopotamia, and almost all of Asia Minor; Lysimachus taking Bithynia and Thrace; and Cassander taking Macedonia and Greece. Thus the kingdom was "divided toward the four winds of heaven; and not to his posterity." The prophecy states explicitly that Alexander's kingdom would not go to his son but to the four generals whose names appear in our history books. How accurate and detailed is the Word of God.

The Reign of Rebellion

Beginning with verse 5 and continuing through verse 35, many details are given regarding the long and bitter struggle between the Ptolemies and the Seleucidae. These wars continued for about two centuries. The rulers are spoken of as the king of the south and king of the north, because of their relationship to Palestine, which was the focal point of prophecy. The other two kingdoms had no bearing on God's chosen people Israel, thus they are not considered in the prophecy. Ptolemy Lagus is "the king of the south," of whom it is prophesied in verse 5 that he would "be strong," but also that "one of his princes" was to become "strong above him, and have dominion." This refers to Seleucas Nicator who was initially subject to Ptolemy but later, following the death of Ptolemy Lagus, Seleucas annexed Babylon, Media, and the surrounding nations, after which he broke his allegiance with Egypt and ruled independently.

Another period of time elapsed, to 250 B.C., when the king of the north and the king of the south sought to make an alliance: "in the end of years they shall join themselves together" (verse 6). This alliance was brought about through the marriage of the daughter of the king of the south, Princess Berenice, to Antiochus Theos, the king of the north. To enter into this marriage, Antiochus had agreed to divorce his wife and to make the first-born child in his new marriage the heir to the kingdom. But the Scripture declares that "she shall not retain the power of the arm; neither shall he stand, nor his arm: but she shall be given up, and they that brought her, and he that begat her, and he that strengthened her in these times." Tragedy soon followed as these prophecies were fulfilled. The king's former wife, Laodice, was the instigator of a plot that resulted in the murder of Berenice and all her attendants. Laodice was reinstated as queen by Antiochus, but, not long after, she poisoned him and her son Seleucus Callinicus was crowned king.

"Out of a branch of her roots shall one stand up in his estate" (verse 7). The one who would "stand up in his estate" was Berenice's brother, Ptolemy Euergetes, who avenged the death of his sister with a mighty army, thus retaliating for the humiliation inflicted upon Egypt. This is foretold in the prophecy of verse 7: "Which shall come with an army, and shall enter into the fortress of the king of the north, and shall deal against them, and shall prevail," and in the next two verses: he "shall also carry captives into Egypt their gods, with their princes, and with their precious vessels of silver and of gold; and he shall continue more years than the king of the north. So the king of the south shall come into his kingdom, and shall return into his own land." As prophesied, Ptolemy did all this. He returned, following his conflicts, with four thousand talents of gold, forty thousand talents of silver, and twenty-five hundred idols and idolatrous vessels. In addition, he lived four years beyond the king of the north.

"His sons shall be stirred up, and shall assemble a multitude of great forces: and one shall certainly come, and overflow, and pass through: then shall he return, and be stirred up, even to his fortress" (verse 10). The two "sons" spoken of here are the sons of Callinicus the king of the north, Seleucus (Ceraunus III) and Antiochus the Great. These brothers assembled "a multitude of great forces" to attack Egypt. Seleucus III died several years later and Antiochus pushed the attack with an army of seventy-five thousand warriors. The attack was successful since the king of the south did not oppose him, but according to verses 11 and 12, the king of the south, Ptolemy Philopator, gave the king of the north a severe defeat at Raphia. Ptolemy Philopator could easily have gone on to achieve military glory, but he gave himself to a life of licentiousness, thus he was "not strengthened by it."

As prophesied, the king of the north refused to give up: "the king of the north shall return" (verse 13). This he

The Reign of Rebellion

did, about fourteen years later, after forming an alliance with Philip II, King of Macedon, as well as enlisting the help of wicked and apostate Jews spoken of in verse 14 as "the robbers of thy people." Antiochus was highly successful in his conquests over the Egyptians (verse 15). His enemy was helpless before his power, "and the arms of the south shall not withstand." According to verse 16, he was to return to "the glorious land," that is, the land of Palestine. This was fulfilled after his Egyptian wars. Antiochus made the whole land subject to himself, though he was considerate and kind toward the Jews because of their support of his armies in attacking Egypt.

Antiochus sought to gain complete control of Egypt, (verse 17): "He shall also set his face to enter with the strength of his whole kingdom, and upright ones with him; thus shall he do." In addition to making a treaty with Ptolemy Epiphanes, Antiochus gave his own daughter Cleopatra to Ptolemy in marriage. It was intended that Cleopatra would support her father and his interest in every possible way. But such was not the case. The prophecy was fulfilled that "she shall not stand on his side, neither be for him." She became a faithful wife to her father's enemy, Ptolemy, thus foiling Antiochus' plan.

Following his failure in Egypt, Antiochus turned in the direction of Greece, as prophesied, "After this shall he turn his face unto the isles, and shall take many." He was successful in getting control of some of the islands off the coast of Asia Minor. But the prophecy states further that Antiochus would be in for trouble: "But a prince for his own behalf shall cause the reproach offered by him to cease; without his own reproach he shall cause it to turn upon him." The word "prince" is really "captain." The one predicted here was Scipio Asiaticus, who was commissioned to meet Antiochus with an army of successful warriors. This he did and defeated Antiochus, sending him home utterly humiliated (verse 19): "Then he shall turn his face toward the fort of his own land: but he shall stumble and fall, and not be found." Antiochus was slain by a band of angry people as he sought to plunder the temple of Jupiter at Elymais. Thus the great king came to a hasty and miserable end.

A further prophecy is recorded in verse 20: "Then shall stand up in his estate a raiser of taxes in the glory of the kingdom: but within a few days he shall be destroyed, neither in anger, nor in battle." The son of Antiochus, Seleucus Philopator, is spoken of here as the "raiser of taxes." He was despised by the Jews because of his attempts to exact money from them. Seleucus reigned only twelve years, which was a "few days" in comparison to his father's reign of forty years. He was poisoned by his tax collector, Heliodorus, thus fulfilling the statement that "he shall be destroyed, neither in anger, nor in battle."

Once again we have seen from the Scriptures that God is speaking to men through the Bible. Every phrase of every verse in these twenty verses in Daniel 11 has been fulfilled in perfect detail. Could this have merely happened? How important that we recognize God's Word as the inspired Word of God!

2. *The Tyrant — verses 21-27.* Once again we are brought face to face with the despicable character of chapter 8, where he is seen as the "little horn" growing out of one of the four horns of the goat. Not only was this person extremely vile and morally wicked, but he was detested most of all because of his extreme hatred of the Jews. Of course, this is Antiochus Epiphanes. Even to this day his name is a reproach in the minds of the Jews. The atrocities perpetrated on God's chosen people easily distinguish Antiochus Epiphanes as one of the most brutal men of history.

After Seleucus Philopator, "in his estate shall stand up a vile person, to whom they shall not give the honour of the kingdom: but he shall come in peaceably, and obtain the kingdom by flatteries." Antiochus Epiphanes had no

The Reign of Rebellion

right to the kingdom, but he obtained it "by flatteries" (verse 21). The word "flatteries" used here means by trickery, not legitimately. After he gained the throne, he preserved his power by military strength, "And with the arms of a flood shall they be overflown from before him, and shall be broken; yea, also the prince of the covenant." The reference to "the prince of the covenant" may mean Ptolemy Philometer, with whom Antiochus made a league in the beginning, but which did not last: "After the league made with him he shall work deceitfully: for he shall come up, and shall become strong with a small people." Only a small number were deceived by Antiochus so that they were willing to fight with him and for him. The prophecy states also "He shall enter peaceably even upon the fattest places of the province; and he shall do that which his fathers have not done, nor his fathers' fathers; he shall scatter among them the prey, and spoil, and riches: yea, and he shall forecast his devices against the strong holds, even for a time." The word "peaceably" means that through lies and frauds he sought to establish friendship with other rulers, whom he soon betrayed. He scattered his spoils among those who supported him, but only to gather their favor. Antiochus Epiphanes has been described well as the one who came into power like a fox but soon ruled as a lion.

According to verse 25 Antiochus Epiphanes would turn toward the south for further conquests: "And he shall stir up his power and his courage against the king of the south with a great army; and the king of the south shall be stirred up to battle with a very great and mighty army; but he shall not stand: for they shall forecast devices against him." This was to be the first invasion into Egypt Antiochus was to make. Ptolemy Philometer was the king of the south at the time. Rallying his forces, Ptolemy Philometer sought to withstand Antiochus, but he was unable to do so, primarily because of the betrayal on the part of his own counselors (verse 26): "Yea, they that feed of the portion of his meat shall destroy him, and his army shall overflow: and many shall fall down slain." Notice "they that feed of the portion of his meat shall destroy him." Philometer's closest aides, even though they were dependent upon him for their livelihood, deceived and humiliated him by defeat. The two kings, Antiochus and Ptolemy, met together to discuss matters further, but their interest was "to do mischief, and they shall speak lies at one table; but it shall not prosper: for yet the end shall be at the time appointed." When these two wicked men met together they came with the express desire to deceive each other. They made promises which were merely lies, as neither proposed to fulfill what he promised.

The action of these two kings was abominable, but what more can be expected from men who have never had a heart experience with God? Is integrity and honesty a product of corrupt hearts? Indeed not! The Lord Jesus in speaking of the hearts of those who had never been born again said in Mark 7:21-23: "For from within, out of the heart of men, proceed evil thoughts, adulteries, fornications, murders, Thefts, covetousness, wickedness, deceit, lasciviousness, an evil eye, blasphemy, pride, foolishness: All these evil things come from within, and defile the man." It is for this reason that man needs a new heart, which can be known by a miracle of God only. Without this new heart, he will be as treacherous and undependable as these two kings.

3. *The Torment — verses 28-31.* After his great success in Egypt, as prophesied, Antiochus Epiphanes headed northward with his army, rejoicing in his riches taken from the Egyptians, "Then shall he return into his land with great riches." Arriving in Judea, once again the wicked king poured out his fury on the Jews, "and his heart shall be against the holy covenant; and he shall do exploits, and return to his own land." Previously it had been reported that Antiochus Epiphanes had been slain

during his Egyptian invasion. The Jews rejoiced greatly upon hearing this welcome news, but the report of their exultation reached the ears of Antiochus who immediately unleashed his wrath upon the people of "the holy covenant." He slew eighty thousand Jews and sold forty thousand as slaves. In abominating the sanctuary, he sacrificed swine and poured the broth of their flesh throughout the Temple. He carried away the golden altar, the golden candlesticks, and all the vessels. This was a never-to-be-forgotten humiliation of the covenant people of the Lord.

Later Antiochus made another invasion of Egypt but it was not as successful as previously, "At the time appointed he shall return, and come toward the south; but it shall not be as the former, or as the latter." In response to the appeal of the defeated Jewish people, "the ships of Chittim shall come against him." These were ships from the Roman navy dispatched to aid the Egyptians in their attempt to check the progress of the ruthless and inhuman Antiochus. Met by a Roman ambassador near Alexandria, Antiochus Epiphanes was commanded, on the authority of the Roman senate, to cease in his intended war with Egypt. He pled for time to consider the matter with his aides, but the Roman ambassador, Popilius Loenas, drew a circle around Antiochus and demanded a reply before he left the circle. Antiochus submitted and retreated, which explains the prophecy, "therefore he shall be grieved, and return." Returning in defeat, Antiochus refused to give up. Again he took his revenge on the Jewish people.

This was another exact fulfillment of prophecy. The Scriptures state that he would "have indignation against the holy covenant: so shall he do; he shall even return, and have intelligence with them that forsake the holy covenant." Those that forsook "the holy covenant" were apostate Jews who readily supported the evil ambitions of Antiochus. On his way north, Antiochus dispatched Apollonius with an army of over twenty thousand men with the command to destroy Jerusalem. This was just about accomplished with another vast massacre. All the Jewish ceremonies in the Temple were brought to a halt. The sacrifices were no longer permitted and the Temple was dedicated to Jupiter Olympius. The prophecy was fulfilled, "And arms shall stand on his part, and they shall pollute the sanctuary of strength, and shall take away the daily sacrifice, and they shall place the abomination that maketh desolate."

4. *The Testimony — verses 32-35.* As is always the case, whenever the people of God are persecuted, there are always faithful ones who remain loyal. This was true during the massacre instituted by Antiochus: "And such as do wickedly against the covenant shall he corrupt by flatteries: but the people that do know their God shall be strong, and do exploits." Antiochus had deceived many Jews by his lies, but God had His faithful remnant that stood true and bore a consistent testimony in spite of the bloody purge. Those who were "strong" were the Maccabees and their followers, who refused to have anything to do with the abominable sacrifices of the desecrated Temple. "They that understand among the people shall instruct many: yet they shall fall by the sword, and by flame, by captivity, and by spoil, many days." This the faithful ones did; they were persecuted in every possible way and slain for their testimony, but they did not waver.

Several years later under the courageous leadership of Judas Maccabaeus a revival took place. The uncircumcised children were circumcised, the idolatrous altars were destroyed, the law was recovered from the hands of the Gentiles, and the work of God was prospered. All this was a fulfillment of the prophecy, "Now when they shall fall, they shall be [helped] with a little help: but many shall cleave to them with flatteries." Wherever you find the good, you may be sure there will be evil. There were apostates who went along with the work of Judas

Maccabaeus, some of whom were anxious to get on the winning side, while others were merely deceivers.

The revival was short-lived but the suffering inflicted upon the Jews was not without purpose: "And some of them of understanding shall fall, to try them, and to purge, and to make them white, even to the time of the end: because it is yet for a time appointed." For His own purposes, unknown to God's beloved ones, the Lord chose to permit suffering. But in it all, God's people were made more holy and pure. Through God's mercy there was a limit on the time of suffering, "Because it is yet for a time appointed."

The sorrows that confront believers are always bound by divine limits set by the sovereignty of God. How assuring it is to know that nothing ever "happens"; it is "appointed." God's purposes, though sometimes painful, are never without purpose. We may rest in the mercies of God, realizing that not only does He know all things but He does all things well. Thus, though you may be weary and worn, trust the Lord. Believe Him, for "God is faithful, who will not suffer you to be [tested] above that ye are able; but will with the [testing] also make a way to escape, that ye may be able to bear it" (1 Corinthians 10:13).

5. *The Terror — verses 36-39.* There is no question about the first thirty-five verses of this chapter and their fulfillment, but considering the passage beginning with verse 36, there is nothing in history to match the prophecies to be found therein. Even Antiochus Epiphanes, who is so vividly portrayed in the previous verses, could not possibly be the willful king of verses 36-39. Thus it seems quite obvious that between verses 35 and 36 there is a lapse of time of hundreds of years. Already two thousand years have passed and the unusual personage described in these verses has not appeared. Who is the king characterized so clearly? There seems to be no question that he is the Antichrist, who will appear during the

tribulation period as Satan's man of the hour. Energized by diabolical power, he will come forth to deceive the people, declaring himself to be the Messiah. Doubtless he will be a Jew who may even be living at the present time.

Let us consider further what verses 36-39 have to say about this mighty king who will terrorize the world, of which Antiochus Epiphanes was merely a type. First of all, he "shall do according to his will." Without regard for either God or man, he will be concerned only with the fulfillment of his own diabolical plans. "He shall exalt himself, and magnify himself above every god, and shall speak marvellous things against the God of gods, and shall prosper till the indignation be accomplished: for that that is determined shall be done." The Antichrist will be a blasphemer of the worst order. Paul speaks of him in 2 Thessalonians 2:4, "Who opposeth and exalteth himself above all that is called God, or that is worshipped; so that he as God sitteth in the temple of God, shewing himself that he is God." The temple in which the Antichrist will sit will be in Jerusalem.

Presently the Jews have no temple, but during the tribulation period the Beast who will be residing in Rome will make a covenant with the Jewish people and the temple will be built in Jerusalem. Following the first three and a half years of the tribulation period, the willful king will establish his throne in this temple, compelling everyone to worship him. Energized by Satan, the Antichrist will have miraculous power. This will be used to deceive the people of the world so that millions will gladly honor and worship him. Supported by the Roman Beast, the political power of the western world, the Antichrist, the mighty religious head guided and led by Satan, will reach his zenith of rulership in the last three and a half years of the tribulation period.

It should be noted that there is a time limit put on the wicked works of the Antichrist: he "shall prosper till the indignation be accomplished: for that that is determined

The Reign of Rebellion

shall be done." From other passages of Scripture it is clear that "the indignation" has to do with the judgment that will be experienced by the unbelieving Jews during the tribulation. Having rejected their true Messiah, they will readily respond to the appeals of the Antichrist, only to bring upon themselves the wrath of God.

As has already been stated, it appears that the Antichrist will be a Jew, for we are told, "Neither shall he regard the God of his fathers, nor the desire of women, nor regard any god: for he shall magnify himself above all." "God of his fathers" is peculiarly a Jewish expression used throughout the Old Testament. Doubtless as used here it refers to his fathers in the flesh, Abraham, Isaac, and Jacob. His teachings will be contrary to theirs regarding God, for he will be a blasphemer and a deceiver. It has been "the desire" of every pious Jewish woman to be the chosen vessel in whom the seed of God might be planted to give birth to the Messiah. The Antichrist will ignore such a hope completely, "for he shall magnify himself above all."

There seems to be only one to whom the Antichrist will give respect: "But in his estate shall he honour the God of forces: and a god whom his fathers knew not shall he honour with gold, and silver, and with precious stones, and pleasant things." Who is this "God of forces... whom his fathers knew not"? It will be the influential military power of his day, the "little horn," the Beast, coming forth from the revived Roman Empire, who will rule the world. The Beast will give the Antichrist protection for which the Antichrist will pay dearly. He will repay the efforts of the Beast with great honor, constructing an image of the Beast from gold, silver, and precious stones. Everyone will bow to this idol or suffer the penalty of immediate death.

Those who acquiesce and worship the image erected in honor of the Beast will be amply rewarded: "Thus shall he do in the most strong holds with a strange god, whom he shall acknowledge and increase with glory: and he shall cause them to rule over many, and shall divide the land for gain." The Antichrist will attempt to imitate the coming Messiah who will honor the faithful and judge the faithless.

It seems certain that the time of the appearance of the Antichrist cannot be far distant. The Apostle John stated in his first Epistle, "Little children, it is the last time: and as ye have heard that antichrist shall come, even now are there many antichrists; whereby we know that it is the last time" (1 John 2:18). Recognizing the works of the spirit of the Antichrist on every hand in apostasy, immorality, hatred, and bloodshed, we believe the time cannot be far distant when the "man of sin" will be revealed, "Who opposeth and exalteth himself above all that is called God, or that is worshipped; so that he as God sitteth in the temple of God, shewing himself that he is God" (2 Thessalonians 2:3-4). It behooves every true believer in Christ to be busy telling the lost not about the deceiver but about the Deliverer, who gives not only eternal life but the hope of meeting Him in the air when He comes for His own.

6. *The Threat — verses 40-44.* The Antichrist will achieve tremendous success in his exploits until his efforts suffer a severe threat at the hands of the king of the south and the king of the north. Let us not overlook the fact that the period given by the divine writer for these conflicts will be "at the time of the end," that is, just prior to the return of Christ to rule and reign on the earth. Incensed by the Antichrist's inhuman treatment of the Jews, as well as his disregard of the authority of the bordering nation, "the king of the south" and "the king of the north shall come against him like a whirlwind, with chariots, and with horsemen, and with many ships; and he shall enter into the countries, and shall overflow and pass over." It was not because the king of the north and the king of the south were brought together in a coalition that

The Reign of Rebellion

they attacked the willful king. In fact, the powers from the north and the south were bitter enemies. But both of these kings were moved with choler against the proud dictator in Jerusalem. The king of the south will strike first, but shortly after the king of the north, the stronger of the two, will launch his attack. There is no question as to the locality where the attack will be made, for the Scripture declares that it will be in "the glorious land," which is unmistakably the land of Palestine.

Nothing more is said in this chapter about the Antichrist. The king of the north comes to the fore in the remaining verses of chapter 11. His attack will not only be concentrated in Palestine but we are told that "many countries shall be overthrown." Furthermore, we note that three countries bordering Palestine will escape his power: "But these shall escape out of his hand, even Edom, and Moab, and the chief of the children of Ammon." Though these countries shall escape from the onslaught of this mighty power from the north, yet Egypt will not escape: "He shall stretch forth his hand also upon the countries: and the land of Egypt shall not escape. But he shall have power over the treasures of gold and of silver, and over all the precious things of Egypt: and the Libyans and the Ethiopians shall be at his steps."

While busily engaged in the destruction of his constant enemy, Egypt, the king of the north will learn of threats to his power coming out of the north as well as the east: "But tidings out of the east and out of the north shall trouble him: therefore he shall go forth with great fury to destroy, and utterly to make away many." Leaving Egypt as quickly as possible, he will overwhelm those who will rise up against him.

It is interesting to consider in the light of the prophetic Scriptures that the king of the north will have great power, but he will not be able to overcome his worst enemy, the Antichrist. God has reserved this right for Himself. The Antichrist will be judged at the return of the

Lord, which will follow the three and a half years of severe persecution and trouble during the bloody reign of the Antichrist. How consoling it is to know that, in spite of the power of men, they cannot supersede the power of God. They may devise wicked plans, even to the intent of completely destroying everyone who names Christ as Saviour and Lord, but they can go only so far. God is still on the throne. Even the powerful king from the north will not be permitted to interfere with the divine plan during the closing days of this age. God is sovereign, and irrespective of how foolish men may become in their attempts to resist divine power, we are assured that "He that sitteth in the heavens shall laugh: the Lord shall have them in derision" (Psalm 2:4).

Sometimes believers fear what man will do to them. Rest assured, nothing can come into the believer's life unless permitted by our sovereign God. We may not always understand why certain things are permitted to cross our paths, but God understands and that is all that is necessary. We cannot pry into His secrets. We are not to pry, but to pray, and to trust the Lord for His providence and grace. In Romans 11: 33-36 the apostle writes: "O the depth of the riches both of the wisdom and knowledge of God! how unsearchable are His judgments, and His ways past finding out! For who hath known the mind of the Lord? or who hath been His counsellor? Or who hath first given to Him, and it shall be recompensed unto him again? For of Him, and through Him, and to Him, are all things: to whom be glory for ever." There is much in life about which God has given us no understanding, but in all these things He remains as "Lord of lords, and King of kings" (Revelation 17:14). Thus the true believer can say with David, "The LORD is my rock, and my fortress, and my deliverer; my God, my strength, in whom I will trust; my buckler, and the horn of my salvation, and my high tower" (Psalm 18:2).

My Father's ways may twist and turn,
    My heart may throb and ache,
But in my heart I'm glad I know
    He maketh no mistake.

My cherished plans may go astray,
    My hopes may fade away,
But still I'll trust my Lord to lead,
    For He doth know the way.

Tho' night be dark and it may seem
    That day will never break,
I'll pin my faith, my all in Him,
    He maketh no mistake.

There's so much now I cannot see,
    My eyesight's far too dim,
But come what may, I'll simply trust
    And leave it all with Him.

For by-and-by the mist will lift,
    And plain it all He'll make,
Through all the way, tho' dark to me,
    He made not one mistake.

                        Author Unknown

God makes no mistakes, and if you are in Jesus Christ and if you know Him as your Saviour and Lord, you have nothing to fear. The God who will control the end time can control your life perfectly if you will let Him do it.

7. *The Triumph — verse 45.* It is not the king of the north who will triumph; rather the King of kings and Lord of lords will triumph over the king of the north: "And he shall plant the tabernacles of his palace between the seas in the glorious holy mountain; yet he shall come to his end, and none shall help him." The king of the north will seek to establish his power between the Mediterranean and the Dead Sea, but he will fail in his attempt, for the Lord will return and subdue not only the king of the north

but every earthly power. We are told in Zechariah 14:3-4, 9: "Then shall the LORD go forth, and fight against those nations, as when He fought in the day of battle. And His feet shall stand in that day upon the mount of Olives, which is before Jerusalem on the east, and the mount of Olives shall cleave in the midst thereof toward the east and toward the west, and there shall be a very great valley; and half of the mountain shall remove toward the north, and half of it toward the south . . . And the LORD shall be king over all the earth: in that day shall there be one LORD, and His name one." Righteousness will triumph over wickedness. The power of the king of the north will be destroyed forever without instruments of warfare of any kind.

But what about the Antichrist, who will be the cause of so much suffering in the world, especially to the Jews, God's covenant people? The answer to this question is given in 2 Thessalonians 2:8 where, in writing of the Antichrist, the apostle declares, "whom the Lord shall consume with the spirit of His mouth, and shall destroy with the brightness of His coming." The destruction spoken of here is not annihilation. We are told in Revelation 19:20, "And the beast was taken, and with him the false prophet that wrought miracles before him, with which he deceived them that had received the mark of the beast, and them that worshipped his image. These both were cast alive into a lake of fire burning with brimstone."

The judgment of hell will be the abode of the Antichrist, but not only of the Antichrist — of all who are possessed by the spirit of the Antichrist, that is, all who have never been born again, who have never received Christ as Saviour and Lord. Hell will be filled with good people, church people, kind people, as well as prostitutes, gamblers, thieves, murderers, drunkards, and the like.

Your attitude toward Christ will be the deciding factor as to whether you will spend eternity in Heaven with the Son of God or in hell with the Antichrist and the devil.

The Reign of Rebellion

Maybe your dearest loved ones are heartbroken because of the hardness of your heart. Let God have His way, that you may come to know the very best in life, His best for you.

Dr. P. W. Philpott, who was at one time pastor of the Moody Memorial Church, and Mrs. Philpott were entertained in a home over which there seemed to be the shadow of some great sorrow. The mother never smiled. While having prayer with the family, Dr. Philpott prayed, "Now, Lord, if there are any members of this family not with us this morning, bless them where they are." As he prayed, the unhappy mother broke out in a sob. Later she told Dr. and Mrs. Philpott this sad story.

"I have only one son. He had disgraced us greatly and frequently because of the curse of the drink habit. Five years ago he and my husband quarreled. Finally, my husband told him to go. He went out through that door and I have never heard from him since. I have believed, however, that my son will be saved. If ever you see him, tell him that I have never missed a night praying for him."

Dr. Philpott said later, "I wish I could find that young man and let him look beneath the blind and see his mother pacing the floor of that little room and crying aloud, 'God, save my son, my only son.' "

It may be that your mother is praying for you at this very moment. For years you have resisted her love and concern in her attempt to point you to the Saviour. She cannot decide for you, she cannot receive Christ in your place. Do not resist your mother's love. Furthermore, do not resist God's love. He declares in Jeremiah 31:3, "I have loved thee with an everlasting love." You have ignored His invitation, you have resisted His grace. But in spite of all you have done, He still loves you and His promise is, "him that cometh to Me I will in no wise cast out" (John 6:37).

Chapter 12

THE RECORD OF RECOMPENSE

Key verse, 2: "And many of them that sleep in the dust of the earth shall awake, some to everlasting life, and some to shame, and everlasting contempt."

This chapter not only brings us to the end of the book of Daniel but clearly presents some of the important details having to do with the present church age. Here believing Israel is seen in her final deliverance from the hands of her persecutors. No longer downtrodden, she enters her final reward.

1. *The Wrath — verse 1.* The first verse of this chapter makes it clear that Israel must face a time of oppression and abuse such as she had never experienced before. God has not left us in the dark as to the time of this severe tribulation, "And at that time shall Michael stand up, the great prince which standeth for the children of thy people." What "time" is the prophet speaking about here? It can only be the time described in the previous chapter, when the Antichrist will rise to the zenith of his power and commit his abominable deeds, at which time also the king of the north will make his entry into the land of God's people, the last three and a half years of the seven-year tribulation period. We are told further that "there shall be a time of trouble, such as never was since there was a nation even to that same time." Other portions of the book of Daniel reveal the heartless and

The Record of Recompense

merciless acts of wickedness that will be unleashed upon the Jews. In the New Testament, the words of our Lord describing this period are almost identical with those of Daniel: "For then shall be great tribulation, such as was not since the beginning of the world to this time, no, nor ever shall be" (Matthew 24:21).

There have been many who have tried to link this period of extreme suffering to the destruction of Jerusalem by Titus. This was a time of extreme persecution as far as the Jews were concerned, far worse than had been known even under Nebuchadnezzar. It is not possible, however, that the time spoken of by Daniel and by our Lord could be the destruction under Titus: "At that time thy people shall be delivered, every one that shall be found written in the book" (Daniel 12:1). The people of God were not delivered during the time of Titus. Daniel's prophecy demands that they be delivered "at that time." Furthermore, "at that time shall Michael stand up, the great prince which standeth for the children of thy people." In a special way the archangel Michael will enter the picture during the time spoken of here for the express purpose of preserving and caring for God's chosen people. There is not the slightest suggestion that this occurred during the destruction under Titus.

But even more conclusive is the fact that in our Lord's prophecy regarding this particular time He declared, "Immediately after the tribulation of those days shall the sun be darkened, and the moon shall not give her light, and the stars shall fall from heaven, and the powers of the heavens shall be shaken: And then shall appear the sign of the Son of man in heaven: and then shall all the tribes of the earth mourn, and they shall see the Son of man coming in the clouds of heaven with power and great glory" (Matthew 24:29-30). Here Christ links His return to this period of extreme and severe tribulation. He did not return during the reign of Titus, but He will return and deliver the Jews when He comes to establish His kingdom at the conclusion of the seven-year tribulation period.

It should be understood, however, that not all Jews will be delivered at this particular time. Deliverance will be for those "that shall be found written in the book." The Prophet Zechariah gives us more light on this fact in chapter 13 of his prophecy, verses 8-9: "And it shall come to pass, that in all the land, saith the LORD, two parts therein shall be cut off and die; but the third shall be left therein. And I will bring the third part through the fire, and will refine them as silver is refined, and will try them as gold is tried: they shall call on My name, and I will hear them: I will say, It is My people: and they shall say, The LORD is my God." These will be spared miraculously in the land regardless of the severity of the persecution. God will preserve His believing remnant in the midst of the severest fire.

As we are made aware of this promise for believing Israel in the midst of the worst tribulation in their history, you and I may take courage in the promises of God for His preservation and care of us in the midst of the trials of life. Even as our Lord will undertake for His own in spite of the sufferings of the tribulation period, so He will see us through our sleepless nights and our anxious days right now. God has not promised to keep us *from* sufferings, but He has promised to keep us *in* our sufferings.

It is said that at St. Margaret's Bay in the southeast of England there is a well that is always covered by the sea at high tide. Strangely enough, however, its water remains fresh and pure, uncontaminated by the briny waters of the sea. Fed from the hills above, it has a constant supply of fresh water pouring into it which effectively prevents the ocean from flowing in. How like the victorious Christian whose life is dominated by the Spirit. The sea of trouble, trial, and adversity may sweep over him, but it can find no point of penetration: the Living Spring is like an inexhaustible well of water within him, ever bubbling up into quietness of soul and peace of mind. How marvelous is God's keeping and sustaining care. Let us not complain in the midst of trouble, because trouble is part of our lot, "For unto you it is given in the behalf of Christ, not only to believe on Him, but also to suffer for His sake" (Philippians 1:29). Let us offer praise and gratitude to God who is always gracious and who never fails to give strength, proving Himself to be "a very present help in [time of] trouble" (Psalm 46:1).

2. *The Wakening — verse 2.* "And many of them that sleep in the dust of the earth shall awake, some to everlasting life, and some to shame and everlasting contempt." Considering this verse in its context, it is obvious that the Holy Spirit is not speaking primarily of a physical resurrection, although I see no reason why this may not be taught from this verse in a secondary sense. But recognizing what is said in verse 1 concerning the "time of trouble, such as never was since there was a nation," which is specifically related to Daniel's people, it would seem that verse 2 has reference to a national and spiritual resurrection of Israel.

During the great tribulation period, many of God's chosen people will realize the truth as never before. For many centuries the Jews have been scattered among the peoples of the world, sleeping in unbelief, but God's remnant will waken "to everlasting life." Suddenly, during the great tribulation period, they will recognize the fact that they have been deceived by the Antichrist and will turn to their true Messiah for refuge. On the other hand, millions of Jews will continue in unbelief, remaining in "shame and everlasting contempt."

There are numerous other passages of Scripture that corroborate the fact of this coming revival and awakening among the children of Israel; for instance, Isaiah 26:19: "Thy dead men shall live, together with my dead body shall they arise. Awake and sing, ye that dwell in dust: for thy dew is as the dew of herbs, and the earth shall cast out the dead." Here is a clear prophecy of the resurrection of the Jews from sin and ungodliness as they turn to the Lord Jehovah. Ezekiel 37 tells of the "dry bones" coming to life, which likewise has reference to the fact of Israel's spiritual resurrection. The Lord declared unto the prophet, "Son of man, these bones are the whole house of Israel: behold, they say, Our bones are dried, and our hope is lost: we are cut off for our parts. Therefore prophesy and say unto them, Thus saith the Lord GOD; Behold, O My people, I will open your graves, and cause you to come up out of your graves, and bring you into the land of Israel. And ye shall know that I am the LORD, when I have opened your graves, O My people, and brought you up out of your graves. And shall put My Spirit in you, and ye shall live, and I shall place you in your own land: then shall ye know that I the LORD have spoken it, and performed it, saith the LORD" (Ezekiel 37:11-14). This prophecy has not yet been fulfilled but it will be when our Lord comes to rule in power and glory at His Second Advent.

There is a sense in which these words of Daniel 12:2 could apply to our present age. Every time someone hears the gospel and believes on Christ, he is raised from spiritual death. All who are without the Saviour remain "dead in trespasses and sins" (Ephesians 2:1). It is through the quickening power of Christ that the unsaved are made alive, raised from spiritual death, and made new creatures in Christ. James declared, "Let him know, that he which converteth the sinner from the error of his way shall save a soul from death, and shall hide a multitude of sins" (James 5:20). What a thrilling privilege is ours in Christ to tell others the blessed gospel story of Christ and His redeeming love, that they might believe and be saved.

Before leaving this passage, think of it for a moment in its reference to physical resurrection. What is said in this verse is confirmed by many other statements of Scripture.

Though not at the same time, the Bible teaches that there will be two resurrections. The Lord Jesus made this clear in John 5:28-29: "Marvel not at this: for the hour is coming, in the which all that are in the graves shall hear His voice, And shall come forth; they that have done good, unto the resurrection of life; and they that have done evil, unto the resurrection of damnation." This is the same truth Daniel taught many centuries before. When will these resurrections take place? The first resurrection for believers will occur when Christ returns to meet His own in the air, as described in 1 Thessalonians 4:16-17: "For the Lord Himself shall descend from heaven with a shout, with the voice of the archangel, and with the trump of God: and the dead in Christ shall rise first: Then we which are alive and remain shall be caught up together with them in the clouds, to meet the Lord in the air: and so shall we ever be with the Lord." The second resurrection will be after the millennium, according to Revelation 20:5, "But the rest of the dead lived not again until the thousand years were finished." John writes of this in Revelation 20:12: "And I saw the dead, small and great, stand before God; and the books were opened: and another book was opened, which is the book of life: and the dead were judged out of those things which were written in the books, according to their works." In verse 15 we have a sobering truth, "And whosoever was not found written in the book of life was cast into the lake of fire." In this same chapter 20 of Revelation, John declared also in verse 6, "Blessed and holy is he that hath part in the first resurrection: on such the second death hath no power, but they shall be priests of God and of Christ, and shall reign with Him a thousand years." How important it is to have Christ in one's heart, to be ready to meet our Lord when He comes.

3. *The Wages — verse 3.* At all times God has His faithful saints who are diligent in their responsibility of sowing the seed of life. There are many professed

followers of the Lord who never witness, but on the other hand, there are those who grasp every opportunity to spread the truth. During the tribulation period, when the blood of the martyred saints will run in the streets, God will not be without His witnesses. Those who will be conscientious in witnessing for the Lord will receive their reward, "And they that be wise shall shine as the brightness of the firmament; and they that turn many to righteousness, as the stars for ever and ever." Among those who will awaken to everlasting life from their spiritual blindness, during the tribulation period, will be a great host of loyal ambassadors for Christ. As God's faithful witnesses, they will go everywhere propagating the truth in spite of the dangers involved. Our text speaks of those who will "turn many to righteousness." A more literal translation would be "they that *instruct* many in righteousness." It is not success spoken of here, in the sense that many unbelievers will be turned to the Lord; rather it has to do with the faithfulness of God's servants in proclaiming the truth. These faithful ones will be rewarded not only in this life but in that which is to come.

Though in the strict sense verse 3 applies to the faithful among Israel, who will be making known the truth to unbelievers in the tribulation period, indeed we of the church age also can take its message to heart and claim its promised blessing. Not all those who come to a knowledge of the truth in the tribulation period will be devoted witnesses; doubtless it will be as we find it in the Body of Christ in our day. Though thousands claim to be saved, only a comparatively few professing Christians are telling the unsaved about the glorious gospel and our gracious Saviour. Daniel identifies those "that be wise" with those who "turn many to righteousness." Truly the wise Christians are the soul-winning Christians. "The fruit of the righteous is a tree of life; and he that winneth souls is wise" (Proverbs 11:30). Often new converts are wiser in this respect than mature saints. The Lord Jesus declared,

"Ye shall be witnesses unto Me" (Acts 1:8). Many new believers heed this and witness for Christ, the Holy Spirit blesses their labors, and souls are won to Christ.

Shame on us who are older in the faith, that we have lost our vision and are remiss in the fulfillment of our obligation to witness. Would you be "wise" with the promise of shining as the "brightness of the firmament"? Then grasp the opportunities our Lord sends to you daily. Soon our time on this side of Heaven will be done, some of us will stand before our Lord empty-handed. Do not miss the supreme joy God has for you in telling others about the Christ who saved you. It may cost you your reputation, comfort, or even property. You may lose some friendships, while suffering ridicule and persecution. But wise believers are busy believers, spreading the truth, regardless of the consequences.

A friend of mine preached in a large evangelical church. Prior to his entry into the pulpit, he was invited to a prayer meeting before the service. One of the old deacons prayed, "Lord, send the unsaved."

In the service that morning was a young man who had not been saved long, but he had a burning heart and a loving concern for the lost. He had risen early and gone into a part of the city where sailors were known to congregate, and in talking with various ones he found five young men willing to come to the service. He drove them to the church, and went in with them. Afterward, he took them to dinner and then back downtown where he had met them.

Which of the two men was more pleasing to God, the one who prayed that the unsaved might come in, or the one who went out and brought them in? God tells us, "Go out into the highways and hedges, and compel them to come in, that My house may be filled" (Luke 14:23). It is not God's responsibility to send the unsaved into our churches; it is ours to go out and witness to them, that they might be saved and want to come to church.

There is no time to be lost in the performance of this important task. In John 4:35-36 we have the words of our Lord, "Say not ye, There are yet four months, and then cometh harvest? behold, I say unto you, Lift up your eyes, and look on the fields; for they are white already to harvest. And he that reapeth receiveth wages, and gathereth fruit unto life eternal: that both he that soweth and he that reapeth may rejoice together." The need is great. No matter in which direction you turn, there are souls that need to be born again. They must hear the gospel. You and I are the appointed ones to tell them of Christ who alone can save. If we are faithful the reward will be great. Souls who were on their way to hell will be turned toward Heaven, and then when we meet our Lord face to face, we shall reap the marvelous promise, "that both he that soweth and he that reapeth may rejoice together." Yes, throughout all eternity we shall "shine as the brightness of the firmament" and "as the stars for ever and ever." Let us be witnesses for the Lord Jesus!

4. *The Writings — verse 4.* The divine messenger had been instructing Daniel about certain events that were to transpire during and following the great tribulation period. The prophet was then told to "shut up the words, and seal the book, even to the time of the end." Why was God's servant told to seal the book? Simply because the events described in this prophecy were not to occur until a time distant. In contrast to this, consider the message the angel gave the Apostle John at the conclusion of the book of the Revelation, "Seal *not* the sayings of the prophecy of this book: for the time is at hand" (Revelation 22:10). Why the difference? Here are two great prophetic books in the Bible dealing with the end time. One of the prophets is told to "seal the book" while the other is told not to seal it. The explanation is this: though Daniel did not know, God knew that many years would intervene prior to the period known as the great tribulation. The Apostle John, on the other hand, was a New Testament

The Record of Recompense

prophet, writing in particular for New Testament believers living during the church age. Since this immediately precedes the tribulation period, the time about which little was known in Daniel's day was to become well known in our day.

Daniel was told also by the angel that "many shall run to and fro, and knowledge shall be increased." Usually this statement is interpreted out of context, referring it to the unusual advances of scientific achievements in the past several centuries. Such an interpretation isolates the statement from the rest of the chapter. Daniel was told to "seal the book" for the present time, but it would not be sealed forever. At "the time of the end" there would be interest such as never known before in seeking the meaning of prophecy. As the events foretold would begin to unfold, thousands would search the Scriptures in an attempt to understand the meaning of the distressing events of the tribulation period. Tregelles says of the phrase, "many shall run to and fro," that it really means, "Many shall scrutinize (the book) from end to end." Thousands who up until the end time had no interest or concern in the Word of God will suddenly turn to the Scriptures in an attempt to seek the answer for the then-present world dilemma.

There can be no question about it, the time of the end is close at hand. The book of Daniel, though sealed at one time, is no longer a closed book. You and I who are in Jesus Christ have an anointing through the Holy Spirit so that we might clearly understand its prophecies. The tragedy is, in the great majority of our churches the subject of prophecy is ignored. Many preachers consider it fanciful, something not to be talked about. God has given us His plan for the ages, yet comparatively few of those in our churches have any interest or concern about prophetic truth.

When I was a student in seminary, one of my professors told us in class that the book of the Revelation was a closed book. "It should not even be read," he said. It is quite obvious that he did not read it, for if he had, he would have found in the third verse of the opening chapter these words, "*Blessed* is he that *readeth*, and they that *hear* the words of this prophecy, and *keep* those things which are written therein: for the time is at hand."

Prophecy should be studied for the reason the apostle gives, "The time is at hand." In Daniel's day, the prophecy was to be sealed up, but in our day the seal has been broken. You and I, if we are to know the why's and the wherefore's of what is happening in the world today, must be students of prophecy. But prophetic truth is not for spiritual babes. Those who would have an understanding of God's prophetic Word must be growing saints. Carnal and defeated Christians are not only plagued by the evil of no interest, but they are lacking in spiritual gift of divine wisdom. If you are a child of God, living in the victory of Christ, take the time you should to study the prophetic Scriptures, not only for your own edification but also for the value you will be able to provide for others.

Eighteen centuries ago a young scholar of philosophy from the Roman colony near ancient Samaria was taking a solitary walk along the shore of the Mediterranean Sea. Thirsting after truth as the one great possession, he had drawn water out of every well of ancient learning and philosophy, only to thirst again. He had gone the rounds of the Stoics, the Platonists, the Peripatetics, the Pythagoreans, and yet had not come to satisfaction and peace. But during his morning walk by the seaside, he met a venerable Christian. They engaged in conversation, and that conversation changed the course of Justin Martyr's life. This unknown friend showed him how the philosophers reasoned about the truth, whereas the Hebrew prophets spoke the truth as men who had been witnesses. He pointed out to him how the prophets had foretold the coming of Christ, and how their predictions were fulfilled in His life and work. Taking the old man's advice, Justin

The Record of Recompense 243

commenced the study of Old Testament prophecies and their confirmation in the New Testament. This convinced him of the truth of Christianity; he became a Christian, one of the greatest defenders of its truth, and most heroic of its martyrs.

The prophetic books are not closed. They are for you, if you love Christ. As we approach the end time, we ought to be men and women of the Book, studying all the Word of God, including the great prophetic books of Scripture. Of course, if you have never come to Christ, as far as you are concerned the entire Bible is a closed book. Let no man think that by his own wisdom he can understand any portion of the Word of God. He needs the Holy Spirit to give him understanding of God's truth. Step number one is to claim Jesus Christ as Saviour and Lord. Ask Christ to come into your life; He will come in. After you receive Him, grow in grace daily by reading His Word and spending time with Him in prayer, while telling others about Him that they might believe and be saved.

5. *The Wonders — verses 5-7.* Wonders never cease for those who love the Lord. The Christian life is a thrilling life, not only because of God's constant providential care, but even more, because of the joyous surprises the believer enjoys along his pilgrim way. Daniel records another surprise God had for him, "Then I Daniel looked, and, behold, there stood two, the one on this side of the bank of the river, and the other on that side of the bank of the river." Suddenly two angels appeared whom Daniel had never seen before. "The river" is the same one spoken of in chapter 10, the Hiddekel or Tigris, and a further mention of "the man clothed in linen." Surely this can be no other than the one who appeared to the prophet at the beginning of this concluding vision.

Let us reflect on the meaning of this awesome scene. It seems conclusive that "the man clothed in linen" was the Lord Jesus Christ. He was standing "upon the waters of the river." "Water" in the Bible usually signifies people. In

Psalm 29:10 we read that "The LORD sitteth upon the flood; yea, the LORD sitteth King for ever." In the New Testament we see Him responding to the need of the distressed, storm-tossed disciples by walking on the sea. Christ possesses power and dominion over all humans, though millions in the world do not realize this. When Christ returns, He will exert His power and every knee will bow to "confess that Jesus Christ is Lord, to the glory of God the Father" (Philippians 2:11). The Lord Jesus standing on the river and the angels standing on both banks of the river suggest God's overwhelming care in every situation. The angels are God's ministering spirits to protect and preserve the people of God. Every situation of life is under the control of Him who is Master of all. No wonder Job declared, "Though He slay me, yet will I trust in Him" (Job 13:15). Because of Christ's constant, watchful care, every believer may trust Him fully, knowing that He will not and cannot fail.

A father tells of being awakened in the night by his little boy who called out in fear.

"Daddy, are you here?"

"Yes, Son, I am here," the father answered reassuringly.

"Daddy," said the voice, a little steadier, "Is your face turned toward me?"

When the father answered, "Yes, Son," the little fellow lost his fear and quietly fell asleep.

How comforting it is to know that after one has experienced salvation through Jesus Christ, the Saviour's face is always turned in his direction. In 2 Chronicles 16:9 we are told, "the eyes of the LORD run to and fro throughout the whole earth, to shew Himself strong in the behalf of them whose heart is perfect toward Him." David declared in Psalm 91:11, "He shall give His angels charge over thee, to keep thee in all thy ways." With Christ in control of every situation as Lord of all and with legions of angels surrounding us, what have we to fear? Let us believe God for all things!

One of the angels "said to the man clothed in linen, which was upon the waters of the river, How long shall it be to the end of these wonders?" In other words, what will be the length of time of the period "of trouble" spoken of in verse 1? Doubtless this question was asked and answered that the Prophet Daniel might record this in his prophecy for the benefit of believers in all ages to come. In response to the angel's question, "the man clothed in linen" declared, "it shall be for a time, times, and an half." As he made this statement he held both his hands up toward Heaven, assuring Daniel that what he had spoken was truth. Again it was made clear, as we have already seen from Daniel 7:25, that the "time of trouble" represented a period of three and a half years or forty-two months. This will be the time of extreme tribulation during which the little horn of Daniel 7 and the Antichrist under Satan's control will reign prior to the return of Christ. "The man clothed in linen" informed Daniel and the angels that this would be the period of time when the ruthless, godless leader will "scatter the power of the holy people." Then, he said, "all these things shall be finished." Indeed, they will be.

At that moment, the great event described by the apostle in Matthew 24:29-31 will come to pass: "Immediately after the tribulation of those days shall the sun be darkened, and the moon shall not give her light, and the stars shall fall from heaven, and the powers of the heavens shall be shaken: And then shall appear the sign of the Son of man in heaven: and then shall all the tribes of the earth mourn, and they shall see the Son of man coming in the clouds of heaven with power and great glory. And He shall send His angels with a great sound of a trumpet, and they shall gather together His elect from the four winds, from one end of heaven to the other." The man of sin will reign in terror, but his reign will be brief, for the Son of man will return to reign in glory.

6. *The Witnessing — verses 8-10* Daniel was left in the dark somewhat after hearing the prophecy of the great tribulation period. Of course, he did not have the book of the Revelation and other important portions of Scripture to clarify his thinking. But he did a wise thing: rather than remain in a state of confusion, he asked a question of the Lord Himself, "O my Lord, what shall be the end of these things?" Actually, he was asking, "What is the meaning of all this?"

Here is a worthy lesson for those of us who would know more about the Word of God. As we carefully and prayerfully study the Scriptures, so often we are confronted with passages hard to understand. What should we do? Where should we turn for help? Ask Him who is the Author of the Word. If you are in earnest and sincerely desire to know the truth, doubtless God will give you the answer.

It may be, however, that what you are asking is not to be made known to you at the time. The Lord may have a greater purpose in this which He does not care to divulge to you. Such was Daniel's experience. God's word to him was, "Go thy way, Daniel: for the words are closed up and sealed till the time of the end." As far as Daniel was concerned, the meaning of the prophecy was not to be made known to him. He was to be the messenger but not the interpreter. He was the vessel used by God at the time to record this important prophecy having to do with the tribulation period. Note, however, that the prophecy was not sealed forever but only "till the time of the end." Then Daniel, as well as all other believers, will have perfect understanding of all prophecy for they will be in that vast company of saints who will return to the earth with Christ when He returns in glory. All the prophecies Daniel received will be understandable at Christ's Second Advent.

Another revelation was given to Daniel in verse 10 portraying moral conditions during the great tribulation: "Many shall be purified, and made white, and tried; but the wicked shall do wickedly: and none of the wicked shall understand; but the wise shall understand." What is said here could apply very well to the conditions in the world from Daniel's day until the time of the end. The Lord Jesus in His parable of the wheat and tares emphasized the fact of the good and bad continuing until His return: "Let both grow together until the harvest: and in the time of harvest I will say to the reapers, Gather ye together first the tares, and bind them in bundles to burn them: but gather the wheat into My barn" (Matthew 13:30).

In concluding the book of the Revelation the Apostle John wrote of a truth similar to that given to Daniel: "He that is unjust, let him be unjust still: and he which is filthy, let him be filthy still: and he that is righteous, let him be righteous still: and he that is holy, let him be holy still" (Revelation 22:11).

It seems obvious from the context that verse 10 refers to the tribulation period. With this in mind, consider the words, "Many shall be purified, and made white, and tried." What does this mean? Souls will be saved even in the midst of abominable wickedness. How will they be saved? In all probability they will come to know Jesus as Lord through the faithful witness to be raised up by God. In spite of dungeon and sword, the Lord will have His faithful ones who will not be "ashamed of the gospel of Christ" (Romans 1:16). Doubtless it will be then as in our present day: not all believers will be witnessing, some will be fearful and remain silent; but He will not be without His faithful ambassadors.

What a difference it would make in our own day if all believers who have been truly born of the Spirit were to be witnesses for God. Our churches, which should be the training ground for evangelism, do not seem to be producing soul-winners. We have much activity, but in many instances little or nothing is being accomplished.

Several years ago a television program showed a machine containing many thousands of moving parts. There were wheels, levers, gears, moving up and down and around. The builder of this machine was interviewed and stated that he had collected the material from many junk yards in many parts of the world. There was a most unusual feature about this machine: it had no purpose or usefulness whatsoever. It had taken a lot of work and effort, but was merely a curiosity piece, serving no benefit at all.

Many churches are just about as productive as the machine which had no purpose. Did not the Lord Jesus declare, "Ye shall be witnesses unto Me" (Acts 1:8)? If we are not witnessing for Christ, we are failing Christ.

In a testimony meeting, a man rose and spoke at length on his religious experience.

"I have spent the last five years on the mountaintop," he exclaimed.

D. L. Moody was moderating the meeting, and broke in immediately, asking, "How many souls have you led to Christ in those five years?"

The man hesitated and finally stammered out that he could recall none.

"Well," said Moody briskly and bluntly, "we don't want that kind of mountaintop experience."

Peter, James, and John spent one night with Jesus on Mount Hermon. The rest of the time they were busy as His ministers to a needy world. It is of the very essence of Christianity that the Christian be a witness, pointing others to the Saviour. Let us not shirk this supreme responsibility that God has committed to us! Determine by God's grace that you will witness to at least one soul each day. Ask the Lord to fill your heart with His love and

The Record of Recompense 249

compassion, that, like Paul, the love of Christ will constrain you to speak for Him who died for you.

7. *The Waiting — verses 11-13.* "The man clothed in linen" continued to speak, "And from the time that the daily sacrifice shall be taken away, and the abomination that maketh desolate set up, there shall be a thousand two hundred and ninety days." In the verse which follows we are told of another time period, "Blessed is he that waiteth, and cometh to the thousand three hundred and five and thirty days." Here are three different time periods commencing with "the abomination that maketh desolate": 1260 days, 1290 days, and 1335 days. A special blessing is pronounced on those who wait and come to the third period of 1335 days.

What is the meaning of these three time segments? If one were to read all the commentators who have written on this subject, he would certainly be confused, for many fanciful interpretations have been given. There can be no question, however, as to the beginning of the time from which these days are to be reckoned. Verse 11 is clear that it is "from the time that the daily sacrifice shall be taken away, and the abomination that maketh desolate set up." In His Olivet discourse, the Lord Jesus made a direct reference to this time: "When ye therefore shall see the abomination of desolation, spoken of by Daniel the prophet, stand in the holy place, (whoso readeth, let him understand:) Then let them which be in Judaea flee into the mountains: Let him which is on the housetop not come down to take any thing out of his house: Neither let him which is in the field return back to take his clothes. And woe unto them that are with child, and to them that give suck in those days! But pray ye that your flight be not in the winter, neither on the sabbath day: For then shall be great tribulation, such as was not since the beginning of the world to this time, no, nor ever shall be" (Matthew 24:15-21). Some have tried to tell us that the abomination of desolation took place under the destruction of Jerusalem by Titus. In Daniel we have read, "Blessed is he that waiteth, and cometh to the thousand three hundred and five and thirty days." Was there any time of great blessing 1335 days after the destruction of Jerusalem? This prophecy can refer only to one period of time, the great tribulation.

But the question is, why are there three periods mentioned following the three-and-a-half-year tribulation period? First of all, consider the fact that the Lord Jesus will return at the conclusion of the first period, 1260 days. At this time, the Beast and the Antichrist will be destroyed. It would seem that during the next thirty-day period the Jews from all over the world will be liberated. At the same time, all the nations of the world will be judged. Furthermore, there is another forty-five-day period in which doubtless all the preparations will be made to set up Christ's kingdom. At the conclusion of this period, all the plans will be finalized and the blessing of God will flow throughout the whole earth. Indeed, this is a time for which every true believer patiently waits. Doubtless there are many other events, of which we are not told, that will take place during the thirty-day and the forty-five-day periods. In brief, it will be a time in which all Israel's enemies will be subdued and God's people will be prepared for millennial blessing.

There is a final word given to Daniel, "But go thou thy way till the end be: for thou shalt rest, and stand in thy lot at the end of the days." Daniel knew little concerning the end time, about which he was writing, but was promised that some day it would all be made plain. Until that time, he would rest in the sleep of death and then his body would be raised to share in the promised blessing. Daniel was an old man when this prophecy was given, perhaps nearly a hundred years of age. He had walked courageously with the Lord through many storms and sorrows, but as "the LORD preserved David whithersoever he went"

(2 Samuel 8:6), so He preserved His fearless servant Daniel. And He will preserve you and me as we fully trust Him in our walk of faith.

It is with this thought that I close our studies from this marvelous book of prophecy. Realize that we have a great God, One who is "able to do exceeding abundantly above all that we ask or think" (Ephesians 3:20). Set your sights high! Expect the impossible, as daily you rely upon the mighty power of your indwelling Lord to enable you to stand against the forces of evil. Let Christ have the pre-eminence in your life! The devil is ceaseless in his efforts to destroy your soul, but if you have committed yourself to the Lord Jesus, you have nothing to fear; victory is assured.

It is very possible that even though you have given careful thought to each of these studies, you may still be an outsider looking in. You have continued as a stranger to Christ. All of us make mistakes, but there is no greater mistake in life than the failure to receive Jesus Christ as Saviour and Lord. Do not be guilty of this grave error, for the price of such a mistake is an eternity in hell. Let me urge you to receive Christ into your heart immediately and then begin a walk of faith with Him.